W9-ASO-446

DISCARD
DISCARD

RANDOM HOUSE
LARGE PRINT

# GOD SAVE TEXAS

# GOD SAVE
## ★ TEXAS ★

## A Journey into the Soul
## of the Lone Star State

## LAWRENCE WRIGHT

RANDOM HOUSE
LARGE PRINT

Copyright © 2018 by Lawrence Wright

All rights reserved.
Published in the United States of America by
Random House Large Print in association with Alfred A. Knopf,
a division of Penguin Random House LLC, New York, and
distributed in Canada by Random House of Canada, a division
of Penguin Random House Canada Ltd., Toronto.

Front-of-cover photograph **Pecos Clouds, FM 1776
South of Coyanosa** by Jeff Baker © 2009
Cover design by Chip Kidd
Illustrations and endpapers by David Danz

The Library of Congress has established a Cataloging-in-
Publication record for this title.

ISBN: 978-0-5255-8954-9

www.penguinrandomhouse.com/large-print-format-books

FIRST LARGE PRINT EDITION

Printed in the United States of America

10  9  8  7  6  5  4  3  2  1

This Large Print edition published in accord
with the standards of the N.A.V.H.

For Steve,
who was there at the beginning
and will be at journey's end

We're oilmen and philosophers
Astronauts and ranchers
Fishermen and roughnecks
And college professors.
We're carpenters and preachers
And artists and physicians
High-tech geeks
And redneck musicians.
We're Church of Christ and Baptist
(Evangelical and Southern).
We're straight and gay and what the hey
We come in every color.
We're Czech and Greek and Mexican,
Vietnamese and Cajun
We sprawl a quarter million miles
We have no common language.

God save Texas
From the well-intentioned masses!
God save Texas
From the posers and jackasses!
God save Texas
He's the only one who can!

—unpublished song by
    Marcia Ball and Lawrence Wright

# Contents

# GOD SAVE
# TEXAS

# ONE

# The Charms, Such as They Are

S ubtle" was the word my friend Steve used as we drove through a spongy drizzle from Austin to San Antonio on a mild February morning. He was referencing the quality of the pleasures one might experience from observing the Texas landscape—small ones, requiring discernment—although the actual vista in front of us was an unending strip mall hugging a crowded interstate highway. Subtlety is a quality rarely invoked for anything to do with Texas, so I chewed on that notion for a bit.

There are some landscapes that are perfect for walking, disclosing themselves so intimately that one must dawdle to take them in; some that are best appreciated in an automobile at a reasonable rate of speed; and others that should be flown over as rapidly as possible. Much of Texas I place in this last category. Even Steve admits that Texas is where "everything peters out"—the South, the

Great Plains, Mexico, the Mountain West—all dribbling to an anticlimactic end, stripped of whatever glory they manifest elsewhere. But in the heart of Texas there is another landscape that responds best to the cyclist, who lumbers along at roughly the rate of a cantering horse, past the wildflowers and mockingbird trills of the Hill Country. Our bikes were in the back of my truck. We were going to explore the five Spanish missions along the San Antonio River, which have recently been named a World Heritage Site.

Steve is Stephen Harrigan, my closest friend for many years, a distinguished novelist who is now writing a history of Texas. We stopped at a Buc-ee's outside New Braunfels to pick up some Gatorade for the ride. It is the largest convenience store in the world—a category of achievement that only Texas would aspire to. It might very well be the largest gas station as well, with 120 fuel pumps, to complement the 83 toilets that on at least one occasion garnered the prize of Best Restroom in America. The billboards say The Top Two Reasons to Stop at Buc-ee's: Number 1 and Number 2, and also Restrooms You Have to Pee to Believe.

But gas and urination are not the distinguishing attractions at Buc-ee's. Texas is—or at least the kind of material goods that reify Texas in the minds of much of the world: massive belt buckles, barbecue, country music, Kevlar snake boots, rope signs (a length of rope twisted into a word—e.g., "Howdy"—and pasted over a painting of a Texas flag), holsters (although no actual guns), T-shirts (Have a Willie Nice Day), bumper stickers (Don't Mess with Texas), anything shaped like the state, and books of the sort classified as Texana. There is usually a stack of Steve's bestselling novel **The Gates of the Alamo** as well.

One image on the T-shirts and bumper stickers and whiskey jiggers has become especially popular lately: that of a black cannon over the legend Come and Take It. The taunt has a long history, going back to the Battle of Thermopylae, when Leonidas I, king of Sparta, responded to the demand of the Persian leader, Xerxes, that the Greeks lay down their arms. In Texas, the reference is to a battle in 1835, the opening skirmish of the Texas Revolution, when Mexican forces marched on the South Texas outpost of Gonzales to repossess a small bronze cannon that had been lent to the town for defense against Indians. The defiant citizens raised a crude flag, made from a wedding dress, that has now become an emblem of the gun rights movement. Ted Cruz wore a "Come and Take It" lapel pin on the floor of the U.S. Senate when he filibustered the health care bill in 2013.

At Buc-ee's, an aspiring Texan can get fully

outfitted not only with the clothing but also with the cultural and philosophical stances that embody the Texas stereotypes—cowboy individualism, a kind of wary friendliness, superpatriotism combined with defiance of all government authority, a hair-trigger sense of grievance, nostalgia for an ersatz past that is largely an artifact of Hollywood—a lowbrow society, in other words, that finds its fullest expression in a truck stop on the interstate.

I've lived in Texas most of my life, and I've come to appreciate what the state symbolizes, both to people who live here and to those who view it from afar. Texans see themselves as confident, hardworking, and neurosis-free—a distillation of the best qualities of America. Outsiders view Texas as the national id, a place where rambunctious and disavowed impulses run wild. Texans, they believe, mindlessly celebrate individualism, and view government as a kind of kryptonite that saps the entrepreneurial muscles. We're reputed to be braggarts; careless with money and our personal lives; a little gullible but dangerous if crossed; insecure but obsessed with power and prestige. Indeed, it's an irony that the figure who most embodies the values people associate with the state is a narcissistic Manhattan billionaire now sitting in the Oval Office.

Obviously, those same qualities also have wide

appeal. Texas has been growing at a stupefying rate for decades. The only state with more residents is California, but the number of Texans is projected to double by 2050, to 54.4 million, almost as many people as California and New York combined. Three Texas cities—Houston, Dallas, and San Antonio—are already among the top ten most populous cities in the United States. The eleventh largest is Austin, the capital, where Steve and I live. For the past five years it has been one of the fastest-growing large cities in America, the metropolitan area surpassing two million people, dwarfing the little college town Steve and I fell for many years ago.

There's an element of performance involved with being "Texan." The boots, the pickup trucks, the guns, the attitude—they're all part of the stereotype, but they're also a masquerade. Stylistic choices such as the way Texans dress or the vehicles they choose to drive enforce a sense of identity, but they also add to the alienation that non-Texans often feel about the state.

Riding on top of the old stereotypes are new ones—hipsters, computer gurus, musicians, video-game tycoons, and a widening artistic class that has reshaped the state's image and the way we think of ourselves. That Texas can't be captured on a coffee mug or a bumper sticker. "I'm the least Texas person I know," Steve once observed. I've never seen him in cowboy regalia, or even a pair of jeans. He hasn't owned a pair of boots since he was six years old. In college, he took horseback riding as a physical education requirement and got an F. He contends that must have been a clerical error, but the last time he was on a horse he fell off and broke his arm.

Neither Steve nor I could have lasted in Texas if it were the same place we grew up in, but we're so powerfully imprinted by the culture it's impossible to shake it off. Still, both of us have considered leaving and often wondered why we stayed. Many times I've considered moving to New York, where most of my colleagues live, or Washington, which is Lotus Land for political journalists. I've never felt at home in either spot. Washington is a one-industry town, and although writers have influence, they are basically in the grandstands watching the action. New York intellectuals sometimes put me off, with their liberal certitudes, their ready judgment of anyone who differs with them. The city is a pulsing hive of righteous indignation. In any case, I think I'm too much of a rustic to survive there. Once, when I was walking up Sixth Avenue in Manhattan, I saw a nicely dressed older man standing in the street beside the curb. He was turning around in small, distracted circles. All my prejudices against the city came up: here was a man in need, but people were walking by, evidently uncaring. In Texas, we wouldn't let a confused old man place himself in danger. I approached him as any gallant Texan would and said, "Sir, are you okay?"

He looked at me in puzzlement. "I'm waiting for a cab," he said.

★

WRITERS HAVE BEEN sizing up Texas from its earliest days, usually harshly. Frederick Law Olmsted, a journalist before he became the designer of New York's Central Park, rode through in 1854. "Horses and wives were of as little account as umbrellas in more advanced states," he noted. In 1939, Edna Ferber arrived on a prospecting trip that led to her novel **Giant**. That book, finally published in 1952, was a sensation. It popularized the image of Texas millionaires as greedy but colorful provincials, whose fortunes were built largely on luck rather than hard work or intelligence. That there was truth in this summation was part of the sting. When the **New Yorker** writer John Bainbridge passed through the state in 1961, gathering material for his book **The Super-Americans**, he found Texans still reeling from what he called ednaferberism. "Few documents since the Emancipation Proclamation have stirred as much commotion," Bainbridge observed; however, he also noticed that the movie had just come out, and it was booked on nearly every screen in the state. In the movie version, Rock Hudson plays the cattle rancher with a spread the size of several states; James Dean is the roughneck, who rises from nothing to build a stupendous fortune; and Elizabeth Taylor is the civilizing Easterner, who acknowledges the exploitation of the Mexicans who do all the labor but fail to reap the profits. It's been three quarters of a century since **Giant** first appeared on bookshelves, but the archetypes that Ferber codified still color the perceptions of Texans by both outsiders and Texans themselves.

Bainbridge observed that the condescension of non-Texans toward the state echoes the traditional Old World stance toward the New. "The faults of Texas, as they are recorded by most visitors, are scarcely unfamiliar, for they are the same ones that Europeans have been taxing us with for some three hundred years: boastfulness, cultural underdevelopment, materialism, and all the rest," Bainbridge wrote. He diagnosed the popular disdain for Texas as a combination of "hostility born of envy" and "resentment born of nostalgia." He added: "Texas is a mirror in which Americans see themselves reflected, not life-sized but, as in a distorting mirror, bigger than life. They are not pleased by the image."

When Bainbridge visited, Texas was in the backseat of the national consciousness, a marginal influence despite its swelling oil wealth and sui generis political culture. By the time Gail Collins, **The New York Times**'s op-ed columnist, arrived to research her 2012 manifesto, **As Texas Goes . . . How the Lone Star State Hijacked the American Agenda,** the accumulation of economic and political power meant that Texas now had a hand on the steering wheel. Alarm had set in. "Texas **runs everything**," Collins wrote, expressing a typical liberal complaint. "Why, then, is it so cranky?"

Steve and I have talked over the question of whether Texas is responsible for fomenting the darker political culture that has crept over our country, which is the charge that outsiders like Collins often make, citing as evidence Lyndon Johnson and Vietnam, George W. Bush and Iraq, Tom DeLay and redistricting, Ted Cruz and the Tea Party—an impressive bill of particulars that has contributed to the national malaise. Steve takes the position that Texas is simply a part of the mainstream. Its influence may seem disproportionate, but it's a huge state and it reflects trends that are under way all across the country. "If you visualize America as a sailing ship, Texas is like the hold," he says. "When the cargo shifts, it's bound to affect the trajectory of the vessel."

I'm less forgiving. I think Texas has nurtured an immature political culture that has done terrible damage to the state and to the nation. Because

Texas is a part of almost everything in modern America—the South, the West, the Plains, Hispanic and immigrant communities, the border, the divide between the rural areas and the cities—what happens here tends to disproportionately affect the rest of the nation. Illinois and New Jersey may be more corrupt, Kansas and Louisiana more dysfunctional, but they don't bear the responsibility of being the future.

★

WE DECIDED TO begin our ride at the farthest of the five missions—San Francisco de la Espada, established in 1731. From there it was about thirteen miles to the oldest mission, the Alamo, in downtown San Antonio.

Texas has had a lot of blood spilled on its soil, and although the term "terrorism" wasn't in coinage during the settlement of the state, people on all sides understood the stakes. Torture, scalping, beheading, indiscriminate and imaginative murders were the nature of the conflict between the native world and the European colonizers. The idea of the missions was to provide sanctuary for the Coahuiltecan Indians, where they could be Christianized and turned into farmers and artisans. "The point was to make them as much like Spaniards as possible," Steve says. Unfortunately for the Coahuiltecans, they were caught in a crossfire between the Spaniards and the Apaches, as well as the Comanches, who ruled the savage plains. "It was like modern-day Syria," Steve observed.

A wedding was going on in the little Espada chapel, so Steve and I wandered over to an out-building where an amateur baseball league was selling barbecue plates. We ate on a bench in a field of purple clover beside the ancient granary and listened to the nuptial music. A waft of incense floated from the tiny sanctuary, and the sun suddenly broke through. Already in February we could feel the breath of July.

Presently, the bride and groom emerged, and as the bells pealed they stood for photographs in front of the Moorish arch of the doorway. History leaves such interesting traces of itself—subtle, as Steve would have it—and here was a remnant of the Alhambra. We talked about how the Spanish colonization of America was an outgrowth of the Inquisition and the ousting of the Moors. After they captured Granada in 1492, the Spanish Catholics took their holy war to the New World. They were rather late in arriving in Texas. Álvar Núñez Cabeza de Vaca was shipwrecked near Galveston Island in 1528. The conquistadors brought with them the entire catalog of European pestilence—bubonic plague, smallpox, measles, influenza—producing one of history's greatest demographic disasters. "Half the natives died of a disease of the bowels and blamed us," Cabeza de Vaca complained. The Indians who rescued the stranded Spaniard demanded that he become their medicine man; thus the first European in Texas found himself attempting to cure the very infections he had caused. Generations later, when Europeans began coming to Texas to stay, the original, thickly settled Indian country had been reduced to the wide-open spaces that greeted the Spanish friars. Their missions are about the oldest material objects in Texas, aside from arrowheads and dinosaur bones.

As we were finishing lunch, I spotted another bride waiting beside the ruined walls; a tall black photographer with a red Mohawk was snapping photos of her, while her plump Mexican mother held her train. Steve and I took a peek inside the chapel, then decided it was time to mount up and ride.

We pedaled along a paved trail beside the river—or what used to be the river before it was channelized following a series of floods in the first half of the twentieth century. In the last two decades, however, there has been a heroic attempt to return life to this waterway. Engineers installed artificial shoals and falls; native plantings now line the shoreline, disguising the reinforcements, so that the river, while no longer natural, has at least become naturalistic. Cormorants perch on the artfully positioned boulders, hanging their wings, like Dracula's cape, out to dry. We passed a number of small farmhouses, where roosters called to us, along with the occasional fussy peacock. These birds, with their incessant screeching, are among the most annoying immigrants to the state. A rancher friend of mine claims that peacocks were first brought to Texas because they were said to be excellent snake eaters. They've become a plague in some city neighborhoods. The best way to silence them, folks have found, is to station a mirror nearby, so that the males spend their time gaping at their own reflection.

The peacock invasion reminded me of the collapse of the great emu bubble of the 1990s, when breeding pairs of the five-foot-tall Australian flightless bird were selling for $50,000 in Texas. Emu oil was promoted as a treatment for cancer and arthritis and was even said to repel mosquitoes. Emu steak was on the menu. Soon more than half a million emus were grazing on Texas ranchland. Ostriches joined the big-bird craze. Then the bubble popped, and the formerly prized emus turned into unwanted tenants that were sold at auction for about two bucks apiece, or simply shooed out the open gate. Some counties had to hire emu wranglers to recapture the fast and notoriously obstinate birds. There are still colonies of feral emus roaming the state.

Texas has practically no laws regulating exotic animals. After a herd of nilgai antelope was released on the King Ranch in 1930, every rancher felt compelled to own a few zebras, or camels, kangaroos, gazelles, maybe a rhinoceros. Hunters decided to breed Russian boars with the feral hogs that are a remnant of the Spanish colonization, and now we've got more than two million of these beasts, each weighing twice as much as a white-tailed deer, with tusks like bayonets, tearing up fences and pastureland and mowing down crops, even eating the seed corn out of the ground before it sprouts. They can run twenty-five miles per hour and smell odors seven miles away.

But at least they're not tigers. The Humane Society of the United States estimates that there are more tigers living in captivity in Texas than the three thousand that are thought to be living in the wild. Some are kept as pets in backyards. During the floods in East Texas in 2016, a tiger escaped in Conroe still wearing its collar and leash. When my wife, Roberta, was teaching kindergarten, she would go to a state teacher supply center to get classroom materials, and one of the options was to check out a few Madagascar hissing cockroaches to amuse the children. That's all we need.

★

WHAT I KNOW about Steve:

He was born Michael Stephen McLaughlin, but his father, a fighter pilot who had won the Distinguished Flying Cross in the Second World War, died in a crash six months before he was born. Steve's name was changed when his mother remarried, so he became Stephen Michael Harrigan. Or else Michael Stephen Harrigan. It's one way on his driver's license and the other on his passport. He's not sure himself what his legal name is.

Steve has always been set in his ways. When he was a boy, a pretty girl gave him a rock, and he kept it in his pocket for two years. One time when we were on another bike ride, Steve confessed that he has difficulty changing gears because his personality is so inflexible.

He's a serial sneezer—I have counted up to fourteen in a row—and he has impressive dexterity, being able to snap all his fingers, and peel an orange with a spoon. He is a somnambulist, who occasionally walks in his sleep, and once even showered and dressed without waking up. He has been known to latch his hotel room door to keep himself from wandering into the hallway in his underwear.

He fathered three adorable daughters and evidently has no Y chromosomes.

He suffers from a crippling civility and is con-
stitutionally unable to enter a door before anyone else. His niceness sometimes gets him into
trouble, but it goes along with his chivalry. Once
he saw a woman being manhandled on the street
and he sprung to her defense, whereupon her boyfriend beat him up while she told him to mind his
own business.

He goes to the movies at least twice a week,
even those known to be awful, which he will
sometimes defend because "it succeeds on its own
terms" or some such inarguable formulation. He
hates clowns and mimes, which scream phoniness
to him, but he's soft on pests, like rats and snakes,
because they can't help being what they are.

Nothing depresses him like good news. He's
always worried about money, but tell him he's won
the lottery and he'll sink into a funk, imagining
all the things that will inevitably go wrong. He
claims he's not a pessimist; he's just anxious about
being taken in by dreamy illusions. When we
got our first movie contract, he glumly observed,
"This could be the worst thing that ever happened
to us."

Steve still has his old interior lineman frame,
but he's bald and his beard is going white. In fashion, he inclines toward survivalist gear. He divides
the world into those who are ready to flee into
the hills on a moment's notice and those who are

liable to find themselves, like Pierre in **War and Peace,** trapped on the field of battle in a swallow-tail coat—to Steve, the most frightening passage in all of literature.

As it happens, Steve and I were born in the same hospital in Oklahoma City, and lived at the same time in Abilene, Texas. Steve's stepfather was an oilman, which brought his family to Texas. We didn't meet until I moved to Austin in 1980 to work for **Texas Monthly** magazine, where Steve was a staff writer. Living such parallel lives, we were destined to get together eventually.

✷

THE WRIGHTS CAME to Texas through a terrible error of judgment. My great-grandfather Edwin Wright was born in Stratford-upon-Avon, one of the most charming and historic villages in all of the United Kingdom. The 1861 British census lists his occupation as "castrator." Why he left is a mystery no one has ever solved. He immigrated to America around the time of the Civil War, lived for several years in Buffalo, where he had an uncle, and filed for citizenship in 1868. We think he went from there to Minnesota, possibly to practice his craft on the local sheep. By then he had a family. Kansas was open for homesteading, and Edwin decided to try his luck there. It was then that he made his colossal mistake.

With no history as a farmer, Edwin brought with him a wooden moldboard plow. We believe he bought it in Buffalo. This was, already, ancient technology, long since replaced by steel, but when my great-grandfather and his family stepped off the train in central Kansas, he was faced with a choice. On one side of the tracks was blackland prairie, which his wooden plow couldn't turn, and on the other side was sandy soil, not much denser than a beach. That's where Edwin Wright made his claim, in the heart of what became the Dust Bowl.

Generations of Wrights were ruined by that cursed decision. My father, John Donald Wright, the youngest of five children, was the only one of his siblings to escape. He worked his way through college and law school, then spent seven years at war, in Europe and Korea. Disgusted with the law, he decided to become a banker, which is how we got to Texas. Daddy was a vice president of Citizens National Bank in Abilene at the same time that Steve's stepfather had his office downtown. We wondered if they might have had coffee together.

In 1960, my father finally got the opportunity to be president of a little independent bank in a strip shopping center in East Dallas, between a drugstore and a beauty salon. He built that bank into a major institution, and used its resources to renovate the declining neighborhood, granting innovative loans to young people willing to apply "sweat equity" to resurrect the old houses. Texas was a place where ambitious young men like Don Wright were welcomed and given a chance to succeed.

Many years after my father had put down roots in Dallas, he paid a visit to Stratford-upon-Avon to see if he could figure out what had caused his ancestor to leave such a civilized spot and move to Kansas, where he lived in a sod house, like an igloo made of dirt. Our ancestral English home, on the other hand, is a tidy brick row house on West Street. My father knocked on the door, but no one was there. Daddy remembered his grandfather as a cantankerous old man who hated children. Perhaps my ancestor's dark mood was colored by regret.

Years later, Roberta and I were in England, hiking in the Cotswolds, and we also made a pilgrimage to the old place. A young man from Bangladesh answered the bell, saying, "Master not here." While we waited for Master to come home, we walked over to the Holy Trinity Church, where Shakespeare is buried. He's inside the chapel, but the churchyard itself is filled with Wrights, the patrilineal mother lode.

We finally did meet the landlord of the two-bedroom house that gave birth to our portion of the Wright clan. He cheerfully confided that it was now an illegal jeans factory—a sweatshop, I suppose, but on a small scale. The rooms upstairs were filled with sewing machines. The landlord gave me a pair of very nice jeans as a souvenir.

I must have inherited some of the restlessness that propelled Edwin Wright to leave the land of his birth and my father to fight his way out of Kansas. By the time I graduated from high school, I was sick of Texas. I did everything I could to cleanse myself of its influence. I had been pious, but I became a bohemian existentialist. I ditched the accent, which I hadn't been conscious of until my first session in the language lab when I heard myself speaking Spanish—with that high nasal twang so typical of North Texas.

I've seen the same thing happen to people who come from other societies with a strong cultural imprint; they reverse the image. But being the opposite of what you were is not the same as being somebody new. As soon as the doors to liberation opened, I fled. I wanted to be someplace open, tolerant, cosmopolitan, and beautiful. I thought I would never come back. I turned into that pitiable figure, a self-hating Texan.

★

STEVE AND I PEDALED to Mission San Juan Capistrano, a plain, whitewashed structure with the traditional belfry. The mission was named after Giovanni da Capistrano, a friar who defended Christian Hungary against the Muslim invasion in 1456. There's a carved wooden icon of the saint inside a glass case; he has a red flag in one hand and an upraised sword in the other. As he gazes heavenward with a beatific expression, one of his sandaled feet rests on the head of a decapitated victim.

Outside, several Indians were taking down a huge tepee, stacking the lodgepoles on a flatbed truck. A young man who was watching the others work told us that there had been a Native American Church ceremony here on the **campo santo**— the graveyard of their ancestors—the night before, with eighty-five people crowded inside the tepee. "It's a lot of work," he said, as the others hefted the giant poles and bore them toward the truck.

"I can see you're doing your part," I observed.

He grinned and said, "I'm with management."

"Is that your altar?" Steve asked, gesturing toward the low mound of red sand that remained from the ceremony. The altar is usually crescent-shaped, signifying the journey from life to death, but this one was angular. An older man leaning on the tailgate of the truck had been watching us with squinted eyes, but he suddenly brightened and acknowledged that the altar was his handiwork—"the Quanah Parker altar," he said, referring to the last great Comanche chief.

Farther down the river we passed the ruins of the old Hot Wells Hotel, a once grand resort where Will Rogers and Rudolph Valentino came to take the waters. A pioneering French filmmaker, Gaston Méliès, set up a movie studio next door in 1910, hoping to turn Texas into what would become Hollywood. That didn't happen, although the first movie to win an Academy Award for best picture—**Wings** in 1927—was filmed nearby on Kelly Field. We rode on, leaving behind the alternate history Texas might have had.

There was a time when Steve and I considered moving to L.A. and going into the movie business—our own alternate history. We had just sold a script to Sydney Pollack, right after he finished directing **Tootsie**, when he was the king of Hollywood. On the first-class flight home, we mulled over what our lives were going to be like from now on. A friend of ours in the trade had warned that writing movie scripts was like raising children for adoption. On the other hand, we'd be consoled by the weather and our enormous wealth.

Sydney made **Out of Africa** instead of our script, but our next project was for Jane Fonda. When we arrived in her office in Santa Monica, she opened the door and stuck out her hand. The collar on her blue blouse was turned up, and it matched the startling blue of her eyes. Her hair was blond and leonine. This was at the peak of her exercise video sensation, and she looked like she could jump over a building. "Hi," she said. "I'm Jane Fonda."

"Hi," I said. "I'm Steve Harrigan."

I don't know why that came out of my mouth. Jane never got us straight after that, always seeming a little anxious in our presence. In any case, Jane married Ted Turner and retreated from the film business, while Steve and I returned to our books and articles. The lure of Hollywood faded, although we each continued to do occasional screen work from afar. Another friend of mine moved back to Austin after spending a couple of years in the screenwriting business. "One day in Los Angeles, I heard a mockingbird imitating a car alarm," she told me. "That's when I knew. I was like a bird that had lost my song."

★

WE DECIDED to save the two prettiest missions, Concepción and San José, for the ride back so we'd have plenty of time at the Alamo. On the horizon we could see the Tower of the Americas, a lonely remnant of the 1968 HemisFair. There was once a bill by a San Antonio lawmaker and professional gambler, V. E. "Red" Berry, to divide Texas in half, with San Antonio becoming the capital of the southern entity and the governor's office placed in the rotating restaurant atop the

tower. South Texas today really is a virtual linguistic province, like Quebec, with San Antonio
playing the role of its bilingual capital.

Soon we were on city streets, passing through
the King William Historic District, with its great
nineteenth-century German houses nested under
massive oaks and pecans, and then into the low-
slung downtown. Unlike other bustling Texas
metropolises, San Antonio still has the look of a
city that might be on a colorized postcard.

We were hot from the ride, and Steve suggested
we indulge in a snow cone. Bees swarmed around
the syrup dispensers at the shaded stand in front of
the Alamo. On the plaza, we examined the Alamo
Cenotaph, which the former lead singer of Black
Sabbath, Ozzy Osbourne, peed on in 1982. (The
conscience-stricken celebrity later apologized for
his actions.) The stone barricade that once enclosed
the mission has given way to parasitical tourist
attractions such as Ripley's Haunted Adventure
and the Guinness World Records Museum. Steve
pointed out the area where the Mexican forces
broke through, near the corner of what had been
the north wall, now occupied by Tomb Rider 3D.

The Alamo itself is a modest construction of
limestone, yellowed by the patina of age, like old
teeth. The primitive symmetry of the facade, with
its arching pediment resembling a child's draw-
ing, is a familiar feature of the Texas imagina-

tion. Steve once described it as "a squat and oddly configured structure that is in almost every way inscrutable." Here in 1836 about 250 men and a number of women and children gathered, determined to block the progress of the army of General Antonio López de Santa Anna, the imperious president of Mexico, who styled himself the "Napoleon of the West." Santa Anna might easily have gone around San Antonio or stationed a small garrison to keep the rebels penned up inside the mission as he pursued Sam Houston's army of insurgents. The hapless defenders were expecting to be reinforced at any moment. "The Alamo guarded the Camino Real, the only road and supply route into Texas from Mexico," Steve observed. "The defenders just got trapped there, and Santa Anna wisely attacked before help could arrive." As for Houston, he never wanted to defend the Alamo; he had proposed simply blowing it up.

The defiant Texians—as they were then called—held off Santa Anna's forces for thirteen days under the command of a prickly young Alabama lawyer, William Barret Travis. With him were Jim Bowie, a land speculator and renowned knife fighter, and David Crockett, a legendary frontiersman and former U.S. congressman who had once been mentioned as a possible presidential candidate. After being voted out of office, Crockett advised his Tennessee constituents, "You may all go to hell and I will go to Texas"—an example followed by many since.

As boys, Steve and I had fallen under the spell of the Alamo legend, having been indoctrinated by the Disney television series **Davy Crockett**, which Steve compares to **Star Wars** and **Harry Potter** in terms of its cultural sway. Like every other boy we knew, we sang "Davy! Davy Crockett! King of the wild frontier!" We owned replicas of Davy's coonskin cap, a fashion statement that is perhaps hard to account for but now seems ripe for revival among the tattooed ironists of the coffee shops. My family had just moved from Abilene to Dallas in 1960 when **The Alamo**, starring John Wayne as Crockett, came to the Capri Theatre. At the time, the movie was widely read as a rallying cry for the right-wing politics that Wayne trumpeted, with the Mexicans serving as stand-ins for the forces of international communism; in Texas, however, **The Alamo** was our creation myth. In some elemental and irresistible manner, the movie told us who we were.

One of Steve's fans is the British rock star Phil Collins, who has amassed the world's largest private collection of Alamo relics, including a rifle owned by Crockett and a knife that belonged to Jim Bowie. As a child, Collins had also been fixated on Davy Crockett and the Alamo myth. His grandmother cut up a fur coat to make him a coonskin cap, which I suppose wasn't as readily available in London as it was in Texas. Collins once told Steve that when he finally saw the Alamo in person—in 1973, when he was the lead singer for Genesis—it was like meeting the Beatles for the first time.

Collins inadvertently triggered a bitter legal and political contest between the Daughters of the Republic of Texas, the jealous guardians of the Alamo for more than a century, and the newly elected Texas land commissioner, George P. Bush, son of the former Florida governor and presidential candidate Jeb Bush. In 2014, Collins offered his artifacts to the State of Texas under the condition that a suitable repository—i.e., a $100 million museum—be constructed to house the Phil Collins Alamo Collection.

George P. muscled control from the Daughters, who had a history of financial trouble, pledging to repair the infrastructure of the building and make the plaza more sober-minded. Given his mother's Hispanic roots, George P. is expected to bring more balance to the legend that the Alamo has enshrined. One hopes that he will address the original sin of the Texas Revolution. Stephen F. Austin founded the Texas colony as a cotton empire, manned by slave labor. Mexico outlawed slavery in 1829, but appeased the colonists by granting an exemption to Texas. The Constitution of the Republic of Texas not only legalized slavery, it prohibited the emancipation of any slave without the consent of Congress. In 1845, with the price of cotton on the floor, the bankrupt young republic faced a choice of being annexed by the United States as a slave state or accepting a bail-out from Great Britain and remaining independent. The loan came with a catch: Texans would have to pay wages for all labor. Despite the chest-thumping Tea Party bluster about secession these days, Texas tossed away its independence when it appeared it would have to surrender on slavery.

As you pass through the heavy wooden door into the hushed sanctuary of the Shrine of Texas Liberty, men are advised to remove their hats. "Be silent, friend," a plaque commands. "Here heroes died to blaze a trail for other men." Since I last visited, the exhibits have improved and the sacristy rooms, where the women and children took shelter during the massacre, have been opened. The relics inside glass cases include Davy Crockett's beaded leather vest, Bowie's silver spoon, and Travis's razor. The garish paintings depicting the battle, which once adorned the walls, have been taken down, revealing the faded frescoes of the original structure.

We passed through the gift shop, which as you would imagine is a kind of Lourdes of Texas kitsch. Coonskin caps are still available for $12.99, along with reproductions of Travis's farewell letter pledging that he will "die like a soldier who never forgets what is due to his own honor & that of his country—**Victory or Death**." All this meets with Steve's approval, to a point. "You don't want to take away everything," he said. "You don't want it to be in 'excellent taste.'" Steve actually owns a tie he bought here some years ago depicting Travis drawing the legendary line in the sand with his sword. He is supposed to have said on the occasion, "Those prepared to give their lives in freedom's cause, come over to me." Travis fell early in the assault, which lasted only ninety minutes; his slave, Joe, was spared, as were the women and children.

It was twilight when we finished our ride. On the way back to Austin we stopped to eat in Gruene, a little German town where, in 1979, my decision to return to Texas began to take shape. I was writing an article for **Look** magazine about the twelve men who walked on the moon. One of them, Charlie Duke, was living in New Braunfels. When I got to town, I checked in at the Prince Solms Inn, named after the military officer who established the German colonies in Texas. There was a rathskeller in the basement. I figured I would have a beer and a kraut and then retire with a book—Saturday night in New Braunfels—but destiny placed an insurmountable obstacle in my path in the person of Frank Bailey, **Texas Monthly**'s restaurant critic. Away we went on a gallivant around the Hill Country, eating at a roadhouse where Frank ordered a three-inch steak, rare, a bleeding brick of meat, and winding up at Gruene Hall, Texas's oldest dance emporium. A band called Asleep at the Wheel was playing Texas swing. A young man named George Strait opened for them. Dancers were two-stepping; the boys had longnecks in the rear pockets of their jeans and the girls wore aerodynamic skirts. There was something suspiciously beguiling about the scene, verging on being staged for my benefit. Memories were stirred. The tunes, the accents, the food— they all felt familiar and yet curated so that they could be properly noticed and appreciated by the susceptible exile.

At the time, my wife and I were living in Atlanta. That night, I called her and said, "Something's going on in Texas." I couldn't put it all into words then. It was subtle.

# TWO

# A Tale of Three Wells

One can't be from Texas and fail to have encountered the liberal loathing for Texanness, even among people who have never visited the place. They detect an accent, a discordant political note, or a bit of a swagger, and outraged emotions begin to flow. Fear is a part of it, as every decade Texas gains congressional seats and electoral votes, while moving further rightward and dragging the country with it. Whereas, for conservatives, Texas is a Promised Land of entrepreneurship, liberals draw a picture of Daddy Warbucks capitalism—heartless, rapacious, and predatory. Even in Norway—that earnest, pacific, right-thinking country—there is the phrase "Det var helt texas!" which translates as "It was totally bonkers." "It's actually said with a touch of admiration," a Norwegian friend assured me.

Texas is invariably compared to California, its political antithesis. California is more regulated and highly taxed, whereas Texas is relatively unfettered, with one of the lowest tax burdens in the country. Every statewide officeholder in California is a Democrat; in Texas, there hasn't been a Democrat elected to statewide office in more than twenty years. The gross domestic product of Texas is $1.6 trillion; as an independent country, its economy would settle in around tenth, eclipsing Canada and Australia. California, with 40 percent more people, has a GDP of $2.6 trillion, making its economy the fifth largest in the world, just ahead of the UK.

Texas has been steadily closing the gap in both population and economic growth, however. Texas exports nearly outrank those of California and New York combined. Yes, a lot of that is from petroleum products, but Texas also tops California in exporting technology. Between 2000 and 2016, job growth in Dallas and Houston expanded 31 percent, which is three times the rate of Los Angeles. Austin employment expansion was over 50 percent during the same period.

All that vigorous growth in Texas had a rope thrown around it when oil prices, which had climbed to $145 a barrel in 2008, slumped in 2014, ultimately falling below $30. In 2016, for the first time in twelve years, Texas job growth lagged behind that of the nation as a whole. Houston alone lost as many as 70,000 energy-related jobs.

California's gross domestic product outpaced that of Texas in the first two quarters of 2016. In the third quarter, however, when oil prices began to stabilize, Texas once again leaped ahead. Critics of the Texas economic model would say that's proof that it's not magic—it's oil.

★

THE MANY LAYERS of subterranean Texas have names that resonate among oilmen and even form a part of the ordinary Texan's consciousness. The Barnett Shale, the Wolfcamp, the Austin Chalk—each held a buried treasure waiting to be discovered. The grand story of Texas oil, however, is really about three wells.

At the beginning of the twentieth century, near Beaumont, on the Gulf Coast close to the Louisiana line, there was a sulfurous hill called Sour Spring Mound. Gas seepage was so noticeable that schoolboys would sometimes set the hill on fire. Pattillo Higgins, a disreputable local businessman who had lost an arm in a gunfight with a deputy sheriff, became convinced that there was oil below the gassy hill. Wells weren't drilled back then; they were essentially pounded into the earth using a heavy bit that was repeatedly lifted and dropped, chiseling its way through the strata. The quicksand under Sour Spring Mound defeated several attempts to make a proper hole. Higgins forecast oil at a thousand feet, a totally made-up figure.

Higgins hired a mining engineer, Captain Anthony F. Lucas, a Croatian American who had studied mining engineering in Austria. Captain Lucas's first well got to a depth of only 575 feet before the pipe collapsed. Lucas then decided to use a rotary bit, a novelty at the time, which he thought more suitable for penetrating soft layers. His drillers also discovered that by pumping mud down the hole, they could form a kind of cement to buttress the sides. These innovations created the modern drilling industry.

Lucas and his team hoped to bring in a well that could produce 50 barrels a day. On January 10, 1901, at 1,020 feet, almost precisely the depth predicted by Higgins's wild guess, the well suddenly vomited mud and then ejected six tons of drilling pipe clear over the top of the derrick. No one had ever seen anything like this. It was terrifying. In the unnerved silence that followed, the flabbergasted drilling team, drenched in mud, crept back to the site and began to clean up the debris. Then they heard a roar from deep in the earth, from another era, millions of years earlier. More mud flew up, followed by rocks and gas, and then oil, which shot 150 feet into the air—a black geyser that spewed from the arterial wound that the drillers had made in the greatest oil field ever seen at the time. For the next nine days, until the well was capped, the gusher blasted 100,000 barrels of oil into the air—more than all the wells in America combined. After the first year of production, the well, which Higgins named Spindletop, was producing 17 million barrels a year.

In those days, Texas was almost entirely rural; there were no large cities and practically no industry; cotton and cattle were the bedrock of the economy. Spindletop changed that. Because of native Texas suspicion of outside corporate interests—especially John D. Rockefeller's Standard Oil—two local companies were formed to develop the new field: Gulf Oil and Texaco (both now merged with Chevron). The boom made some prospectors millionaires, but the sudden surfeit of petroleum was not entirely a blessing for Texas. In the 1930s, prices crashed, to the point that, in some parts of the country, oil was cheaper than water. That would become a familiar pattern of the boom-or-bust Texas economy.

In August 1927, Columbus Marion Joiner, a prospector and beloved con man widely known as Dad, began drilling in East Texas, near Henderson, on the Daisy Bradford lease, named after the widow who owned the land. Joiner had practically no money and even less luck. His first two wells went bust. To entice investors to back yet another well, he drew up fake geological reports indicating the presence of salt domes and oil-bearing anti-clines. The phony report predicted that at 3,500 feet the well would tap into the greatest oil field in the world. Once again, a wild prediction would turn out to be absolutely true.

Dad Joiner was targeting the Woodbine sand, which sits above a layer of Buda limestone, thick with fossils of the dinosaurs and crocodiles that had plied the shallow Cretaceous seas. Over millions of years, plankton, algae, and other organic materials buried in the sandy layer transformed into oil or gas. Joiner scraped by for three and a half years, paying his workers with scrip and selling $25 certificates to farmers to raise enough money to complete the rickety well. When Joiner reached 3,456 feet, a core sample showed oil-saturated sand. Thousands gathered to watch the roughnecks drilling and swabbing through the night. Imagine the scene: farmers in bib overalls, women in dresses sewn from patterns out of the Sears catalog, all of them dreaming of a life in which they would be strolling down a grand boulevard in fine clothes, pricing jewels and weighing investments—a dream that was about to come true for many of them. In the late afternoon on October 3, 1930, a gurgling was heard; then, two nights later, oil flew into the air in a great and continuous ejaculation. People danced in the black rain; children painted their faces with it.

Overnight, new prospectors arrived, along with major producers. Within nine months of the Daisy Bradford No. 3 strike, a thousand wells were up and running in the East Texas field, accounting for half the total U.S. demand. Saloons and hotels sprang into existence to accommodate the rough-necks, along with the "man camps" that invari-ably blossom in the booms. Cities such as Tyler, Kilgore, and Longview suddenly found them-selves in a forest of towering derricks, which rose out of backyards and loomed over downtown buildings. In one city block in Kilgore, there were forty-four wells. It was said you could walk from derrick to derrick without touching the ground. Texans pumped so much oil out of the Woodbine that prices fell from $1.10 a barrel to thirteen cents. The governor shut down the wells in an attempt to staunch the decline.

Besieged by lawsuits because of his years of reck-less promises, Joiner sold his interest in the lease to H. L. Hunt, who would eventually become the richest man in the world. Dad Joiner died broke in Dallas in 1947.

By the mid-nineties, the oil business in the U.S. was lagging. The industry seemed to be on the verge of peak oil—the moment when at least half of all the recoverable petroleum in the world has been exploited. On the other side of that peak lay an unyielding slope of diminishing returns.

The major oil companies began concentrating their exploration efforts outside the U.S., whose reserves were deemed to be more or less used up. The end of the fossil-fuel era was not exactly imminent, but it was no longer unimaginable.

The situation was brutally clear to George Mitchell, one of Texas's most famous wildcatters. His father, Savvas Paraskevopoulos, was a goat-herder from a little village in Greece, who opened up a shoeshine stand in Galveston and changed his name to Mike Mitchell. George worked his way through Texas A&M, studying geology and petroleum engineering, graduating at the top of his class. In 1952, he acted on a tip from a bookie and optioned a plot of land in Wise County, an area in North Texas that was known as the "wild-catter's graveyard." He soon had thirteen produc-ing wells, the first of the ten thousand he went on to develop in his career.

In 1954, Mitchell secured a lucrative con-tract to supply 10 percent of Chicago's natural-gas needs—up to 200 million cubic feet per day. However, as the years passed, the wells operated by Mitchell Energy & Development were declin-ing. He needed to discover new sources of petro-leum, or else.

Mitchell was under the sway of an influential report, published in 1972, by an international team of scientists, led by Dennis L. Meadows at MIT,

titled **The Limits to Growth.** The scientists examined a number of variables—population, food
production, industrialization, pollution, and con-
sumption of nonrenewable natural resources—all
of which were increasing exponentially. "**Under
the assumption of no major change in the present
system,**" the authors emphatically warned in the
section dealing with declining natural resources,
"**population and industrial growth will certainly
stop within the next century, at the latest.**" Even
under a more optimistic scenario, in which the
available natural resources doubled, pollution
would overload the capacity of the environment
to absorb it, leading to the same dire outcome:
"**The basic behavior mode of the world system
is exponential growth of population and capital,
followed by collapse.**" The only way to halt the
march to disaster is to achieve what the authors
call "equilibrium." That would mean sacrificing
certain liberties, "such as producing unlimited
numbers of children or consuming uncontrolled
amounts of resources."

As the father of ten children, Mitchell certainly
hadn't done much to control population, but he
was deeply engaged with the concept of responsible growth and environmental welfare. In 1974,
he founded a planned community outside Houston, called The Woodlands, designed to be eco-
logically mindful. (It is now the home to more

than 100,000 residents and a number of corporate campuses.) Mitchell began holding conferences there, inspired by the ideas in **The Limits to Growth.** He and his wife, Cynthia, formed a foundation that is largely dedicated to promoting ideals of sustainability.

In 1980, Mitchell predicted that there were only about thirty-five years of conventional sources of petroleum remaining in the U.S. The obvious alternative was coal, which had dire implications for the environment. Natural gas, on the other hand, was far cleaner, almost an ideal fuel, in Mitchell's opinion. But was there enough gas remaining to prevent the world from returning to a time when coal-burning fireplaces coated the cities in black ash and smog filled the air with dangerous pollutants?

Mitchell still faced the immediate problem of fulfilling his contract with the city of Chicago. His company's main assets were the leases that he held on 300,000 acres seventy miles northwest of Dallas, in the region known to oilmen as the Fort Worth Basin. A mile and a half below the surface was a formation called the Barnett Shale. Geologists had speculated that the Barnett, which extends five thousand square miles and spreads through seventeen counties, contained the largest gas reserves of any onshore field in the United States. The problem was that nobody knew how to

extract the gas. Porous formations, like the Woodbine sands that Dad Joiner had tapped, allow the
flow of liquids and gases, but the Barnett Shale
is "tight rock," meaning that it has very low per-
meability. In the mid-twentieth century, prospectors attempted to liberate petroleum reserves by
pulverizing tight rock. Imaginative techniques—
using dynamite, machine guns, bazookas, and
napalm—were tried, without success. In 1967, the
Atomic Energy Commission, working with the
Lawrence Livermore Laboratory and the El Paso
Natural Gas Company, exploded a twenty-nine-
kiloton nuclear bomb, dubbed Gasbuggy, four
thousand feet underground, near Farmington,
New Mexico. More than thirty other nuclear
explosions followed, in what was called Project
Plowshare. Natural gas, it turned out, could be
extracted from the atomized rubble, but the gas
was radioactive.

A safer and more precise method, developed in
the seventies, was to use jets of fluid under intense
pressure, to create microcracks in the strata, typically in sandstone or limestone. Expensive gels or
foams were typically used to thicken the fluid,
and biocide was added to kill the bacteria that can
clog the cracks. A granular substance called "proppant," made of sand or ceramics, was pumped
into the cracks, keeping pathways open so that
the hydrocarbons could journey to the surface.

The process came to be known as hydraulic fracturing, or fracking. It certainly did jostle loose the captured oil or gas molecules, but as far as Mitchell was concerned, it had a fatal flaw: it was too costly to turn a profit in shale. His quest was to find a way to liberate the gas and save his company—and, perhaps, the world.

In 1981, Mitchell drilled his first fracked well in the Barnett Shale, the C. W. Slay No. 1. It lost money. Year after year, Mitchell continued drilling in the Barnett; he sank $250 million into this venture, hoping to formulate a cheaper and more effective fracking formula. Seventeen years later, Mitchell's company was in real trouble. His shareholders had begun to think he was a crank—the company was heavily in debt, and its share price had plunged from thirty dollars to ten. And yet Mitchell kept drilling one unprofitable well after another.

To cut costs, one of Mitchell's engineers, Nick Steinsberger, began tinkering with the fracking-fluid formula. He reduced the quantity of gels and chemicals, making the liquid more watery, and added a cheap lubricant, polyacrylamide, which is used in the manufacture of face creams and soft contact lenses. The resulting "slick water"—aided by a dusting of sand for the proppant—worked beautifully. It also cut the cost of fracking by more than two-thirds.

Mitchell combined this new formula with horizontal drilling techniques that had been developed offshore; once you bored deep enough to reach a deposit, you could steer the bit through the oil- or gas-bearing seam, a far more efficient means of recovery than just going straight down. In 1988, after about three hundred attempts, Mitchell's company finally made a profit on a fracked well in the Barnett, the S. H. Griffin No. 4. The shale revolution was under way. The same fracking innovations that Mitchell had pioneered in gas were almost immediately applied to oil.

For the third time in Texas history, the state transformed the energy business in ways that would shake economies and stir political quarrels all over the globe. In July 2008, oil prices had reached an all-time peak, $145.31, but the frackers were just getting started. By 2010, there were more than fourteen thousand wells in the Barnett alone, and the economic formula of past Texas booms held: a sudden fortune, a glut, a crash in prices. By January 2016, oil had fallen to less than $30 a barrel.

"We're back where we were in 1931," Robert Bryce, an author and journalist who writes frequently about the energy business, told me. "Texas drillers are once again determining the price of the marginal barrel in the world market."

"Two things are going on," Mack Fowler, an

oilman and philanthropist in Houston, told me, as he laid out several graphs for my education. The first showed the U.S. production of crude oil. In 1970 American oil production reached nearly ten million barrels a day; that summit was followed by a long, slow slide, decade after decade, touching bottom in 2008 at little more than five million barrels a day. The decline was marked by oil embargoes, price shocks, gas lines, shifting geopolitical alliances, wars in the Middle East, and the fear of the world economy being held captive to oil states that were often intensely anti-American. Then, around the time Barack Obama was elected president, something startling happened. U.S. production shot back up, approaching its all-time high. On the graph, it looked like a flagpole. "In the span of five years, we go from 5.5 million barrels a day to 9.5 million, almost doubling the U.S. output," Fowler said. It was the fastest growth in oil production ever seen. The difference was fracking and horizontal drilling techniques.

Five thousand energy-related companies make their home in Houston, the world's energy capital, and the effect of the crash in prices caused by the shale oil boom was evident in the slowdown in home sales, empty office buildings, and diminished traffic on the freeways. One Houston restaurant in the storied River Oaks neighborhood, Ouisie's Table, began offering a three-course meal each Wednesday night pegged to the price of a barrel of oil—when I visited in the spring of 2016, it was about $38. At oil's peak in June 2014, that meal might have cost $115. Between January 2015 and December 2016, more than a hundred U.S. oil and gas producers declared bankruptcy, half of them in Texas. That doesn't count the financial impact on the pipeline, storage, servicing, and shipping companies that depend on the energy business, and the colossal debt—$74 billion so far, much of it unsecured—that these failures leave behind.

Recently, I drove to North Texas to visit the well that started the revolution, the S. H. Griffin No. 4. It stands amid a little community of pre-fab homes and tidy brick bungalows, marking the extended reach of the Fort Worth suburbs. The town used to be called Clark, but a decade ago the mayor made a deal with a satellite network to provide ten years of free basic service to the two hundred residents in return for renaming the town after the company, using all capital letters, as in the company logo. Satellite dishes still sit atop many houses there, and even though the agreement has expired, the town's name remains—DISH.

This part of Texas is flat grassland dotted with scrubby mesquite. You see a lot of heavy industry associated with pipelines and drilling. Tanker trucks, which carry the millions of gallons of water required to frack a well, and tractor trailers known as SandCans, which haul silica to the site, have worn down the roads. Each drilling rig is huge and arrives disassembled, in a dozen truckloads of parts. There's also the four-inch metal pipe for the hole, which comes in thirty-foot lengths weighing six hundred pounds apiece; the concrete to encase the pipe; and the carbon-steel transmission pipes, between two and three feet in diameter, that transport the gas to storage containers. About 1,200 truck deliveries are needed for every well that is fracked.

Before the fracking comes the drilling. In the Barnett, holes go down about six thousand to eight thousand feet, substantially below the water table. Once the desired depth is reached, the drill slowly bends until it becomes horizontal, for as much as another ten thousand feet.

There is a science-fiction quality to the fracking process. Several tubes, called perforating guns, are snaked to the end of the well bore. The guns contain explosives that rupture the surrounding strata. Meanwhile, on the surface, twenty or so trucks line up on either side of the well. Pipes and hoses emanating from the trucks connect to a metal apparatus known as a manifold, which looks like a giant alien insect. A mighty sound suddenly erupts as the trucks begin pumping eight hundred gallons of fluid and proppant a minute into the manifold and down the well, opening up fresh microfractures in the shale. The process is repeated again and again until the entire horizontal plane of the well has been blasted open. It takes about a month to bring a well into production.

The S. H. Griffin No. 4 is in a grassy field inside a cage of chain-link fencing. It looks small and inert on the surface, and few neighbors seem to appreciate its historic significance. Unlike an oil well, there is no pump jack. Instead, the well is capped by what is known in the industry as a "Christmas tree"—a bunch of pipes and valves that control the flow of gas and direct the emissions into olive-green condensate tanks.

On the northern horizon, there was a cloud of black smoke, perhaps from an oil fire or a gas flare.

Fracking is a dark bounty. It has created enormous wealth for some. The flood of natural gas has lowered world energy costs and blunted the influence of traditional oil economies, such as Saudi Arabia and Russia. It has also despoiled communities and created enduring environmental hazards. As in many Texas towns where fracked wells have become commonplace, the citizens of DISH were anxious. In 2010, the little town paid $15,000 for an air-quality study. It found elevated amounts of benzene, a carcinogen, and other harmful chemicals, but not at levels that are known to endanger health. "If you drew a circle of a mile around my house, there were probably two hundred wells inside it," the former mayor, Calvin Tillman, told me. His children started getting nosebleeds when gassy odors were present. "One of my boys got a nosebleed that was all over his hands," Tillman recalled. "There was blood dripping down the walls. It looked like a murder scene. The next morning my wife said, 'That's it.'" They sold their house at a loss and moved to a community that is not on the Barnett Shale. The nosebleeds went away. (Since then, additional emission controls have been installed on the wells around DISH.)

The frackers advanced fifteen miles northeast, to the city of Denton. It is now thought to be the most heavily fracked city in the country. Wells have been drilled near schools and hospitals, and on the campus of the University of North Texas. In 2008, multiple earthquakes were recorded in the area, and according to a study conducted at Southern Methodist University, in Dallas, more than two hundred quakes have followed. The study concluded that the quakes have most likely been caused by the 1.7 billion barrels of wastewater that have been pumped into the region's 167 "injection" wells, which are used to dispose of fracking fluids. Even after environmental activists recorded twelve earthquakes over a twenty-four-hour period in and around Irving, where Exxon-Mobil is headquartered, in January 2015, energy executives and state regulators maintained that the earthquakes were a natural phenomenon.

"I started sounding the alarm pretty early," Sharon Wilson, who once worked in the energy industry, told me. In 2008, she sold the mineral rights on a small horse ranch that she owned in Wise County. "My air turned brown and my water turned black," she said. "I moved to Denton, thinking that my family would have some level of safety there." As she was unpacking, she noticed a well being drilled across the street from a nearby city park.

George Mitchell had been reluctant to admit that the fracking revolution that he unleashed had damaging consequences for the environment. "He was caught off guard by the backlash," his son Todd, a geologist, recalls. Todd informed his father that, although natural gas caused less air pollution than coal, industrial leakages of natural gas—especially of methane, a potent greenhouse gas—could render it no better than coal in terms of global warming. Mitchell also came to appreciate the damage caused by the industrialization of the landscape in communities subjected to intensive drilling. In 2012, the year before he died, he and New York City mayor Michael Bloomberg coauthored an op-ed for **The Washington Post**, arguing for increased regulation. "The rapid expansion of fracking has invited legitimate concerns about its impact on water, air and climate—concerns that the industry has attempted to gloss over," they wrote. "Safely fracking natural gas can mean healthier communities, a cleaner environment and a reliable domestic energy supply." Mitchell expressed himself more succinctly to his son-in-law Perry Lorenz, an Austin developer. "These damn cowboys will wreck the world to get an extra one percent" of profit, Mitchell said. "You got to sit on them." Unfortunately, Mitchell's plea has gone largely unheeded in Texas.

Sharon Wilson began volunteering in Denton for Earthworks, a national environmental organization with a focus on accountability in the oil and gas industry. Earthworks joined forces with a local organization, the Denton Drilling Awareness Group. Their campaign led, in November 2014, to a ban on fracking in the city limits. "It should send a signal to the industry that if the people in Texas—where fracking was invented—can't live with it nobody can," Wilson said at the time.

In short order, the state legislature, which is slavishly devoted to the oil-and-gas industry, passed a law prohibiting any such ban. Now cities in Texas have almost no recourse when frackers move in. There are three hundred wells in Denton already, and a third of the landmass of the city has been platted for future wells, now that the legislature has given the green light. "People think there are health consequences," Ed Soph, who used to teach jazz studies at the university, told me. "Kids were getting asthma. There were nosebleeds and headaches. The silica coated the neighborhood in dust. There was the odor, the noise. The kids couldn't play outside—they would get sick. It's that simple."

In October 2015, unable to stop fracking in the city, the Denton Municipal Electric utility announced its intention to derive 70 percent of its electricity from renewable resources by 2019, making it one of the cleanest energy providers in the state.

★

IF YOU HAVE ever flown over West Texas, above the region surrounding Midland and Odessa, you may have noticed something that looks like graph paper stretched across the flatland prairie for hundreds of square miles. This is the Permian Basin, and each intersection on the graph marks an oil or gas well. No region on earth has been more thoroughly drilled. Nearly 30 billion barrels of "sweet" low-sulfur oil known as West Texas Intermediate have come out of this field, roughly the size of South Dakota, and more than that remains. Because of the fracking revolution, it is once again the hottest oil and gas play in the world.

For the first time ever, the United States holds

more proved oil reserves than either Saudi Arabia or Russia. More than half of the U.S. total is in shale. New technology has decreased the cost of production to the point that fracking is becoming competitive with traditional means of extraction. Production in the Permian Basin has doubled in the last five years, to 2.4 million barrels a day, and the break-even cost of a fracked well has plummeted to as low as $25 a barrel. This has had dramatic consequences for more expensive means of production, such as coal-tar extraction and ocean drilling.

In September 2016, Apache Corporation, a Houston-based oil and gas exploration company, announced the discovery of an entirely new field in the Permian Basin, called Alpine High, estimated to contain 75 trillion cubic feet of gas and 3 billion barrels of oil. That was followed in November by an announcement from the U.S. Geological Survey that the Wolfcamp formation within the Permian Basin contains an estimated 20 billion barrels of oil—"the largest continuous oil accumulation that USGS has assessed in the United States to date," according to the agency—plus an additional 16 trillion cubic feet of natural gas. Within a decade, the assessment of newly discovered recoverable oil in the Permian Basin alone has increased by more than 800 percent. Moreover, productivity per well has shot up; according to Robert Bryce, the amount of oil produced by a new well in the Permian stayed flat from 2007 to 2013, at about one hundred barrels per day. But from 2013 to 2016—while the rig count was falling dramatically—the productivity of a new well rose to five hundred barrels a day, a fivefold increase in three years. Multiply that rate of productivity by the newly discovered oil, and factor in the declining cost of recovery, and you will have a rough calculation of the future of energy.

The little town of Balmorhea lies within the vast Apache field, as does one of the most glorious spring-fed swimming holes in the state, an oasis more than an acre in size, which attracts tourists from all over the world. Aside from the natural beauty, the pool is home to two endangered species of fish. Locals are concerned that the water table will be contaminated by leakage from a disposal well, or an earthquake (the town happens to sit on a geological fault line). Apache, which maintains that its methods are "safe and proven," promises not to drill within the town limits or beneath the state park that contains the swimming hole, but it's hard to imagine that there won't be considerable environmental consequences from the five thousand wells envisioned to extract all that oil.

Those costs have to be measured by other benefits—the decent jobs that will come to the region, for instance, and the taxable income that will support city services. There are also undeniable geopolitical advantages in reducing American dependence on foreign oil and lowering the cost of energy. Because of fracking, there is an abundance of natural gas, which is killing demand for coal, a trend that the Trump regime is unlikely to be able to stop. Gas burns far cleaner than coal, and as a result, greenhouse gas emissions in the United States are at their lowest point in a quarter century.

Texas is the only state to have its own electrical grid, which was created largely to avoid federal regulations. The state invested $7 billion in high-voltage transmission lines to carry wind power through the shrub-covered plains eastward toward the cities. Because of the intense energy needs of the oil and gas business involving oil refineries and petrochemical plants, Texas uses far more electricity than any other state—67 percent more than second-place California. And yet electricity in Texas is cheaper than the national average, in some places actually free at night. That's because Texas gets about 17 percent of its electricity from wind power, and wind generally blows more at night, when demand is lower. The plains and caprock mesas of West Texas, as well as the coastal region south of Galveston, are lined with regiments of wind turbines. They are so heavily subsidized by the federal government that the wind-energy producers sometimes pay companies to take the energy off their hands in order to receive their federal tax credits. On some days, wind satisfies half of the state's electricity demand. In the first quarter of 2017, wind generation accounted for 23 percent of the power generated in the state. In October, Jeff Bezos, the founder of Amazon, broke a bottle of Champagne atop a three-hundred-foot turbine to inaugurate a vast new wind farm in Scurry County, in northwest Texas, which will provide another million megawatt hours a year to the grid. Solar energy is also growing, but has been slower to catch on, despite abundant and intense sunshine. Austin gets nearly a fourth of its power from renewable sources and aims to double that in ten years. Georgetown, just north of Austin and one of the most conservative suburbs in the state, already gets all of its electricity from renewable sources.

Nick Fowler, the younger brother of Mack Fowler, the oilman I met in Houston, operates a petrochemical plant in Odessa. Nick is a ruddy man whose strikingly white hair and moustache look like a disguise. He is what is known as a "downstream" oilman. Upstream are the people who find the oil and the money to drill. Midstream are the pipeline operators and people who move the product to refineries and to market. At the end of the stream, Nick makes a kind of plastic that is a by-product of the refining of gasoline. "We take a hydrocarbon and turn it into a polymer," he explained, as he showed me around the plant, with its inscrutable towers and a maze of pipes and gangplanks. I remembered as a child seeing plants like this lit up at night on the flat horizon like some kind of **Mad Max** skyscrapers.

Nick handed me a sample of his end product, a malleable glob, which in the trade is called a "potato," although it more closely resembles a pregnant ravioli. "It's a form of polypropylene used for hot-melt adhesives," he told me. I recognized it then as the same substance I use in a hot-glue gun. When melted, the potato becomes spreadable. "The biggest use is in the assembly of non-woven materials, like in feminine hygiene products, disposable diapers, panty liners, adult incontinence," Nick said. "Our adhesives hold the layers together. Diapers are a very complicated structure."

Unfortunately, on the day I visited, the plant was on the blink. As he drove me through the facility, Nick rolled down the window and stopped to talk to his three engineers. A train car was waiting to take the next shipment of polymer to market, and who knows how many fortunes were being lost, but the engineers were unfazed. Actually, they all seemed a little amused and excited. They had an interesting problem to work on. The lead engineer, J. J. DeCair, speculated about what might be wrong, possibly a water leak in a condenser. Nick drove on, praising his crew. J.J. was self-taught, "an American genius of the same ilk as Wilbur and Orville Wright." It takes a lot of ingenuity to run a petrochemical plant. Here they were, in one of the most desolate parts of Texas, on a hundred-degree day, having a pretty great time.

Later that afternoon, Nick drove me to the Odessa Country Club for dinner. On the highway next to a strip club there was a large lot where unused oil rigs were stored. Every Friday at noon, Baker Hughes, a giant oil-field-services company in Houston, releases a "rig count": a measure of how many new wells are being drilled in the U.S. It is the most closely watched barometer of the drilling industry's health. On that Friday evening in June 2016, when Nick and I went to dinner, only 421 rigs were being put to use in the U.S., less than a tenth of the 4,500 rigs that were at work in December 1981, the highest count since records began to be kept. In the lot that Fowler and I passed, there were 47 unused rigs lined up in parallel ranks. "They cost fifteen to eighteen million dollars apiece," Nick observed. He estimated the total investment of the idle rigs to be as much as $850 million.

We sat in the empty dining room watching a storm blow in across the flayed landscape. Golfers raced into the clubhouse as lightning lit up the giant black sky like war. The rain itself was paltry, typical of the noisy, uncharitable storms of this part of Texas.

Through the picture window, the idle rigs on the horizon, illuminated by the blinding flashes, looked like ideal lightning attractors. There have long been dreams of harvesting the electrical power of Texas's many lightning strikes. In 2006, a company called Alternative Energy Holdings announced its intent to create lightning farms, and it actually set up an experimental lightning-capture tower in Houston, where there are lots of electrical storms and a huge demand for power. Nothing came of it, but I was reminded of the scene in **Back to the Future** where Marty McFly has to capture energy from a lightning bolt on the clock tower in order to power his DeLorean back to present time.

I asked Nick if he ever thought of leaving Odessa. "Only on mornings when the sun rises in the east," he admitted. "When the weather's nice, it's delightful, although it's still not very attractive." On the other hand, he liked being in a place where "the people at the laundry know your name." Mainly, he was comforted by the 210 good jobs he provided.

Fracking saved the economy of the Permian Basin, Nick observed, but it wasn't going to last forever. When he and Mack were boys, their parents took them on vacation to Colorado, and they stopped in Leadville, headquarters of the great silver boom in the 1880s. Leadville then sported a dozen theaters, including the grand Tabor Opera House, where Oscar Wilde and Harry Houdini performed. The lobby floor of a hotel was paved with silver dollars. After Denver, it was the largest city in the state. Only a few thousand people live there now. It's a meager tourist stop, gateway to the gold-mining ghost towns in the mountains. At best, Nick said, the Permian Basin has another twenty-five years before it follows the same path. "Fortunes change. People move on. How can it be any different in Odessa?"

★

I REMEMBER after the great bust in the 1980s there were bumper stickers reading "Please, God, Send Me One More Oil Boom. This Time, I Promise Not to Piss It Away." That bust lasted for nearly twenty years.

Societies that depend on natural resources tend to have certain inherent problems. The centralization of wealth—whether from oil, coal, diamonds, or any extractable commodity—often leads to corruption and authoritarianism. Venezuela, Saudi

Arabia, and Louisiana are primary examples. In such a society the economy rises and falls by a single measure. Where money comes out of the ground, luck and a willingness to take risks are the main factors that determine one's future, not talent or education or hard work. Money so easily acquired comes to seem well deserved, because those who have it must be either uniquely perspicacious or divinely favored.

In good times, a kind of forgetfulness falls over the land. It's easy to make money when the price of oil skyrockets and building cranes loom over the cities like praying mantises and the malls are jammed and you can't get a dinner reservation. Then the reckoning arrives.

The central fact about boom societies is that they inevitably go bust. The collapse of oil prices, beginning in the early 1980s, then falling into an abyss in 1986, put an end to one of the most expansive periods in Texas history, bringing down the savings-and-loan industry and puncturing the real-estate bubble that had created so much illusory wealth.

In the Age of Money, Roberta and I watched many of our friends sending their children to private schools named Saint This or Saint That. They spent their evenings going over architectural plans, and generally lived life as it is glimpsed in magazine ads. Occasionally, we made the mistake of going out to dinner with them. We spent more on the tip than Roberta and I would ordinarily spend on a meal.

A few years into the decline, I was serving on a jury in Travis County, which includes Austin. During a recess, I walked out of the courthouse to get some air, and there was a mob of people on the steps, pushing themselves forward to grab a paper that was being handed out. I had gotten used to signs of economic distress by then. Department stores were shuttered. Vacant skyscrapers were called "see-throughs." Out-of-state interests bought up our newspapers and banks, so that we lost control of our sources of information and finance. Now Serving Breakfast banners foretold the next restaurant about to close. One of my neighbors, an engineer who worked for the city, lost his house and moved into his Volkswagen van. But I had never seen foreclosed properties for sale on the courthouse steps.

My father, who was a retired banker by this time, watched many of his friends and colleagues in Dallas go through bankruptcy. They had been some of the most respected people in the city, the money men who had raised Dallas fifty stories into the air. One of Daddy's friends, Jim Toler, a jovial former college football star, was the mayor of Garland, near Dallas. At Christmas, we always got a burlap bag of pecans, inscribed Nuts to You from Jim Toler. He had made a fortune on a crazily speculative suburban condominium development along the I-30 corridor. Some of the properties were sold as many as eight times in a day, starting at $100,000 in the morning and winding up at a million bucks by nightfall. There was a lot of fraud involved. Savings-and-loan associations, once known as "thrifts" because they were supposed to be more cautious financial institutions, had been deregulated in the Carter administration, and they became the piggy banks for the speculators. They were making loans on properties at 110 percent of the grossly inflated values, meaning that buyers, instead of putting money down, got a cash bonus when they signed the loan. You'd walk away with thousands of dollars in your pocket. The concept spread like a virus, infecting S&Ls all over the Southwest. When the scheme collapsed, more than seven hundred financial institutions in the country were shuttered. Toler was eventually convicted on forty-one counts of conspiracy, racketeering, and bank fraud. Daddy used to visit him in prison.

Our former governor John Connally, who had been secretary of the Treasury under President Nixon, suffered a humiliating bankruptcy auction. He sat gallantly with his wife, Nellie, over the four days it took to dispose of their luxurious possessions, including his ceremonial saddles, extensive gun collection, Persian rugs, and even a Santa Claus cookie jar. At the end, Nellie salvaged a cardboard box so that Big John could have a bedside table for his alarm clock.

Texas was riveted by the Connallys' plight, but they were merely the grand marshals of the bankruptcy parade, which included Denton Cooley, the great heart surgeon in Houston, who owed $100 million on his unprofitable real-estate holdings; the Hunt brothers—William Herbert, Nelson Bunker, and Lamar—who were $1.5 billion in debt, after two of them tried to corner the market in silver; and the owner of the Dallas Cowboys, Clint Murchison Jr., who died broke. Even Willie Nelson was wiped out, owing nearly $32 million in back taxes, one of the largest individual tax liabilities ever generated by the IRS. The government seized almost everything he owned, except his guitar, which he hid at his daughter's house. That still didn't pay the tax collector, so he made a record to pay off what he could. It was called **The IRS Tapes: Who'll Buy My Memories?**

One day in 1989, while our children were in Saturday-morning music classes in Austin, Roberta was talking to some of the other parents about real estate. We had invested in a little rent house with a friend, paying $62,500 for it only four years before. Now it was worth half that. Roberta asked one of the mothers about the house she had had for sale for months. "Well, we deeded it back to the bank," the woman said. "It cost us a hundred thousand dollars, but at least it's off our backs." Then another mother asked, "Oh, how do you do that?" It turned out that every single parent in the group was thinking the same thing. They were all looking for some relief from their crushing financial burdens.

I knew about the fall of financial titans. I had read about the sleazy dealings of some of our most prominent political figures, and the corruption and mismanagement of our financial institutions. But when the bill for these misdeeds came due, it was paid mainly through the suffering of ordinary people. For some, the downturn passed by unnoticed. That same mother who told Roberta about deeding her house back to the bank recalled that the very next day her son was picked up for a concert by a friend in a Rolls-Royce with mink-covered seats.

I looked around at the legacy of the great oil-fueled boom of the 1970s and early 1980s that had come to such a crashing end. Where were the cultural institutions, the schools, the public art? What I saw instead were cruddy strip shopping centers, garish beach communities, the ugly sprawl of car lots and franchise chicken joints and prefab warehouses that issued out of the heart of every city and crawled along our highways like poison vines. Texas in the wake of the boom was revealed to be a civilization built on greed and impermanence, a civilization that was here to take, not to give. It was odd, because Texans were always talking about how much they loved the state, but I wondered where was the evidence of that love.

I thought about what had brought us to this point. What was the source of the greed, the blunders, the bullheaded arrogance that had led to this monumental crack-up? It was clearly a culture that confused wealth with value, where every notable personality had to be a millionaire. Even during the downturn in the eighties, **Texas Monthly** published an annual review, called "The Texas 100," of the wealthiest Texans. To strike it rich is still the Texas dream, although the state has never been rich in the way that Maryland and Connecticut and other old money Eastern states are. Even Nebraska has more millionaires per capita than Texas. And yet, when people all over the world think of Texas, they still think of big money. You can tell the oil is gushing when they start selling those oversized dollars in the airport souvenir shops.

I considered leaving Texas then. I don't know why I didn't. But something important happened in the wake of that mighty crash. There was a stronger sense of community as people hunkered down. The national schadenfreude that greeted the downfall of the Texas economy was sobering. Our political and business leaders began to realize that the state couldn't compete without strong institutions and educated people. We had to diversify. Tolerance and openness were not notable Texas qualities, but they were vital for creating a resilient society in the modern world.

Maybe God, in His mercy, will spare Texas another oil boom.

# THREE

# Houston, We Have a Problem

On Thanksgiving morning my friend Steve and I hopped on our bikes again to go see the new African American history monument at the Texas capitol grounds in Austin. There are two bronze wings on the monument, with a frieze depicting the evolution and struggle of black Texans. On the far left stands Esteban the Moor, a slave who had been a part of Cabeza de Vaca's expedition. Esteban was the first black person in Texas and, according to Steve, likely the first Muslim in America. On top, there is a pair of freed slaves, one holding the torch of liberty and the other with a copy of the Emancipation Proclamation. On the day that the monument was unveiled, a small group calling themselves White Lives Matter protested the event, reminding everyone that the sentiments that led to civil war still resonate in some minds.

Nearby, in the gateway to the capitol grounds,

stands a massive Confederate shrine, topped by a statue of Jefferson Davis, the Confederate president. There is also a monument to John Bell Hood's Texas Brigade, one of the most valiant units in Robert E. Lee's army. Out of 4,400 men in the brigade, only 600 were still standing at the end of the war. A Confederate flag is inscribed in the shaft. Closer to the capitol building is a monument to Terry's Texas Rangers, who were the shock troops for the Battle of Shiloh and other significant engagements. On the building itself is a plaque, which was placed there in 1959, titled the Children of the Confederacy Creed. It pledges to honor the veterans and the ideals of the Confederacy, as well as "to study and teach the truths of history (one of the most important of which is that the war between the states was not a rebellion, nor was its underlying cause to sustain slavery)." That the state would dignify such lies by placing them on the capitol is shameful.

You can find Confederate monuments all over the state. In 2015, the University of Texas at Austin, bowing to student demands, removed a statue of Jefferson Davis from the campus, together with one of Woodrow Wilson. Then, in the middle of the night, on August 20, 2017, workers removed the remaining Confederate statues: Robert E. Lee, General Albert Sidney Johnston, and John Reagan, who served as the postmaster general for the

Confederacy. James Hogg, a progressive governor, who was the son of a Confederate general, was also taken down. The empty pedestals remain.

Steve and I both have ancestors who fought for the Confederacy. Steve's great-grandfather was a cavalry officer in Bradford's Regiment, assigned to guard Galveston against a federal invasion. He is thought to have been in the Second Battle of Sabine Pass, when the Yankees attempted to invade Texas in 1863. It was the most lopsided victory the Confederates enjoyed during that war. My great-grandfather on my mother's side, Robert L. Peacock, was injured at the Battle of Chancellorsville. I have the cane a fellow invalid carved for Sergeant Peacock while he was recovering, as well as his pardon, granted at Appomattox Court House. I keep his powder flask on my desk. On my bedroom wall, as a child, I had a portrait of General Lee on his revered gray mount, Traveller. The historical memory of the Confederacy, and the lingering legacy of racism and separatism, have always been a part of my consciousness. I went through my entire education in Texas public schools without a single black classmate. I still feel ashamed of the prejudices that I struggled to shed. As a young reporter, I covered the civil rights movement, which was, after the writing of the United States Constitution, the greatest triumph of democracy in our country's history. I had hoped that my generation would be the last to deal with racial discrimination, but hatred is a potent addiction.

Just inside the doors of the capitol building stand the marble statues of Stephen F. Austin, the entrepreneur who brought the first Anglo colonists to Texas, and Sam Houston, the first elected president of the republic. Both men were slaveholders, despite their stated opposition to the institution. Austin inherited the Texas project from his father, Moses Austin, who died of pneumonia shortly after gaining a grant to settle three hundred families in the portion of Mexican territory that was still mostly Indian country. Stephen was an unlikely frontiersman; he was short and slight, with curly hair and a fair complexion. He was better suited as a diplomat, and had it been up to him, Texas would have remained part of the Mexican nation. Although he was initially opposed to slavery, most of his colonists came from the South, and they insisted on the need for bondage. "The idea of seeing such a country as this overrun by a slave population almost makes me weep," Austin remarked. The colonists got around the fact that slavery was illegal in Mexico by having their slaves sign a document, before entering Texas, that they were indentured servants. They remained slaves in all but the law.

The statue of Houston looks like a Roman emperor, in buckskin, gazing into the middle distance, where destiny awaits. I much prefer the gargantuan version outside Huntsville, which is sixty-seven feet tall, depicting the old soldier with a cane, staring out at I-45. Inscribed on the bronze plaque is Houston's admonition to future Texas leaders that they should "govern wisely, and as little as possible."

★

ONE SPRING DAY I walked around Sam Houston Park, in Huntsville, with a group of rambunctious seventh graders from The Woodlands, who were on a field trip for their mandatory Texas history class. We peeked through the window of the "Steamboat House" at the bed where Houston died, on the evening of July 26, 1863, spurned by the Texas he had created after laboring to spare it the fate that secession would inevitably impose. The clock on the mantel had been stopped at 6:15 p.m., the hour of his death. The kids groaned when the docent explained the function of the chamber pot next to the bed.

Houston was a product of the populist revolt in America in the 1820s, a period that in many respects resembles our current era. A protégé of fellow Tennessean Andrew Jackson, the founder of the Democratic Party, Houston was elected to the U.S. House of Representatives in 1823, the same year that Jackson went to the Senate. Four years later, Houston was elected governor of Tennessee. He was a political star, ruled by the populist credo that the people are always right. At this point, one could easily have imagined a different path for him, one that would have led directly to the White House, following in Jackson's footsteps; certainly, many people expected as much from him. But a disastrous romance would change the course of Houston's life, and that of the nation.

A friend of mine, historian H. W. Brands, maintains that the founding of Texas was largely the result of the shocking divorce between Houston and his first wife, Eliza Allen, whom he had married in 1829. Houston was thirty-five, tall, handsome, vain, and powerful. Eliza was nineteen, refined, fashionable, and delicate. Eleven weeks after their wedding, Eliza returned without explanation to her parents' house. Houston resigned as governor, citing "sudden calamities." The mystery of their estrangement has never been solved. Houston threatened violence against anyone who cast doubt on Eliza's virtue. He is said to have told a friend that Eliza's parents had pushed her into the marriage, although she actually loved another man. "Cursed be the human fiends who force a woman to live with a man whom she does not love," Houston supposedly remarked.

Another theory suggests that Eliza recoiled at

the sight of Houston's disfigured body, which bore three nearly mortal wounds that he sustained in the Battle of Horseshoe Bend in 1814, as part of General Jackson's war against the Upper Creek Indians. Early in the battle, an arrow struck Houston in the thigh. He demanded that another soldier rip out the barbed shaft, which created a gaping hole. Jackson ordered him out of the fight, but Houston stumbled to his feet and assaulted the Indian breastworks, only to be shot twice, in the right shoulder and arm. The doctors decided he was certain to die, so they turned their attention to possible survivors. The next morning, when he was found still alive, the surprised surgeons finally treated him. The massive shoulder wound never actually healed, continuing to drain throughout his life.

After his marriage dissolved, Houston fled into Indian country to live with the Cherokees. They called him the Big Drunk. He became a Cherokee citizen and took a native wife. In 1832, like so many with shipwrecked ambitions, he headed to the Mexican colony of Texas to make a new start. Soon he found himself leading a kind of rebel mob that called itself an army. There was little chance that Houston's forces could defeat the larger, well-trained Mexican forces; but in April 1836, weeks after the Alamo fell, Houston caught the Mexicans napping at San Jacinto.

There is a painting in the Texas capitol of the surrender of Antonio López de Santa Anna. Houston is shown lying on the ground, leaning against a moss-draped live oak, his right ankle bandaged from a stray bullet wound that would render him permanently lame. The camp surgeon sits on his medical box at Houston's feet. Santa Anna, the greatest general in Mexico's history, and the most dominant political figure in his country (he would serve eleven terms as president), stands before Houston, hat in hand. He had fled the battle, carrying a box of chocolates, but somehow got unhorsed and was discovered the next day hiding in the grass, wearing the uniform of a private. Behind the dignitaries in the painting stands a white flag with a lone star in its center. That star would become a symbol of the Republic of Texas, and then of the state, representing its defiant sovereignty. The Texian soldiers, without uniforms, wear the rough clothes of frontiersmen. Some of them look ready to lynch the Mexican leader; indeed, one of them has a length of rope. The slaughter at the Alamo had been followed, three weeks later, by the execution of more than four hundred prisoners in Goliad, on Santa Anna's orders. "Remember the Alamo! Remember Goliad!" was the cry of Houston's bedraggled army as they massacred the Mexicans in turn at San Jacinto. It was all over in eighteen minutes.

There's another story that Texans tell about the capture of Santa Anna, which has long been regarded as mere legend. Recent scholarship, however, makes it more likely that Houston's victory at San Jacinto came about in part because of the sly distraction on the part of a serving girl, Emily Morgan. "Why, historians ask, did Santa Anna choose an untenable encampment on the plains of San Jacinto, with the Texan Army in front of him and a bayou prohibiting his retreat?" Steve once wrote in **Texas Monthly**. "Why, on the afternoon of April 21, when he knew that Houston's forces were only half a mile away, was his army taking a siesta? The answer resounds through the ages: Santa Anna was in a hurry to get into the sack with Emily Morgan." Whether the legend is true or not—and even Steve has doubts—she is memorialized by the Emily Morgan Hotel, next to the Alamo.

There is a lesson to be drawn from Houston's career as a populist leader. He would twice be elected president of the Republic of Texas, which his decisive victory had secured. After Texas entered the Union, on December 29, 1845, Houston became one of the first two U.S. senators from the state of Texas. He clearly envisioned the disaster that the proposed Southern Confederacy would inflict on the nation and on Texas: "I see my beloved South go down in the unequal contest, in a sea of blood and smoking ruin." In 1860, on the eve of the Civil War, he was elected governor as a Unionist, but the secessionists were more powerful. Houston's faith in populism as a force for progress was shattered. "Are we ready to sell reality for a phantom?" Houston vainly asked, as propagandists and demagogues fanned the clamor for secession with deluded visions of victory. To those who demanded that he join the Confederacy, Houston responded, "I refuse to take this oath . . . I love Texas too well to bring civil strife and bloodshed upon her." Houston was evicted as governor, and the bloodshed came.

★

HOUSTON'S NAMESAKE CITY was founded in 1836, months after his victory at San Jacinto. Two New York real-estate-developer brothers, Augustus and John K. Allen, commissioned Gale Borden Jr., a publisher and surveyor who would later invent condensed milk, to lay out a grand metropolis in the lowlands around Buffalo Bayou. They named the swampy new town after the hero of San Jacinto, but the brand was about the only thing to commend the place for settlement. "Houston (pronounced Hewston) has a reputation of being an unhealthy residence," Frederick Law Olmsted, a New Yorker, disdainfully remarked on his trip through the state in 1854. He took note of the slave markets and the numerous venomous snakes. "Alligator holes are an additional excitement, the unsuspicious traveler suddenly sinking through the treacherous surface, and sometimes falling victim, horse and all, to the hideous jaws of the reptile."

After Spindletop hit, Houston discovered itself as the capital of an oil empire. By 1913, there were a dozen oil companies located in the city, including Humble Oil, the predecessor of ExxonMobil. "Houston was a one-industry town," Stephen Klineberg, the founding director of Rice University's Kinder Institute for Urban Research, said over coffee at a French bakery. "We did oil the way Detroit did cars."

Klineberg has been conducting an annual survey of the city for the last thirty-five years. When the study began, oil and gas accounted for more than 80 percent of the city's economy; now, it's half that. The medical center alone—the largest medical complex in the world—has more than 100,000 workers, in fifty-nine institutions, occupying an area larger than Chicago's Loop. Houston's port is the second-busiest in the country. The city added more than 700,000 jobs between 2000 and 2014, almost twice the number of jobs created in New York City. "People complain about the weather and the flying cockroaches, but the latest survey shows that eighty-one percent say life in Houston is excellent or good, even with the downturn," Klineberg told me. "They say that Houston is a crappy place to visit but a wonderful place to live."

When I was growing up in Dallas, we looked upon Houston as a blue-collar cousin, a fine place to go if you liked country music and barbecue. That's still true, but Houston is now rated (by **The Washington Post**) as one of the five best restaurant cities in the United States. It has an excellent opera, and claims to have more theater space than any city except New York—achievements that mark Houston's aspiration to be an international cultural center. "There was this ad in **Texas Monthly**," Lynn Wyatt, the long-reigning queen of the Houston social scene, told me. "It said, 'Houston is'—what's that awful word? **Funky**. It said, 'Houston is **funky**.' I called them up at once! I told them, Houston's not **funky**! You make it sound like Austin or some such place. Houston is a world-class city."

★

I SPENT SOME TIME in the early 1980s writing about the space program, so I hung around the Johnson Space Center, which is in the Clear Lake area of Houston. A massive Saturn V rocket—the kind that took the astronauts to the moon—

reclines on its side at the entryway, like some fallen colossus of an ancient world.

After the glamour days of the race to the moon, the space program had become more prosaic, more workaday, more lunchboxy. I remember seeing the **Columbia**—the first of the shuttle fleet to fly into space—as it passed over our house, in 1981, piggybacked atop a 747, on its way to Cape Canaveral. It was exciting and pitiable at the same instant. **That's** a rocket ship?

A new generation of astronauts had arrived, and the tone of the space center changed. For one thing, they weren't all white men. Franklin Chang-Diaz was a plasma physicist from MIT; he was born in Costa Rica and was part Chinese. He showed up on his first day at the Johnson Space Center driving a rusted-out Renault sedan, its doors held shut with ropes, and occupied the same spot where the legendary Wally Schirra, one of the original Mercury Seven, once parked his Maserati. There were still some dashing test pilots among the new group, drawn from the military ranks, like Charles Bolden, a cheerful Marine who would one day become the first black administrator of NASA. Sally Ride, a physicist, was the first American woman in space. Judith Resnik, the first American Jewish astronaut, was a classical pianist and an electrical engineer. Ronald McNair got his doctorate in laser physics from MIT; he had a black belt in karate and played the saxophone. What really impressed me was that he had integrated the library in Lake City, South Carolina, where he grew up, refusing to leave until he was allowed to check out books. His mother and the police were called, but he was finally allowed to become the first black child to borrow books. He was nine years old.

I was a little infatuated with the whole group. They were bright and fit; you could see them running around the track like ponies. There was an emergency-room surgeon from Murfreesboro, Tennessee, Rhea Seddon, who took me to lunch in her Corvette. She was also a jet pilot and probably had other skills, such as speaking Mandarin or playing the xylophone. As we raced down NASA Road One, I looked over at Dr. Seddon, with her long blond tresses tossed about like an advertisement for Clairol, and an unfamiliar thought leaped into my mind: **I want to have your baby.**

I quickly pushed that aside.

I wrote a profile of one of the early women in the astronaut corps, Mary Cleave, a diminutive woman with an infectious cackle and gray-green eyes that were twice as sharp as normal—pilot's eyes. But her specialty was sanitary engineering, one area that the geniuses at NASA had never really figured out. The first American in space,

Alan Shepard, had to pee in his space suit. After that, there were diapers and a "fecal collection bag" that fit over the hips like a pair of Bermuda shorts. Most astronauts in the early days forced themselves to wait until they got home to defecate. The first true space potty featured a seat that the astronaut could strap himself into. A fan created differential air pressure to simulate gravity, and air jets directed the feces away from the anus. For urination, there was a funnel that fit over the penis. But the potty still needed to be modified to accommodate women. And that's where Mary came in.

She joined the astronaut corps in May 1980; a year later, she got to see the first launch of **Columbia**, which went flawlessly, except for the fact that the potty broke. When my profile of her came out in **Texas Monthly**, Mary was on the cover, in her astronaut suit, with that giant globed space helmet in her hand. I blithely signed a form obligating me to pay for the helmet if it broke as I ferried it over to the photographer. Half a million dollars.

The astronauts represented the best of America, it seemed to me. They were marvelously accomplished but surprisingly modest; serious but upbeat; and of course their courage was unquestioned. Many of them had sacrificed high-paying positions at universities or in medical practice to take a government job at a fraction of their previous earnings.

To a person they were motivated by grand visions of moving humanity into space.

My friend Steve had also covered the space program, so we decided to write a screenplay. It was called "Moonwalker," about one of the old Apollo guys who gets back into the program and falls in love with a new woman astronaut. Like so many Hollywood scripts, it was always on the verge of getting made. We went to Cape Canaveral to watch the launch of STS-9, along with our friend Gregory Curtis, then the editor of **Texas Monthly**. For each of us, it was one of the most thrilling sights we had ever witnessed, despite the fact that the stands were three miles away from the launch pad. "What had been the hazy blip on the horizon suddenly began spewing flames so intense that even at such a distance, you wondered if watching them would damage your eyes," Greg later wrote. "Huge, roiling clouds of water vapor, pure white, billowed up from the base of the rocket, and then the sound arrived."

The sonic shock made the ground tremble and knocked shorebirds out of the sky. The spacecraft finally tore itself free of the earth and climbed into the sky, executing a roll that I thought must be dangerous but was of course a natural part of the launch. "When it finally disappeared into the clouds," Greg wrote, "you continued to watch, with all your nerves revving."

To our dismay, Steve and I discovered that we had both applied to be the first "journalist in space," a program that NASA had cooked up to generate public interest, which had plummeted once space flight became routine. I was jealous of Steve, who I was certain would be chosen, and he was jealous of me. We made a deal: whichever one of us actually did get picked would place the other's latest book into orbit.

Before the journalist in space, however, there was a teacher in space. I had suggested to Roberta that she might want to apply, but she was nonplussed by the idea. Christa McAuliffe, a social studies teacher from Concord, New Hampshire, got the nod.

Steve and I were working on a rewrite of "Moonwalker" on January 28, 1986, when Roberta came down to my office. She had the flu and wasn't teaching that day. "Did you hear about the **Challenger?**" she asked. The twenty-fifth space shuttle mission had exploded. The flight lasted seventy-three seconds, then it simply blew to pieces. Weirdly, the announcer continued to broadcast the velocity and distance, even as the capsule, containing those noble lives, fell into the Atlantic Ocean. At least some of the astronauts may have been alive until the capsule hit the water, at more than two hundred miles per hour.

Among the dead were Christa McAuliffe, the

first teacher in space; Judith Resnik, the Jewish American piano-playing physicist; and Ronald McNair, the saxophonist and physicist. They named the library he integrated in South Carolina after him.

★

HOUSTON'S FAMOUS ASTRODOME was for sale, so I hurried over to size up the property, arguably the most historic building in Texas aside from the Alamo. No city in America may aspire to greatness without sports teams, but the tropical heat and torrential rains played havoc with Houston's mighty ambition. In 1965, Roy Hofheinz, a former mayor who was called the Judge because of his brief tenure as a county official, opened what was then called the Harris County Domed Stadium. The former "Eighth Wonder of the World" has been home at various times to the Houston Astros, the Houston Oilers, the Houston Rockets, and the Houston Livestock Show and Rodeo, but when I visited it had been sitting empty for eight years, after all the teams ran off to newer venues and the fire department jerked the venue's certificate of occupancy. It was a little sad, honestly, to see this noble landmark out on the streets, as it were. The city had turned its back on the iconic building that made civilization in Houston—and

Texas at large—seem somewhat plausible in the first place.

Judge Hofheinz was an ideal expression of the Texas go-getter. He gained control of the Colt .45s, a National League expansion team, which he renamed the Astros. The team had only agreed to come to Houston because of the Judge's promise to build a covered stadium. Hofheinz claimed to have been inspired by the Roman Colosseum, which in ancient days was shaded by an awning during matinee gladiatorial contests. If the Romans could do it, why not the Houstonians? But shade wasn't enough for the Judge. He set out to construct the world's largest air-conditioned room.

Such a structure had never been built before. Overheated Texans used to cool their churches and restaurants by placing fans over tubs of ice. Then, in 1923, the Second National Bank became the first air-conditioned building in Houston. By the 1950s, Houston laid claim to being "the air-conditioning capital of the world," which included the PlazAmericas, the first fully air-conditioned mall. But the building of the Astrodome was a civic leap of faith. It still stands imposingly beside the freeway, "like the working end of a gigantic roll-on deodorant," as Texas author Larry McMurtry noted with his unsparing eye. Hofheinz moved into an apartment inside the dome that occupied seven floors of the right-field bleachers and was equipped with a chapel, a bowling alley, a shooting gallery, and a private bar called the Tipsy Tavern. Bob Hope observed the decor and pronounced it "early King Farouk." Hofheinz dressed the stadium ushers—attractive young women called Spacettes—in quilted golden outfits suitable for the frigid interior climate. The grounds crew, who wore orange jumpsuits with space helmets, were called Earthmen. "It was like having your own planet," the Judge's widow, Mary Frances Hofheinz, later recalled.

Another county judge, Ed Emmett, inherited the Astrodome dilemma when he took office in 2007. Most Houstonians said they'd prefer to have the old stadium torn down and made into green space, and they decisively rejected a bond proposal of $213 million to convert the structure into a multi-use event facility. However, Judge Emmett decided it didn't make financial sense to raze the Astrodome. "It's solid," he told me, as we walked around the vast interior. "When Hurricane Ike came through [in 2008], every other structure in this area was damaged, but not this place. Plus, it's already paid for."

Emmett turned to the public for suggestions. About a hundred ideas were submitted, some scribbled on bar napkins: make it a parking garage, a ski slope, a science museum. One suggestion was to flood the arena, which is two stories below ground level, and reenact naval battles. Another group proposed turning it into a gigantic movie studio. "None of these ideas came with any money attached," Emmett noted, as we stood in what had once been shallow center field, near the spot where Muhammad Ali knocked out Cleveland Williams in 1966. Judy Garland, Elvis Presley, Billie Jean King v. Bobby Riggs—there's an endless roster of memories here. I have a friend who scattered his father's ashes on the playing field. Except for a brief birthday party for the stadium on its fiftieth anniversary in 2015, the last time the public was admitted was in 2005, when refugees from Hurricane Katrina took shelter here.

Emmett favored making the Astrodome's 350,000 square feet of floor space into a giant indoor park, or else simply providing a space for festivals and special events. It's a minimal plan, he admits. "We could have the state archery contest here," he said. "The Texas horseshoe tournament. I've also got ties to the cricket community." It seemed a long way from opening day, April 9, 1965, when the Astros beat the Yankees 2–1, and Mickey Mantle hit the stadium's first home run.

I got a tour in a golf cart with a flashlight

through the home team's old locker room, where the hot tub was still intact. Judge Hofheinz also used to prowl around late at night in his golf cart, exploring his creation. The playing field was now given over to storage, much of it from the larger, sleeker NRG Stadium next door. There were stacks of stadium chairs, turnstiles, and a hut for a parking-lot attendant. Two hundred feet above us was the roof with its geometric plastic tiles. When the stadium opened, there was reasonable concern that outfielders wouldn't be able to see the ball, so someone stood on the catwalk overhead and dropped baseballs as Joe Morgan and Rusty Staub raced around struggling to catch them. To reduce the glare, the Lucite panels were painted with a translucent coating, but that killed the grass. Hofheinz had the dead grass painted green until he was able to replace it with AstroTurf, a grass-like carpet, which was now lying in massive rolls like haybales on the concrete stadium floor.

The retractable pitcher's mound was buried under a couple of steel plates. Two of my favorite ballplayers, Nolan Ryan and J. R. Richard, once stood on this spot. They were briefly teammates, although Ryan was the one who got the first million-dollar contract in baseball history, creating resentment on Richard's part. Both could throw hundred-mile-an-hour fastballs and breaking balls at almost that speed, but the six-foot-eight Richard was by far the more intimidating pitcher. I never saw a pitcher so thoroughly over-power hitters. At the moment he released the ball, his right foot was almost off the mound and his hand seemed to be right in the batter's face. His slider was probably the most difficult pitch in the game to hit. It was thrilling to watch him.

In both 1978 and 1979, he struck out more than three hundred hitters, a feat that only Nolan Ryan and Sandy Koufax had accomplished in consec-utive seasons in the modern era. The following year was expected to be the season that Richard firmly proved himself to be the most dominating pitcher in baseball. He was thirty years old, and getting better every year. He won ten of his first fourteen starts. But then he began complaining about a "dead arm," along with stiffness in his shoulder and back. He took himself out of several games when he couldn't see the catcher's signs. For weeks he complained of dizziness and pain. Because of his very public gripes about Ryan's contract, fans turned against him, believing he was "loafing," although he hadn't missed a start in five years. Even the team doctors and staff didn't believe him. The Astros reluctantly put him on the disabled list. "They said it was all in my head," Richard later recalled. "They said I was unhappy, pouting about Ryan."

On July 30, 1980, with an earned run average

of 1.90, Richard suffered a major stroke from a blood clot in an artery leading to his right arm. Doctors had finally detected it several days earlier but decided it was stable, and so they did nothing. Richard never played in the big leagues again. After a couple of bad investments and two divorces, he was financially ruined. In January 1995, while Ryan was preparing to start his twenty-seventh season in the major leagues, a reporter for **The Houston Post** found Richard living under a bridge, about three miles from the Astrodome.

Ryan went on to the National Baseball Hall of Fame and served as president of the Texas Rangers. He is said to be worth $60 million. He is one of the most popular Texans of all time. Richard became a minister and got involved in serving the homeless population in Houston. They were two great players, but I wonder how their destinies would have differed if their plights had been reversed. One imagines that Nolan Ryan, the million-dollar man, and white, would have been treated as soon as he reported his symptoms. No one would have accused him of being a malingerer and a malcontent. No doubt he would have been rapidly attended to. Perhaps he would have been given better financial advice. On the other hand, Richard was always solitary and difficult. He was known to be using cocaine in his playing days. He was not as easy to make into a hero. Still . . .

I asked Judge Emmett if the fate of the Astrodome was that it, like its predecessor the Roman Colosseum, would become a venerable ruin. Emmett said he didn't see that happening. Indeed, a few months after my visit, Emmett persuaded the Harris County commissioners to put up $10.5 million to design the redeveloped facility, which would include underground parking and a vast festival area. "The Astrodome's days of sitting idle and abandoned are over," the Judge promised. "I'm confident we can do it without a tax increase. A hundred million dollars more or less is easily doable in a county with a larger population than twenty-five states."

★

HOUSTON IS the only major city in America without zoning laws. You can build pretty much anything you want anywhere you want, except in designated historical districts. You'll see some odd sights, such as a two-story family home adjacent to a roller coaster, or an erotic nightclub next to a shopping gallery, or a house made of beer cans. Solo skyscrapers suddenly pop up in residential neighborhoods. The absence of zoning is an artifact of the anticommunist hysteria of the 1950s and 1960s, when zoning was viewed as a communist plot. But there was another group, of blacks and liberals, who saw an advantage in siding with the ultraright. "Zoning would have been used to keep people out," Bill White, a former mayor, observed.

According to **City Journal**, a publication of the Manhattan Institute for Policy Research, Houston now has the highest standard of living of any large city in America, and among the highest in the world: "Personal household income has risen 20 percent since 2005 in Houston, compared with 14 percent in New York, 11 percent in Los Angeles, and less than 9 percent in Chicago." Parks are being renovated and expanded, and housing is affordable—60 percent below the average in Los Angeles, for instance.

Houston grew by 35 percent between 2000 and 2013, an astounding figure for an already mature city. It will soon bypass Chicago to become the country's third-largest metropolitan area, behind New York and Los Angeles. "All the growth has been Latino, African American, and Asian," the Kinder Institute's Stephen Klineberg said. "Houston is now the single most ethnically diverse metro area in the country." One out of four Houstonians is foreign born, and no single racial or ethnic group constitutes a majority. "We speak one hundred forty-two different languages," Sylvester

Turner, Houston's second black mayor, told me. "We're seeking to be even more inclusive."

For many years Texas led the nation in the number of refugees it admits. In 2016, Texas took in 8,300 of the 85,000 refugees that came to America, a close second to California. (Under President Trump, the number of refugees permitted into the country has been capped at 45,000.) Houston accepts more refugees than any city in the country. At last count (2010), Texas has the largest number of Muslim adherents in the United States. However, the governor decided in September 2016 to withdraw from the federal resettlement program.

Like other cities in Texas, Houston has become more progressive over the years; for instance, 81 percent of Houston's citizens favor background checks for all gun owners, and a majority approves a path to legal citizenship for undocumented immigrants. The proportion of Houstonians identifying themselves as Democrats was 52 percent in Klineberg's latest survey, while the number saying they are Republicans declined to 30 percent—the largest gap in the history of his polling. Those numbers are not at all reflected in the political leadership of the state, which is far more right wing than the general population.

Nearly 40 percent of Houston's population is under twenty-four—it's an incredibly youthful town—so education is a pressing issue. More than half of that youthful cohort are Latino, and nearly 20 percent are African American; they are the future of Houston and also the most likely to be undereducated. Texas is near the bottom on education spending and academic achievement. These failures will have national consequences, since one out of ten children in the United States is a Texan—more than seven million of them. One in four Texas children lives in poverty.

There was a time when oil, cotton, and cattle were the only real sources of wealth in the state, and education wasn't such a crucial predictor of success. "The question is whether older, wealthy Anglos are willing to invest in a Texas future that is predominately not Anglo, when it's not a mirror of Europe but a microcosm of the world," says Klineberg. "The hope for Houston and Texas is that it is in our basic DNA to do what is needed to succeed." Houstonians know that they are at a crossroads. "This place could be either London or Lagos," my friend Mimi Swartz, a longtime **Texas Monthly** writer, told me.

★

IN EARLY AUGUST 2017, an atmospheric formation known as a tropical wave stirred into life off the western coast of Africa and began its journey across the Atlantic Ocean. By the time the disturbance neared the Lesser Antilles, on August 17, it was designated a tropical storm and named Harvey. Two days later, Harvey bumped into a wind shear in the eastern Caribbean, and it subsided once again into a wave. The National Hurricane Center stopped providing advisories as it appeared that the storm with its rather amusing name had simply petered out.

The Texas Gulf Coast acts as sort of a catcher's mitt for the tempests that are hurled across the sea. And yet, with all the predictions about global warming generating more frequent storms of increased severity, we hadn't had a direct hit since Hurricane Ike hit Galveston in 2008. Ike was rated only a Category 2 hurricane, but it was one of the most destructive storms in Texas history, bringing a twenty-foot storm surge and killing eighty-four people. Many of our complacent political leaders doubt that the climate is changing—or if it is, that human activity has anything to do with it. In light of widespread scientific consensus on these matters, it is difficult to read the political resistance as anything other than abject submission to the oil and gas industry, which is headquartered right in the Gulf Coast hurricane strike zone.

The depleted storm named Harvey lumbered across the Yucatán Peninsula into the Gulf, where it gathered enough strength to be termed a tropical depression—meaning that it had winds of thirty-eight miles per hour or less. Suddenly, in the space of fifty-six hours, Harvey exploded into a Category 4 hurricane, thanks to abnormally warm waters in the Gulf.

Harvey made landfall at 10 p.m. on August 25 at Rockport, a little fishing village and art colony north of Corpus Christi, with sustained winds of 130 miles per hour, wiping out city blocks in Rockport and leveling smaller towns in the area. But it wasn't the wind that would do the real damage; it was the rain.

As the storm veered northwest, toward Houston and Beaumont, meteorologists began to panic. "All impacts are unknown & beyond anything ever experienced," the National Weather Service tweeted on August 27. William Long, director of the Federal Emergency Management Agency (FEMA), predicted that the storm would be the worst disaster Texas had ever seen.

Governor Abbott urged residents from Corpus Christi to Houston to evacuate, but Mayor Turner and Judge Emmett quickly overruled him. "You literally cannot put 6.5 million people on the road," the mayor said at a press conference. He referenced Hurricane Rita in 2005, when an evacuation order had been given. About 2.5 million people fled inland, creating the worst gridlock in Houston's history. Steve Harrigan got his eighty-five-year-old mother out, and it took him nine hours to drive to Austin, usually less than a three-hour drive. His brother-in-law left two hours later, and the same trip took thirty-two hours. People who were stranded on the highway died of heat stroke. There were traffic accidents. Fights broke out. A bus carrying evacuees from a nursing home caught fire. More than a hundred people died in the thwarted exodus. The uncomfortable truth about Houston is that there is no escape in the face of a major hurricane.

Harvey had become indolent; it just sat on top of Houston and the surrounding region, pouring more rain than any storm in U.S. history—measuring 51.88 inches at Cedar Bayou, just east of Houston, a record. An estimated 34 trillion gallons of rain fell on East Texas and western Louisiana. Nearly a hundred thousand homes were flooded, and as many as a million vehicles were destroyed. Dr. Joel N. Myers, the president and chairman of AccuWeather, predicted, "This will be the worst natural disaster in American history. The economy's impact, by the time its total destruction is completed, will approach $160 billion, which is similar to the combined effect of Hurricanes Katrina and Sandy."

★

AS IT HAPPENED, I was supposed to be in Houston rehearsing a new play. I had planned to drive down on Sunday, August 27, but Harvey got there before me. All the roads were blocked. My actors had already arrived for costume fittings, and they were marooned in the hotel. I had a video chat with them on Monday, and they kept looking away from the screen to the window, where the storm continued to rage. Their eyes were filled with awe.

My play is called **Cleo.** It's about the making of the movie **Cleopatra.** Elizabeth Taylor and Richard Burton are the main characters. Their illicit romance began on the movie set in Rome in 1962 and became the most scandalous love affair of the twentieth century. I was radiated by their romance, which happened to coincide with the onset of puberty. I have been working on the script, off and on, for twenty years. Bob Balaban, the actor, is our director, and we had a reading at the Alley Theatre in January 2016, on the little Neuhaus stage downstairs. The audience was wonderful, and after the reading, Gregory Boyd, the artistic director of the Alley, offered us a production.

The roads to Houston were just beginning to open up when I drove down on August 30. The Colorado River was well over its banks, and the sodden fields under the heavy sky appeared unnaturally lush, like an Irish landscape. Some of the access roads were still flooded. I saw an eighteen-wheeler trapped under an overpass; only the top of its cab was above the waterline. I wondered what had happened to the driver. There were only a few cars on the interstate, including some free-lance rescuers towing swamp boats. Nathan Rott, a reporter for NPR, ran into a bunch of guys with oversized four-wheel-drive pickups who were forming up in Columbus, seventy miles from Houston. One of them told Rott, "It's moments like these—and only moments like these—that America truly appreciates its rednecks."

When disaster strikes Texas, one of the most effective first responders is a local chain of grocery stores, H-E-B, which dispatches a convoy of fifteen vehicles, including mobile kitchens that can produce 2,500 meals an hour, fuel tankers, portable generators, and Disaster Relief Units that contain pharmacies, ATMs, and business services equipment. By the time Harvey made landfall in South Texas, the convoy was already on the way to Victoria and Rockport. Over the next several days, various units headed to Houston. On Thursday, August 31, the Beaumont emergency management coordinator called H-E-B to say that the city was marooned. There was no water pressure. No supplies were getting in. And the state wasn't able to help in a timely fashion. The H-E-B convoy charged through. That's my idea of enlightened Texas capitalism.

As soon as I got into Houston, I went over to the theater. It's on Texas Avenue, in the heart of the Theater District, only three blocks from Buffalo Bayou, which marks the northern edge of downtown. I had seen photos and videos that cast members had sent me during the storm. Texas Avenue had essentially merged into the bayou. The water was five feet deep in front of the theater. When I arrived, the streets were mostly dry, with jumpable puddles along the curb. The storm had moved off to Beaumont, but the wind was still gusting through the canyon of skyscrapers. I was prepared for the worst, I thought.

The Alley had its first performance in 1947, in an unheated (and certainly uncooled) dance studio on Main Street that accommodated eighty-seven people. A sycamore tree grew through the roof. A high-school drama teacher named Nina Vance was the founder. That same year, director Margo Jones created America's first nonprofit resident theater in Dallas. Until then, theater outside New York was largely made up of touring Broadway productions, but it is because of visionaries like Vance and Jones that the flow reversed. Most original works—such as **Cleo**—now start in regional theaters, where they can be developed and find an audience.

The Alley opened in its current, brutalist-style building in 1968. It looks to me like a fifteenth-century Venetian fortress, with turrets that have also been compared to anti-aircraft emplacements. It's not the kind of building to concern itself with hurricane winds. On the street in front of the theater was a vacuum truck, a sort of tanker that is used in the oil fields to suck fluids and slurry out of fracked wells. It had been going for twenty-four hours, the driver told me, but so far had only gotten two feet of water out of the theater.

I followed the suction line inside, where the chief engineer, Daniel Naranjo, greeted me. Daniel's regular flashlight was out of batteries, so we relied on my iPhone. Upstairs was the recently renovated 774-seat Hubbard Theatre, where **Cleo** was intended to be staged; it was untouched. We could have put on the play that afternoon, except for the fact that the utilities were all drowned.

We headed down a spiral staircase toward the little theater below, but we only got a few steps before the water greeted us. The Alley had been flooded before. The previous high-water mark came from Tropical Storm Allison, in 2001—the worst rainstorm to hit an American city until that time. Harvey eclipsed that mark by a solid two feet. Below the submerged stage was a basement, which contained the dressing rooms, restrooms, laundry, wardrobe department, and about a hundred thousand props from the seventy years of the Alley's existence, all of it buried under millions of gallons of water like a sunken ship.

It would take ten days to drain the theater before the demolition could begin. The main problem, Daniel explained, was the electrical panels, which were custom made, and would require at least six weeks if not several months to replace. **Cleo** was supposed to begin performances in three weeks.

One had to wonder at the wisdom of rebuilding. Initially, it was thought that the water had gotten in through the subterranean tunnel system that underlies downtown Houston, as had happened during Allison. Since then, submarine doors had been installed, which worked during Harvey. This time, the floodwaters rose high enough to enter through an air vent the size of a sewer drain and blew out the reinforced concrete wall leading to the power vault. That sheared off a sprinkler head, which added another million gallons of water to the gusher coming in from the street.

Hanging over our rehearsal was the obvious question of whether we would actually have a production. Alternative venues were either damaged or booked. Bob Balaban was stuck in New York since the Houston airports remained closed. We were waiting for the ax to fall.

★

THE NEXT MORNING, I walked over to the George R. Brown Convention Center, where eight thousand refugees had taken shelter.

The initial chaos of the first days of Harvey had subsided into an impressive sense of order and gentility. The giant halls of the convention center were divided into dormitories for families, families with animals, single men, and single women. There was food in every aisle. I spoke to Scott Toncray, an official with the Red Cross. "I did Katrina with FEMA," he said. "This one is a whole lot calmer."

The death toll from Hurricane Katrina, which wrecked New Orleans in 2005, was estimated to be over 1,800 people, but no final tally has been made, since 135 people are still listed as missing. Looters took over the streets. The New Orleans police disgraced themselves with their civil rights violations. Doctors at one hospital became so desperate as they waited for rescue that they intentionally hastened the deaths of their patients. FEMA was unequal to the urgency and scale of the disaster. In one of Governor Rick Perry's finest moments, he opened Texas to the refugees, and a quarter million of them came to Houston. As many as forty thousand of them became Houston citizens, aided by a multimillion-dollar resettlement program the city put in place.

I walked past a line of people waiting to file claims with the dozens of FEMA counselors. Volunteers were sorting mountains of donated clothing. Actors in Disney costumes (**The Lion King, Frozen**) wandered around, looking for children. There were phone-charging stations, a table full of consuls from South and Central America, massage therapists, face painters, and yoga instructors. It was almost like a street fair.

Rhonda Wilson, a Houston police officer, observed that, when she first got to the center during the storm, "it was a sea of helpless, desolate victims." Seventy-seven people had died, but that was a fraction of those who had been lost in Katrina and even less than the figure for Rita. "There are still people being evacuated, and the rivers keep rising. I'm living my life in twelve-hour shifts," Wilson said. The night before she had finally gotten a chance to turn on the television, and she had broken down. Like other police officers, her badge was masked, in memory of their colleague Sergeant Steve Perez, who drowned in the flood while trying to report for duty.

★

"THIS CITY SPRAWLS over six hundred square miles, an area so big that Chicago, Philadelphia, Baltimore and Detroit could all fit within it simultaneously," Manny Fernandez, the

Houston bureau chief for **The New York Times,** wrote on Sunday, September 3, when the city was still partly submerged. "The nine-county Houston metropolitan region, covering more than ten thousand square miles, is almost as large as the entire state of Massachusetts." Eighty-five percent of homeowners had no flood insurance.

Harvey calls into question the future of Houston. It has endured more flooding over the last forty years than any other city in America, and yet it continues to grow by four hundred people a day, building forty thousand houses a year to accommodate the influx, many of them in the floodplain, and continually paving over the grassland prairie that sponged up the deluges of the past. Harvey made the cost of the absence of zoning shockingly clear.

"Everybody got hit," Judge Ed Emmett told me when I visited him again, this time in his county office in downtown Houston. "Geographically, demographically—it doesn't matter whether you were rich or poor. If we're going to continue to have this large urban area on the Gulf Coast, we're going to have to deal with flooding."

Houston had come into its own after the Great Storm of 1900 wiped out Galveston, then the major seaport in the state. "The Ellis Island of the West" was the point of entry for tens of thousands of immigrants, especially European and Russian Jews. Wealthy and complacent, Galveston refused to address the hazards of its location—for instance, by building a seawall. The city was only eight feet above sea level at its highest point. The weather bureau did not heed the warnings from Cuba that a major hurricane was on its way. When the storm arrived, it brought a surge fifteen feet high, drowning the island and wiping out the city almost entirely. The death toll was estimated between six thousand and eight thousand people. It is still the deadliest natural disaster in American history. The survivors rebuilt the city with great determination, raising it seventeen feet higher, but chastened investors wanted a safer port.

They turned to Houston.

The seeds of a great city had already been planted. Houston had streetcars and a railroad connection to New Orleans. A philanthropist named George Hermann gave a tract of land for a charity hospital, which would eventually become the foundation of the Texas Medical Center. The bayou had already been dredged to facilitate the lumber trade, but that work quickly expanded when Spindletop came in the year after the Great Storm. President Woodrow Wilson officially opened the Houston Ship Channel in November 1914 by pushing a button on his desk in the White House that was supposedly connected to a cannon in Houston.

But Houston had to face its own destiny in 1935, when downtown flooded. "That's what got every-body spurred into action," Judge Emmett told me. A flood-control district was established. Two large reservoirs were built to contain floodwaters; at the time, they were twenty miles from down-town. "They were out in the middle of nowhere," Emmett said. Since then, some fourteen thou-sand houses have actually been built inside those catchments, a fact that may not have been dis-closed to the homeowners. Those reservoirs were now filled to the brim, many houses within were flooded, and the Army Corps of Engineers was releasing water to keep the levees from breaching, adding to the flooding of the hundreds of homes that had been built around them.

"I'm not a hydrologist, I'm not an engineer, but something didn't work," Emmett said.

I asked Emmett, a Republican, if he was a climate-change skeptic. "The seas are rising, we have to deal with it," he said. "I'm more con-cerned if we're at a new normal. We've had three five-hundred-year floods in less than a three-year period, so our definition of a five-hundred-year flood is probably wrong. Either that, or we get fif-teen hundred years off."

Emmett laid part of the blame on his own party for being anti-intellectual and failing to take climate change seriously. "We've got too many people in our party who believe that the earth is less than ten thousand years old," he said. "Some of the political leaders are so afraid of this extreme element in the party. Periodically, just for fun, I go back and watch the movie **Inherit the Wind**"—about the Clarence Darrow–William Jennings Bryan "monkey trial," which featured a debate about the biblical account of creation versus the science of evolution. "I can't believe we haven't gone any further than that."

★

GREG BOYD FINALLY ASKED to speak to me and the cast about the fate of **Cleo.** The pain in his face reflected the bad news he was carrying. The lower part of his theater was being demolished at that moment. There were dumpsters lined up outside, crammed with drywall, moldering carpet, props, and rows of theater seats. Several of the city landfills were flooded and there was no place to put the debris. Similar piles of rubbish were all over town, where homeowners had stripped their houses of furniture and floors and had taken the walls down to the studs. I was touched by their determination to rebuild as soon as possible, but I also took note of the number of For Sale by Owner signs that had sprung up in neighborhoods like Meyerland, a predominately Jewish section, which had been badly hit once again. Members of the Alley staff had also lost their homes or suffered significant damage. (Greg would step down after the turn of the year amid charges of abuse. It's been quite a rocky season for the venerable old theater.)

It wasn't a surprise when he said he had to cancel the production.

I admit that my involvement in the theater world is tangential. I am a nonfiction journalist, deeply curious about the world outside but not so much affected by the interior landscape. Actors are a little mysterious to me. Their emotionality, their expressiveness, their intuitive genius—all of this is about as far from who I am as nuclear engineers or trapeze artists. When I'm with them, I feel like I'm visiting a foreign country—a friendly place, but one with unfamiliar folkways. I once made the mistake of uttering the word "Macbeth" during a rehearsal in New York, and the actors marched me outside on a cold winter day, made me turn around three times on a crowded sidewalk, and then beg for readmittance. The Scottish play, you are supposed to say.

When Greg delivered the news, the cast nodded, then one of them spoke up, saying, "Yes, well, we just want to keep rehearsing." They all agreed. It was totally unrealistic. There was no venue for us. The Alley was facing millions of dollars in damage. Even when the theater got back on its feet, there was no room in what remained of the season. Greg began to weep. The next day, the Alley staff somehow managed to find space for **Cleo** the following spring.

Shortly before I returned to Austin, there was an ad in **The Houston Chronicle**. "To our friends in Texas," it began:

Twelve years ago, you took in hundreds of thousands of us. You opened your homes, closets, and kitchens. You found schools for our kids and jobs to tide us over. Some of us are still there. And when the rest of the world told us not to rebuild, you told us not to listen. Keep our city and traditions alive . . .

The way of life you love the most will carry on. You taught us that. Your courage and care continues to inspire our whole city. We couldn't be more proud to call you our neighbors, our friends, and our family. Texas forever.

We're with you.

It was signed, "New Orleans."

# FOUR

# Culture, Explained

Texas enjoys the singular blessing that every distinct culture must have: a sense of its own apartness. It is in the sound of our voices, the flavors of our food, the rhythms of our music. Whether through the visual arts, literature, theater, architecture, music, dance, or cuisine, culture is a mirror of a million facets reflecting the society it contains. Primitive cultures reflect nothing more than that. Unauthentic, phony cultures mainly reflect societies other than their own. A great culture is aware of the world beyond but is constantly turning back on itself, searching for its roots, examining its direction, criticizing and talking to itself—in short, taking itself seriously.

From my lifelong field studies spent among Texans, I have formulated a theory of cultural development. Despite the legendary qualities of boorishness, braggadocio, greed, and overall tackiness associated with my state, there is a lot to love about the traditional elements of our culture. If Texas is ever to approach cultural greatness, it will be because of the juice we get from the basic stuff we recognize as Texan. We might call this Level One of Texas culture. It is the bedrock, the foundation that supports everything to come.

Level One is aggressive, innovative, and self-assured. It erupts from the instinctive human reaction to circumstance. The paisano presses his tortilla, the slave mixes his corn bread, the cattleman rubs prairie sage on the roasting steer, and a cuisine is irrepressibly born from the converging streams of traditions and available flavors. Spanish priests mortar limestone rocks with river mud; bankrupt Georgia farmers, remembering the verandas of their plantation empire and mindful of the withering sun, build high-ceilinged houses with broad, shaded porches; thus a native architecture arises. In scores of county seats laid out in the 1880s, the Virginian idea of the central courthouse square meets the Spanish idea of the town plaza and the Victorian idea of wedding-cake masonry, creating an idiom of civic democracy. The imagination chases after memories of cattle drives and Indian wars and the mighty geysers of oil spewing depreciable assets out of the ground, and from these come the stories that power our mythology and inform our literature. The whine of the wind across the plains finds an echo in the nasal twang of our speech and the bending guitar strings, and so even today our songs holler back to the once empty spaces where suburbs now sprawl. All of our culture overlays this primitive template, just as the Houston freeways inscribe the same routes once traced by ox wagons headed for Market Square.

The persistence of Level One in Texas is what makes it unique. You can still find the Tex-Mex Regular Dinner on the menu, and there are steak houses that haven't changed since the introduction of bacon bits on the baked potato. Pickup trucks are as common on the city streets as yellow cabs in Manhattan. (One-fourth of all vehicle sales in Texas are pickups; we buy more than any other state, more than California, Florida, and Oklahoma combined, and nearly every manufacturer has a special Texas edition.) When people think of Texas, these things inevitably come to mind.

Throughout my life in Texas, the state has been torn between Level One and Level Two, which occurs when a primitive culture casts its eye on other societies to see what they have to offer. This stage coincides with the arrival of money. Whereas Level One is aggressive and rooted and sure of itself, Level Two is consumed with longing. Expansive, neurotic, uncertain of its own goals but deeply embarrassed by its naive origins,

Level Two is the stage of sophisticated imports. It is in love with the au courant, which is to say the passing and quickly discarded fancies of more polished cultures. It is a voluptuous and rather bogus stage of development.

It is easy to sneer at Level Two, but it is a necessary stage that any great culture must endure. It is a time of travel, education, and acquisition—the never-ending process of widening one's horizons. Level Two cleans the dirt from under its nails and turns to the humbling work of civilizing itself. Classical music, Renaissance art, Elizabethan theater, foreign philosophies, and exotic cuisines: the world pours in and swamps the little craft of Level One. The undergraduate bohemian reading Chekhov is indulging in the joys of Level Two as surely as the arbitrageur discussing the Matisse exhibit at the Contemporary Arts Museum over a plate of sashimi. This is all wonderful, but it is also in its way destructive, as one can easily see from the homogenized Level Two culture that has franchised itself and spread all across America, leaving so little of the original cultural imprint that made one place stand apart from another.

The most explicit and enduring example of the influence of Level Two in Texas is the architecture of our cities, which have practically obliterated their own native charms in order to become showplaces of other people's ideas. In the rush to build to the sky, cities have scraped away their histories and sucked the life out of their downtowns. When I moved to Austin in 1980, there were shops and cafés and department stores along Congress Avenue, and the majestic capitol dominated the landscape, as it was designed to do. Now Congress Avenue is shadowed by undistinguished office towers, which rudely leapfrog the three-story historic buildings that remain. The effect is like the mouth of a child, full of baby teeth and permanent teeth and awkward gaps in between. There is grandeur in the shimmering new skyline, but the human scale has been obliterated as Austin becomes just another big city.

Philip Johnson and I. M. Pei brought architectural acclaim to Houston and Dallas, and these cities can think more highly of themselves now that **The New York Times** and **Progressive Architecture** have put their imprimatur on them. The buildings that have come to define the urban centers of Texas—the Williams (formerly Transco) Tower, Pennzoil Place, the Morton H. Meyerson Symphony Center, to name several of the most elegant and successful of these—have added energy and an air of self-importance that characterizes any great city. They are "world class," to use a phrase that characterizes Level Two thinking. But there is nothing Texan about these buildings, nothing that refers to the history or responds to the environment in which they are placed. One could just as easily see them in Boston or Sydney—but that's the whole point of Level Two, which is the achievement of a high level of sameness.

It is easy to forget who we are in Level Two. We have wandered far from home and gotten lost in the cultural forest. What had seemed so secure in Level One—that is, our rootedness and a sense of what we stand for—has been torn away and made to seem tacky and inconsequential. In many ways, however, Level Two is a noble and adventurous stage, full of delightful cross-fertilizing discoveries. For me, the first, gratifying step into Level Two began with the arrival, in Abilene, of Kentucky Fried Chicken, a momentous and longed-for departure from meat loaf at the officers club at Dyess Air Force Base on Sundays after church. Abilene was dry in those days, so whenever my parents made a trip to San Angelo, ninety miles away, to load up on liquor, we'd stop at the Lowake Steak House, which was situated in a cow pasture with a dirt airstrip running across the road. We were a family of five but would order steaks for three and then bag up the leftovers. Mother liked to have a beer, which they brought in a goblet she could barely lift. This was pure Level One Texas.

When we moved to Dallas, in 1960, I encountered my first pizza. It took place at Campisi's Egyptian Restaurant—which was, despite the

"Egyptian" moniker, the first pizzeria in Texas. The only actual "ethnic" restaurant I can recall in the city at the time was La Tunisia, which was notable mainly for the seven-foot-tall, fez-wearing doorman, along with cocktail waitresses dressed as harem girls. There was no such thing as a fajita in Texas until Ninfa Laurenzo introduced the dish in her revered Houston restaurant—Ninfa's—in 1973. (I'm aware of the scholarship on this matter, which proposes that the fajita was actually an indigenous Tex-Mex creation of the mid-nineteenth century, which migrated south and ingratiated itself into the kitchens of Coahuila, Mexico, before returning in its full beer-marinated, sizzling-plattered, sour-cream-dolloped glory.)

Level Two is marked by the rise of cultural institutions—the opera houses, ballet companies, symphonies, music halls, museums, galleries, libraries, theaters, and schools that have proliferated in the last several decades. These institutions begin by importing other people's culture and, one hopes, end by fostering their own. To understand the anxiety that floats beneath the boasts of Level Two, we have only to visit the vaulted sepulcher of the Dallas Museum of Art. Solemnly designed by Edward Larrabee Barnes, it opened in 1984, boasting "the finest collection of post-war American art" in the Southwest. It also laid claim to the country's "finest collection of Japanese-influenced American silver," "the largest display of Chinese export porcelain," "the largest Robert Rauschenberg painting," the "largest painting by Mexican artist Rufino Tamayo," and finally, "the world's largest indoor sculpture by Claes Oldenburg." Only in Texas is Large Art an aesthetic category.

The DMA also houses the Wendy and Emery Reves Collection. Wendy Russell Reves was a leggy blonde from Marshall, Texas, who became a New York fashion model and the longtime lover of a wealthy European publisher, Emery Reves, whom she finally married in 1964. She was the Jerry Hall (from Gonzales, Texas) of her day. Wendy became the chatelaine of a villa on the Côte d'Azur formerly owned by Coco Chanel. Winston Churchill spent months at a time there, to paint, and to drink in Wendy's charms. His wife pointedly refused to join him. Noël Coward observed in his diary that Churchill was "absolutely obsessed with Wendy Russell . . . I doubt if Churchill has ever been physically unfaithful, but oh what has gone on inside that dynamic mind?"

After Emery died in 1981, Wendy offered to donate his $30 million collection of impressionist and postimpressionist art to the new Dallas museum, which was still in the planning stage. Museums in France and elsewhere avidly courted the widow, but they were unwilling to accommodate her intransigent demand that her residence be faithfully reproduced in order to showcase the art.

Thus, one leans into the roped-off rooms in the DMA's version of a Mediterranean villa to see life as it was lived by a Hungarian playboy with his spirited Texas mistress. Here in their dining room, with still lifes by Courbet and Cézanne, are the Reveses' china plates and silverware all laid out on the immense banquet table. (Housewares occupy center stage in this exhibit; the art is mere decor.) A nude Degas pastel looms over the tiger-skin boudoir chairs in the master bedroom, and the bed itself is mounted on a kind of presentation dais. At the foot of the bed is a pair of Wendy's not-exactly-Cinderella-sized slippers.

★

STANLEY MARCUS WAS the great Level Two proselytizer in Dallas. He was the only liberal, and practically the only Democrat, that I was aware of in the city when I was growing up. This was a city so hysterically anticommunist that the Dallas Symphony had to cancel a program of Shostakovich because he was Russian, and the Park Board ripped out a bed of poppies because they were red. Marcus fought against the absolutism and paranoia that dominated Dallas politics, creating space for ideas to breathe. Through

Neiman Marcus, the marvelous department store that he oversaw, he tutored the newly affluent city, not only on how to dress and what to buy but also on how to behave. He raised the standard of cuisine in the city when he hired Helen Corbitt to run the store's restaurant, the Zodiac Room. He almost single-handedly desegregated public facilities by welcoming black citizens to shop in the store and, in 1961, by serving two black couples in the Zodiac Room. The word went out in Dallas that desegregation had arrived. Marcus hired Eddie Bernice Johnson, a nurse, as an executive assistant, on the singular condition that she run for office. In 1972, she was elected to the Texas legislature—the first black woman from Dallas ever elected to anything. Since 1993, she has served in the U.S. House of Representatives. Stanley Marcus changed Dallas. Few individuals have ever had such a profound and beneficent effect on the city in which they lived.

Houston had its own great cultural modernizer in Dominique de Menil, the French heiress of the Schlumberger oil-field-services company. She and her husband, John, immigrated to Houston in 1941, following the Nazi occupation of Paris. They brought with them a sensibility that was practically unknown in Texas, intending to plant a flag of cosmopolitanism far from the volatile capitals of Europe. The de Menils collected more than seventeen thousand paintings and other works of art, centering on cubism, surrealism, pop—a totally alien aesthetic for the place and time. "What I admire, I must possess," Dominique once admitted. They brought artists and filmmakers, such as Marcel Duchamp, Max Ernst, Roberto Rossellini, Michelangelo Antonioni, and Bernardo Bertolucci, to speak and teach. They put a cowboy hat on René Magritte and took him to a rodeo.

Dominique commissioned Renzo Piano to design a serene museum to house her vast art collection, his first American building. The museum is cool and gray and perfect. Nearby is the de Menils' most memorable contribution, the Rothko Chapel, a meditative space that provides a brooding counterpoint to the headstrong city. In front, there is a Barnett Newman sculpture, **Broken Obelisk,** which was intended to grace the Houston City Hall, but when the de Menils insisted that it should be dedicated to the memory of Martin Luther King Jr., the city turned the gift down.

"Houston is a major philanthropy center, and they were the start of that," Tommy Napier, the assistant communications director of the Menil Collection, told me, as he took Roberta and me through the de Menils' home, which is now used for museum events. Designed in 1950 by Philip Johnson, the house is a flat-roofed, pale-brick, one-story affair, with a nearly windowless front, which some Houstonians initially mistook for a dentist's office. "It was the first modern house in Houston," Napier said. Certainly it provides a flagrant contrast to the antebellum-esque mansions of River Oaks. Across the back of the house is a long bank of windows, which in the Houston climate were fogged over like a shower stall. The furnishings, by the fashion designer Charles James, are riotously lush, not at all in keeping with the austere Johnson style. The dark living room has black Mexican floor tiles and a vivid yellow Rothko that nearly jumps off the charcoal-gray wall. The bar is a kind of enlarged Joseph Cornell box, filled with colored highball glasses and stuffed birds on a shelf under a Matisse and a Max Ernst. There is a phone booth with a schoolteacher's pencil sharpener on a tiny desk, along with a Sunday missal and books of poetry by Anna Akhmatova. The door to Dominique's bedroom is covered with red velvet, and yet the room itself is like a cloister. The de Menil aesthetic is informed by a monkish devotion to simplicity and an absolute rapacity for beauty.

The best museums in Texas are in Fort Worth. The Kimbell, gracefully designed by Louis Kahn—his last and maybe finest work, using parallel concrete vaults that ingeniously reflect natural light—is one of the most acclaimed buildings of modern times. It set a standard for the future, which was matched by Tadao Ando's exquisite Modern Art Museum. The Amon Carter Museum of American Art (designed by Philip Johnson) houses a distinguished collection of Western art. These buildings showcase the artistry of Level Two and its power to elevate a culture; and yet the walls are practically bare of any great Texas artists.

There is a third level in my analysis, which is when a culture matures and, having absorbed the sophistication of Level Two, returns to its primitive origins to renew itself. One night recently in Houston, I had dinner with friends at One Fifth, a new restaurant opened by Chris Shepherd. He grew up in Tulsa and came to Houston to culinary school. Captivated by the diversity of cultural influences, he began prowling through the city markets and cafés, discovering a mix of cuisines that were all a part of the city around him. Shepherd was drawn to what he called the "underbelly" of the vast city. Just driving west on Bellaire Boulevard is like taking a world tour, through Central America, Thailand, Korea, and the Philippines. Suddenly the street signs are in Chinese characters. In 2011, Shepherd opened a restaurant in a former lesbian nightclub that he calls Underbelly. He subtitled it "The Story of Houston Food." The menu changes every day, depending on what is available from the local farms, Vietnamese bakeries, the catch that day from the Gulf, and the whole animals that are brought to his in-house butchery. His wine list is annotated by the local rapper Bun B. He folds all of these influences into a cuisine that reflects the city that Houston is now. "I wanted to go from simple regional cooking to hyper-regional," Shepherd told me.

Shepherd is a bear-sized man with bristling brown hair and an expression of intense concentration. His new restaurant, One Fifth, reflects the restlessness and imagination that he brings to re-creating a native cuisine. "I wanted to do the corners of Texas," he said. "You've got East Texas, which is Creole, with the field greens and okra. In West Texas you have the Hispanic influence and the chiles. North Texas, you had the cattle drives. In the south and the Gulf, I wanted to give the sense of a true Southern fishing camp. Then in Central Texas you have the Czech and German influences." To accomplish all that, he decided that he would reinvent the restaurant each year.

Its current incarnation was a steak house. We had ordered the chef's board, which was brought to us by two waiters and stretched across the entire table—crispy pork shoulder, lamb Wellington, brisket, collard greens and bacon, sweet potato au gratin. I have to say that my favorite part of the meal was dessert—apple pie, cooked in a wood-burning stove so that the crust was slightly charred but the apples were still firm.

Transcendence is always rare, and the best examples of Level Three tend to be origin stories. Beyoncé's album **Lemonade** absorbed the street talk and country music and the church choir of St. John's United Methodist Church in Houston, and enlarged the tablet of popular music. The National Wildflower Research Center, in Austin, quotes the limestone arches and tin-roof barns of the countryside to create an environment that is both familiar and new. One can look at the jubilant choreography of Alvin Ailey's masterwork **Revelations,** for instance, which is a sumptuous re-creation of Ailey's experiences in a black Baptist church in the flyspeck Central Texas community of Rogers. It is as if the artist had split the atom of consciousness and released its energy into the universe. Robert Rauschenberg, who studied pharmacy at the University of Texas before discovering himself as an artist, used the images of his native Port Arthur—windmills, derricks, even a bubbling tub of oil-field mud—to give a new language to modern art. He commented on the recession in Texas in the 1980s, caused by the crash in oil prices, to create what he called "gluts": tire tracks, crumpled gas-station logos, and highway signs riddled with bullet holes, the detritus of the car culture that rules—and despoils—America.

"I think of the Gluts as souvenirs without nostalgia," Rauschenberg commented. This is what Level Three is all about: returning to one's roots with knowledge, self-confidence, and occasionally, forgiveness.

★

**PERIODICALLY,** Larry McMurtry erupts to deprecate the state of literature in Texas, which he has called "disgracefully insular and uninformed," and produced by "a pond full of self-satisfied frogs." He particularly singled out the overworked cowboy myth for undermining the literary project of the state, before producing the best cowboy book ever, **Lonesome Dove,** four years later. In his essay "Ever a Bridegroom," published in the **Texas Observer** in 1981, he singled out only one writer in the entire state worthy of his unequivocal admiration: Vassar Miller, a little-known poet in Houston.

McMurtry is one of my favorite writers, and after his article came out, I conceived what I thought was a hilarious idea. Every year, the Texas legislature selects a writer to be the poet laureate of the state—typically, back in those days, an elderly schoolteacher from Port Arthur or Burkburnett. I decided to start a political action committee and lobby legislators to pick a real poet for the post. POPAC, I called it. Steve nominated Glenn

Hardin, a talented poet known to be cantankerous and profane and certainly not in the mold of
the usual laureate. Steve used to publish him in a
poetry magazine he founded called **Lucille**. My
object was to see how much money it would take
to get my candidate accorded the state's highest
literary position—its only one, in fact.

Just then, rather suspiciously in my opinion,
the Texas Senate decided to formalize the selec-
tion process, sabotaging my scheme to bribe the
legislators. Jack Ogg, a handsome senator from
Houston, convened a panel, proclaiming that
its purpose was to "select the next poet lariat of
Texas." After that, every speaker who addressed
the panel carefully spoke of "lariats," not "laure-
ates." A few days after this perfunctory panel, the
senators announced they had chosen a new poet
lariat: Vassar Miller. This was the only time in
Texas history that literary criticism has had an
effect on state affairs.

One book often nominated as a candidate for
the Great Texas Novel was **The Gay Place**, by Billy
Lee Brammer. It's actually three novellas pressed
together, with a single towering figure, Governor
Arthur "Goddam" Fenstemaker, based on Brammer's real-life mentor, Lyndon Johnson. Billy Lee
had worked for Johnson in Washington, when he
was Senate majority leader.

Billy Lee had died of a methamphetamine overdose by the time I moved to Austin, so I never got to meet him. In the book, the only one he ever published, he captured a brief moment in Texas history, in the late 1950s, when liberals had a foothold in the capitol and Austin was a highly sexed beatnik outpost (that hasn't entirely changed). It was the first novel to stake a claim on modern, urban Texas. Billy Lee was unfortunately too chaotic to produce another book that might have secured his reputation as a true Level Three artist. I once had lunch with one of his ex-wives, Nadine Brammer, who remembered the time she took Billy Lee to a hypnotist to try to cure his smoking habit. As they were going up on the elevator, she suggested that maybe Billy Lee should also try to get rid of his kleptomania. "No, I want to keep that," he said.

Billy Lee wrote for the **Texas Observer,** the muckraking liberal rag in Austin that had been home to Willie Morris, J. Frank Dobie, and a number of writers I admired. In 1971, I drove down to Austin from Dallas for an interview. Roberta and I had just returned to the United States from Egypt, where we had taught for two years at the American University in Cairo. We were living with my parents while I searched for a job.

The **Observer** was a beacon for ambitious, smart-ass youngsters like me. It was co-edited by Molly Ivins and Kaye Northcott. Molly was six feet tall, red-haired and big-boned. At her side was a black dog named Shit. Molly could spin out resonant Texas witticisms that became classics as soon as she uttered them. Jim Mattox, the attorney general, was "so mean he wouldn't spit in your ear if your brains were on fire." Kaye was Molly's physical opposite—diminutive, with small, fine features and large, scholarly eyeglasses. They were the Mutt and Jeff of Texas liberals, respected even by the politicians they lampooned, because the **Observer** made Texas politics into a recognizable genre, something to be savored. It set us apart. Perhaps because of Molly's continental education, the **Observer** began to resemble a left-wing French publication, with its satire and scathing exposés. We all became a little more Parisian, more amused by ourselves, and disdainful of newcomers who couldn't crack the code. I desperately wanted to be a part of the scene, but my interview with Molly went nowhere. I had no experience and nothing to show, so I drove back home, despairing of ever becoming a writer.

Molly refined Texas stereotypes into an art form, like a Jewish comedian in the Catskills. Her 1991 collection of columns spent twenty-nine weeks on the **New York Times** bestseller list, making her a national celebrity at the same moment that Ann Richards got elected as governor. They were lashed together in the public imagination, the pair of them defining a particular kind of Texas woman—earthy, progressive, sharp-tongued, and unafraid of men, no matter how big their belt buckles.

McMurtry hasn't delivered another broadside on the current state of Texas letters, so I asked Steve what he thought. "The state of Texas literature is defined by writers worrying about the state of Texas literature," he said grumpily. "Why is everyone in Texas so anxious about defining a regional literature when nobody else feels the need to do that? Anything you say reinforces the provincialism. Just let it be what it will be."

★

AFTER I HAD BEEN WRITING in Texas for several years, I was nominated to be a member of the Texas Institute of Letters. All the best people were in it, I was told, and so I naturally wanted to be one of them. But the friend who had submitted my name reported that I had been rejected, at least at that time. When my name came up, one of the board members advised, "Let him spend another year on the cross."

I had been a small part of a very minor literary scene when we lived in Atlanta, nothing so formal as the TIL. We were all regional writers, and whoever had a single nostril above the waterline of total obscurity was regarded with reverence and green-eyed jealousy. When my first book, **City Children, Country Summer,** came out, in 1979, an autograph party was held for me at the Old New York Book Shop on Piedmont Road, which was the unofficial hangout for the Atlanta literati. My book was about minority children from New York City—mainly, black and Hispanic kids from Harlem and Bedford-Stuyvesant—who spent part of a summer with Amish and Mennonite dairy farmers in central Pennsylvania. The venerable charity that sponsors the program is the Fresh Air Fund. The book got no notice at all, followed by zero sales. It was appropriate that the party took place in an antiquarian bookstore, because mine was a rare book from the moment it came off the press. A friend of mine aptly described the publication experience as "the calm before the calm."

But I was a published author at last. A well-known Atlanta writer, Marshall Frady, who had just written a best-selling biography of Billy Graham, was my host and sponsor. Like most Southern writers I knew, Marshall was addicted to the bon mot. When we arrived at the party, he told Roberta, "You look positively lambent tonight"—a cherished compliment she's never forgotten.

The party itself was memorable mainly because the police arrived with reports of an attempted homicide. The victim was a drunken lout, likely a poet, who had been amusing himself by pouring cheap champagne down ladies' dresses. Marshall took him outside and administered some rough justice. "A mere schoolyard scuffle, officers," he said, when the black-and-white pulled up, although Marshall had actually broken his own hand during his inexpert pummeling. Imagine what the cops thought when they learned they had stumbled upon an autograph party for a book about the Amish.

When it came to pass that the golden gates to the Texas Institute of Letters finally opened, I could see what McMurtry was complaining about, although he didn't have Georgia as a point of comparison. McMurtry himself was the speaker at one of the first meetings I attended. He complained about the burdens of fame, eliciting little sympathy. At that same event, I also met Cormac McCarthy, a laconic Tennessean who was living in El Paso at the time and therefore qualified as Texan. He had already published **Suttree** and **Blood Meridian,** but I had not yet read him. None of his books had sold more than five thousand copies, despite impressive reviews. He didn't even have an agent. When we were sitting on the carpet of the hospitality suite with a bottle of bourbon between us, I asked how he was able to make a living. "I've always been fortunate in that people have given me quite a lot of money," he said. He first became aware of his good fortune when he was living in a barn, surviving on corn bread, and didn't have enough money to buy toothpaste. One day, he went to look in the mailbox and found a complimentary tube of Pepsodent. "A few days later, a man came to the barn and gave me a check for twenty thousand dollars from a foundation I had never heard of," he said. And only recently, he remarked, he had become a MacArthur Fellow. He really was a very lucky guy.

Sitting in an easy chair in that cramped hotel suite was the grand old man of Texas letters, John Graves, who wrote an extraordinary book, **Goodbye to a River**, in 1960. The river in question, the Brazos, runs from the high plains to the Gulf of Mexico, serving as the unofficial border between East and West Texas. The Spanish named it Los Brazos de Dios, the arms of God. Upon learning of plans to erect five dams along the Brazos, creating a string of reservoirs, John decided to travel by canoe down a twisty portion of the river in what he thought would be a fruitless protest:

In a region like the Southwest, scorched to begin with, alternating between floods and drouths, its absorbent cities quadrupling their censuses every few years, electrical power and flood control and moisture conservation and water skiing are praiseworthy projects. More than that, they are essential. We river-minded ones can't say much against them—nor, probably, should we want to. Nor, mostly, do we . . .

But if you are built like me, neither the certainty of change, nor the need for it, nor any wry philosophy will keep you from feeling a certain enraged awe when you hear that a river that you've known always, and that all men of that place have known always back into the red dawn of men, will shortly not exist. A piece of river, anyhow, my piece.

McMurtry had summed John up as neither journalist nor novelist but ruminator. He was an ex-Marine with a glass eye, the memento of a Japanese grenade on Saipan. He had grown up in Fort Worth and on his grandfather's ranch in South Texas, but like most of us with any literary pretensions he had fled to where the writers and readers were—to New York, where he got a master's degree in English; then to Europe, where he bummed around, aping Hemingway. "It's heartening to think that he might once have been as uncertain as the rest of us," Steve said, when he gave John's eulogy in 2013, "that his majestic self-possession was something he had to earn and grow into." John returned to Texas in 1957 to take care of his dying father. "It was in Texas that he finally found his voice," his last editor, Ann Close (who also edited this book), observed.

We were all mystified by him. His prose was incantatory, and his attachment to the place we lived in was so much keener and more revelatory than ours. He used the money from **Goodbye to a River** to buy four hundred thin-soiled acres in Glen Rose, fifty-something miles southwest of Fort Worth, that he aptly named Hard Scrabble. After that, he just seemed to disappear into the land. He wrote occasional essays that were collected and admired. He often showed up at literary events, where he was genial and not superior despite the reverence that always attended him. He wore heavy horn-rims that were purposely positioned halfway down his nose so he could tilt his head down and peer over the frames with his one good eye (the other one tended to wander), as he did while Cormac and I chatted at his feet, with his divided glance—I always had to remind myself which eye to respond to. He always seemed to be more like a fan or a contented spouse, never invoking the authority he had over us, preferring to listen. "You always felt that, in some quiet way, he was measuring you and recording your worth," Steve observed. Perhaps his failure as a novelist kept him from venturing more deeply into the craft. Maybe he thought he could never match that first book, so why try. Maybe he didn't care enough about his gift, even though those of us who admired him would often dip into his book for inspiration, when our own words refused to flow and his seemed to come so effortlessly.

Steve ended his eulogy by quoting John's own report of encountering Hemingway in Pamplona during the San Fermín festival, surrounded by acolytes, "holding court at a sidewalk table in the main square, using his sport coat as a cape while still another collegiate American served as bull and charged him." John held back. "I had not yet proved myself as a writer, a real one," he wrote, "and until I managed that I didn't feel I had the right to impose myself on established authors, however much I might admire their work."

"It's an introduction long overdue," Steve concluded. "Mr. Hemingway, meet Mr. Graves."

★

ACCORDING TO THE LEGENDS we tell ourselves, Texans get ahead by relying on luck, nerve, and instinct. These are good qualities. They might be sufficient in a culture of wildcatters and poker players, but not for engineers or city planners or educators—the kinds of people who actually build urban civilizations, but cities don't fit comfortably into the Texas myth.

Central to this myth is bigness. I'm not talking just about the drive from Beaumont to El Paso. Texans themselves are supposed to be big people. I recall the 1960 Boy Scout Jamboree. I went there with a delegation of scouts from Dallas. Along with us came Big Tex, the fifty-foot-tall fiberglass statue that stood outside the State Fair in Dallas—or, I should say, Big D. Big Tex loomed over our tent city, and all of us, I believe, felt proud to be singled out and set apart from the scouts from other states and countries. Somehow we participated in his bigness.

Texas is a macho state. We love sports. We call our teams Cowboys and Rangers and Mavericks and Rockets and Oilers and Spurs—there are no Blue Jays or Dolphins playing ball in Texas. The downside of the machismo is that we turn away from the feminine side of our nature. It is evident in the indifference to beauty and a sort of loathing for compassion, as manifested in our schools, our prisons, our mental health facilities, and our lack of concern for the environment. I recall the panic that hit the Texas legislature in the 1980s when a bill was put forth to ornament our license plates with wildflowers. What could be more representative of our state than our native bluebonnets and primroses? But that proposal was buried as lawmakers turned to the important business of trying to get beef declared the official meat of the Olympics.

Hollywood adored the Texas myth. On the silver screen, "Texas" was not a real place, it was a symbol for the unbridled West, a playground for the frontier legend, made over and over again in the epic westerns of John Ford, William Wyler, and Howard Hawks. "Texas" was an arena of the soul, where a man comes face-to-face with death and destiny. It occupies the same emotional territory as the wilderness of Judea, only without God. When we're in "Texas," the actual film may be shot in Monument Valley, Utah (**Stagecoach, The Searchers**), or in the rolling Canadian wheatfields (**Days of Heaven**). There's a forgettable thriller called **The Swarm,** in which a train crosses a range of mountains to enter the coastal city of Houston. Even in **The Alamo,** the archetypal Texas movie, San Antonio is set on the banks of the Rio Grande, which in fact is two hundred miles south.

Seeing these movies made me feel special as a Texan, but in a fraudulent sort of way. I imagine that every Texas man of my age has experienced the dissonance of failing to live up to the legend in people's minds. Once, when I was teaching in Egypt, I went horseback riding in the desert near the Pyramids. When the owner of the stables learned where I was from, he exclaimed, "Oh, Texas! Have we got a horse for you!" Three handlers led out a rearing stallion, with pulsating nostrils, who pawed the air as if he could rip it apart. He hadn't been ridden in two years. I was no John Wayne, but to save face I mounted this brute, who rocketed past the Sphinx and took me halfway to Libya before I could coax him to turn around.

The Kennedy assassination put an end to the era of heroic Texas movies; after that, the state represented everything Hollywood thought was vile and wrong with America. "Texas" was Slim Pickens as Major "King" Kong, riding the hydrogen bomb to apocalypse in **Dr. Strangelove** (wickedly written by Texas native Terry Southern). Now "Texas" was an asylum of rednecks, yahoos, drifters, and chainsaw massacrers.

The Texas I actually lived in finally did break into the movies, first with **Hud,** based on McMurtry's first novel, **Horseman, Pass By.** The book was about the end of the western frontier and the men who made it. The movie, with Paul Newman in the rapscallion title role, made the antimythic story into a legend of its own. A few years later, there was a terrific film called **Midnight Cowboy,** which opens on the Big Tex Drive-In, in Big Spring. The hero, Joe Buck (Jon Voight), works as a dishwasher, but he has a poster of Newman in **Hud** on his wall. Joe Buck tries to live out the myth by dressing up in movie-cowboy clothes and seeking stardom in New York, where he becomes a failed gigolo. I was teaching in Cairo when the movie came out, and one night during Ramadan I took my class to see it after the evening meal. To me, **Midnight Cowboy** was about the neurosis of wanting to live up to a myth. I came out of the film exhilarated, but my students were shaken.

For the first time, I realized how much the rest of the world valued "Texas," what a rich legacy it is, and how universally appealing the myth is. Perhaps Texas really is a place that exists more fully in film than in real life.

The fear besetting Texans, including its writers and filmmakers, was that, by leaving the myth behind, "Texas" would be crushed by ordinariness. And yet, it's exactly that quotidian quality of life in the small towns and featureless suburbs that becomes so luminous and heartbreaking in the plays and films of Horton Foote, such as **Tender Mercies** and **The Trip to Bountiful**; it also awakens the comedy of Mike Judge's animated series **King of the Hill** and his cult classic movie of the corporate software culture in Austin, **Office Space**. Richard Linklater became the chronicler of the ongoing dialectic of the Austin streets with his first commercial movie, **Slacker** (1991), and then in **Dazed and Confused, Waking Life**, and many other independent films. His tour de force **Boyhood** follows a child who actually grows up in Texas during the twelve years it took Rick to make the film, tracing the evolution of the boy's consciousness as he approaches maturity. The myth has diminished, assuming a more modest place in the Texas psyche. It may never disappear entirely, nor would I wish it to. The myth has gone through hard times before and come back to life—although each time, I think, with a little less reality. The danger in holding on to a myth is that it becomes like a religion we've stopped believing in. It no longer instructs us; it only stultifies us. And besides, what do we want with a myth that makes us into people we don't want to be?

Level Three requires shaking off the mythic illusions and telling new stories about who we really are. The noble quality of Level Three is that it returns us to the familiar. The songs we heard as children, the sounds of our labor, the primal smells of the kitchen, the legends of our ancestors, the phrases and intonations we cling to in our language, the colors of our land, the cloud shapes in our sky—all are folded into the art of Level Three. It feels like home. And isn't that the point of culture, to come home again with a clear and educated eye?

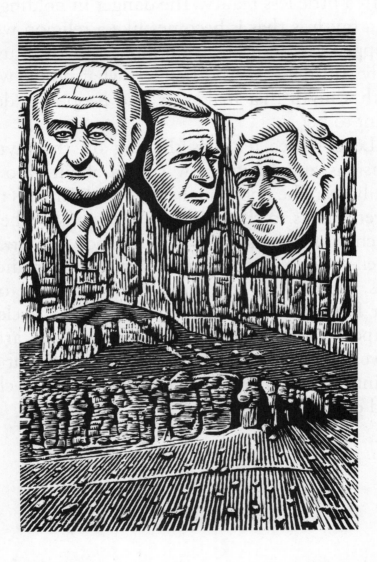

# FIVE

# The Cradle of Presidents

The LBJ Ranch is now a national park, and one early summer day as I was driving west I decided to stop in. The bluebonnets and Indian blankets along the roadsides had faded, replaced by purple thistles and Mexican hats. Lyndon Johnson used to race down these narrow roads in his Lincoln convertible, with a scotch and soda in hand, terrifying visiting heads of state as he careened into the curves. The Lincoln was equipped with a special lever-action horn that bellowed like a rutting bull in order to capture the attention of the heifers in the pasture. Johnson would be trailed by a station wagon full of Secret Service agents, and periodically he would slow down and rattle the ice in his styrofoam cup outside his window until an agent dashed over and refilled his drink.

Johnson was the only president I can recall who really loved cars, especially convertibles. There's a little museum at the end of the airstrip housing a 1934 Ford Phaeton, which he outfitted with a gun rack and a wet bar; the Corvette he gave his daughter Luci for her eighteenth birthday; an antique fire truck; and a little blue Amphicar, a chimerical cross between an automobile and a boat, which Johnson bought as a practical joke. He would drive his guests down to the banks of the Pedernales River and pretend that his brakes had failed as he plunged the vehicle into the water.

There is a one-room schoolhouse, where Johnson signed the Elementary and Secondary Education Act, one of the pillars of the Great Society; and beyond that, a walled cemetery, shaded by massive live oaks, where Lyndon and Lady Bird rest. Finally, there is the house itself, made of limestone, with a broad veranda overlooking the sweep down to the river, handsome but not majestic, the home of a Texas squire on a working ranch, with cow patties decorating the lawn. The last thing Lyndon liked to do at night was to stand on his porch, look at the stars, and pee.

On the wall beside Johnson's desk are portraits of his two beagles, Him and Her, commissioned by Barbra Streisand. In the easy chair is a pillow embroidered with the sentiment "This is my ranch and I do as I damn please." The living room has a bank of three television sets, one for each of the networks that existed during his presidency, and a domino table where he liked to play 42. The kitchen floor is yellow linoleum; there's a copy of **The Joy of Cooking** on a shelf. On the back porch are a massive freezer and a beer tap. It was in the small den under the stairs that the staff gathered on November 22, 1963, to be told by the Secret Service, "You are now in the house of the president of the United States." They had been busy preparing for the reception that night for John F. Kennedy.

Lyndon Johnson was Kennedy's opposite in so many ways. Where Kennedy was polished, Johnson was vulgar—fantastically and unself-consciously so—picking his nose, scratching his ass, eating off other people's plates. He once held a staff meeting in his bedroom while he was getting an enema. Kennedy went to Harvard, he had a Pulitzer Prize, and his friends were movie stars. Johnson went to a teachers college in San Marcos. Kennedy was beautiful and Johnson was ungainly, with immense features—his nose, his ears, and his cock, which he named Jumbo. Kennedy seemed to be a liberal because of his background and rhetoric, but in fact he was a business-oriented conservative and a Cold Warrior. He expanded defense spending by 20 percent. Among his accomplishments were the creation of the Peace Corps, a tax cut, and a nuclear test-ban treaty, but his most enduring legacy was the Vietnam War. Kennedy was the kind of president people would have expected a Texan to be. Johnson, despite his retrograde political past, became the most progressive president since Franklin Roosevelt, and yet the Kennedy acolytes in the Eastern Establishment sneered at him. "The greatest bigots in the world are the Democrats on the East Side of New York," Johnson complained.

The liberal tradition that Johnson embodied is practically extinct in Texas now, but so much of the country we live in was fashioned by his administration, including Medicaid, Medicare, the Civil Rights Act, public broadcasting, federal aid to the arts and education, the War on Poverty, the Immigration and Nationality Act, the Voting Rights Act, even the Gun Control Act. Kennedy had neither the mandate nor the skill to enact such a transformative agenda. Despite these accomplishments, Johnson's presidency sank under the weight of the war. The Kennedy men in Johnson's cabinet told him the only way out was forward, and Johnson was too cowed by their intellect to change course. His resentment against the "Harvards" and the Eastern Establishment socialites would sometimes flare up with a startling bitterness. After Martin Luther King Jr. was assassinated, an aide warned him that black protestors in Washington might march on Georgetown and burn it down. "I've waited thirty-five years for this day," Johnson said.

Texans agonized through the Johnson presidency, sharing in his humiliation, but also enduring the mortification of his hillbilly manners and cornpone accent. The hatred heaped upon him splattered over the rest of us. LBJ was the lens through which we were viewed. And to be fair, Texans were as resentful of the Eastern Establishment as it was of us. It's a cultural divide in this country that has never been bridged. LBJ was hounded out of office by young people, including me, who protested the war, but also hated who he was and where he came from. I wouldn't change my opposition to that war, but I wish we had been kinder to him.

★

WHEN STEVE'S NOVEL **The Gates of the Alamo** came out, there was a dinner for him at the LBJ Library. He and I were seated on either side of Lady Bird as George Christian, who was Johnson's press secretary, recalled the trip LBJ had made to Korea. Johnson told the American troops stationed there that his great-grandfather had died at the Alamo. Christian was half asleep in the back of the room, but when he heard LBJ say that, he sat bolt upright. A Texan making such a claim is a bit like a Muslim saying he is descended from the Prophet Muhammad. "There were only three reporters there, and none of them seemed to take notice," Christian said. He was relieved that the president had gotten away with a whopping lie. But one of the radio reporters, Sid Davis, had recorded the speech, and he played it for the press pool, which included several Texans. They all knew the truth.

Christian went to Lyndon and said he was in hot water because he had claimed his ancestor died at the Alamo.

"I never said any such thing," Johnson replied.

"Well, sir, I heard you."

"I don't care what you heard, I didn't say it."

"But Sid Davis recorded it."

"I don't care what he recorded, my great-grandfather didn't die at the Alamo," the president said.

The Alamo story hit the press, and it became a great embarrassment for Johnson, especially in Texas. At another event a few months later, when the controversy was still raging, Johnson complained that he had never gotten to finish the story: his great-grandfather didn't die at the Alamo; he died at the Alamo Hotel in Eagle Pass.

All through the telling of the anecdote, Lady

Bird chuckled. By that time, she had been a widow for nearly thirty years.

Like Lyndon, Lady Bird suffered in comparison to her glamorous predecessor. Jackie was the most famous woman in the world—chic, beautiful, and iconic in her grief—whereas Lady Bird was "a little brown wren," as her daughter Lynda once described her. As first lady, she was best known for promoting the Highway Beautification Act, derided as "Lady Bird's Bill" by opponents, but it was just one of two hundred laws concerning conservation and the environment that have her stamp on them. Because of her, the plague of billboards that infested our roadways was sharply diminished, and junkyards were removed or screened off. It was her noble goal to let nature shine through.

In Austin, Lady Bird was the driving force in creating the hike-and-bike trail around what is now called Lady Bird Lake—a body of water that was itself created by Lyndon, as a young congressman, when he succeeded in getting the federal government to dam the Colorado River to bring power to the Hill Country. The trail now functions as a kind of town square for fitness enthusiasts. Lady Bird had been inspired by a trip to London, where she admired the walking path beside the Thames. In the 1980s and 1990s you would often see her on the trail, wearing her bonnet, discreetly followed by her Secret Service bodyguard.

Lady Bird founded the National Wildflower Research Center (now also renamed after her) in Austin in 1982, on her seventieth birthday, and it's largely because of her that the roadsides of Texas are so brilliantly carpeted. My father served as head of the Beautify Texas Council in the 1980s, and he worked with Lady Bird. After he passed away, I found a letter from her thanking him for the seeds for the hike-and-bike trail. I had run around that trail thousands of times and never known about that connection.

When the research center opened, wildflowers were still so uncultivated that they were difficult to propagate. Lady Bird herself would prowl the state scouting for hardy specimens. One particularly dry spring she came upon a hillside in Central Texas that was spilling over with pink evening primrose—which she describes in her book (with Carlton B. Lees) **Wildflowers Across America** as "the most exquisite and feminine of all wildflowers!" A young man was plowing them under. Imagine how startled he must have been to see the former first lady throw herself in front of his tractor and yell, "Stop!" She rented the pasture until the flowers went to seed so she could harvest them.

She was the most self-deprecating woman in

public life I ever knew. Once I was at a party in honor of Shakespeare's birthday, given by her erudite nephew, author Philip Bobbitt, who is a law professor at the University of Texas. Lady Bird and I were seated together at dinner, and she asked me to pass the salt, which was in front of her. She was then nearly ninety and suffering from macular degeneration. The only way she could still enjoy her beloved wildflowers was by examining them with a magnifying glass. But she was game and even bemused by her condition. "Just now, during cocktails in the music room, I was trying to carry on a conversation with this gentleman," she told me. "He was so unresponsive, although I was being my most charming self. Finally, I realized I was speaking to a bust of Shakespeare."

★

PAST JOHNSON CITY, you're in the German part of the state, with sturdy stone cottages surrounded by peach orchards and vineyards. Franciscan friars began producing wine in Texas in the 1650s. In the late nineteenth century, when aphids wiped out French vineyards, it was rootstock from Texas vines that rescued the industry. History-minded Texans look upon French wines as Texas wines with French labels on them.

Outside of Ozona, the interstate was lined with a vivid low-lying flower called a mountain pink, another of Lady Bird's favorites, not just for its color but because it grows in the most obdurate conditions, such as roadside gravel. I felt as if I were driving through one of those early, super-saturated Technicolor movies. I turned north at Iraan, named after Ira and Ann Yates, who owned the ranch where one of the great Texas oil booms played out. Once you cross the Pecos River, pump jacks and windmills stretch to the horizon.

In 2004, someone quietly began acquiring ranches in West Texas, near Van Horn, using shell corporations to hide his identity. The fact that anybody was buying up land in Van Horn was a little puzzling, especially at the prices offered. Parched, scalped, remote, the land is certainly not prime real estate. Moreover, the state was in the middle of a punishing drought. The mystery buyer soon became one of the largest landholders in the state. But the question wasn't so much the who as the why.

Finally, in 2005, Jeff Bezos, the founder of Amazon and one of the wealthiest men in the world, admitted to being the purchaser. He needed the land—nearly 300,000 acres by then, with more to come—to build a launching pad for rockets into space. He had become infatuated with space travel when his family moved to Houston in the 1960s, during the NASA glory era, a time when Houston called itself Space City USA. "For me, space is something I've been in love with since I was five years old," Bezos told **The Washington Post,** after he purchased the paper in 2013. "I watched Neil Armstrong step onto the surface of the moon, and I guess it imprinted me."

Bezos's space company, Blue Origin, launched its first rocket from West Texas in 2011. That one crashed, but in September 2015 the company not only sent a rocket into space but managed to retrieve it in a historic vertical landing at the Van Horn facility. Bezos expects to send "test passengers" into space soon. "The vision for Blue is pretty simple. We want to see millions of people living and working in space," he said after the successful launch. "Do we want to go to Mars? Absolutely, but we want to go everywhere." Meantime, Elon Musk, the PayPal cofounder and the creator of Tesla, the electric automobile, has a rocket test facility near Waco and is building his own launching site for an astronomical venture, SpaceX, on the Texas Gulf Coast, near Brownsville. The Texas skies will soon be jammed with rockets.

In most of West Texas, there is really nowhere to look except up. In the hills near Fort Davis is the McDonald Observatory, where Roberta and I once got to see the rings of Saturn, and somewhere far back in time, a white dwarf. Amateur astronomers settle out here in ranchettes and build their own backyard observatories with retractable roofs. Living in West Texas is like being close to the ocean, with the sky serving as a natural point of focus for the contemplation of eternity.

On the side of I-40 you come upon Cadillac Ranch—ten vintage, graffiti-covered Caddies buried nose down in the dirt, tail fins to the sky. It is certainly the most famous art installation in the state. Stanley Marsh 3, an arts supporter and prankster, commissioned the work in 1974. He also liked to put up phony traffic signs, such as Road Does Not End and You Will Never Be the Same. Like a lot of rich Texas eccentrics, he kept exotic animals—a lion, a zebra, a camel, etc. When a developer threatened to build a suburb next to Marsh's property, Stanley erected a billboard on his property line saying:

FUTURE HOME
OF THE
WORLD'S LARGEST
POISONOUS SNAKE FARM

★

JUST SOUTH OF AMARILLO is Palo Duro Canyon, a red gash in the landscape a thousand feet deep and 120 miles long, ranging from half a mile to 20 miles in width. Only the Grand Canyon is larger. Palo Duro was the heart of the

Comanchería. The last band of southern Plains Indians who refused to submit to the dominion of the white colonizers gathered there, in what they believed was a divinely protected space. In 1874, a group of troopers from the Fourth U.S. Cavalry crept into the sanctuary, catching the Indians by surprise. The Indians—Comanches, Kiowas, and Cheyennes—fled on foot. They were not pursued; instead, the soldiers rounded up the Indians' horses and led them to slaughter—the defining moment at which the Texas frontier finally came to an end. The following year, the Comanche leader, Quanah Parker, surrendered the remnants of his depleted, starving band at Fort Sill.

In 1878, Parker was permitted to lead a small group of Indians off the reservation in Oklahoma in order to go on what would be their last buffalo hunt, in Palo Duro. The land was then owned by Charles Goodnight, the most famous rancher in Texas history. The thought that the vast canyon could belong to a single man was hard for the Indians to comprehend. In a journey of about two hundred miles, they hadn't seen a single buffalo. Only then did they realize how thoroughly their way of life had been vanquished.

Evidently, their plight made an impression on Goodnight. He found a few stray buffalo and began breeding his own herd. They were practically the only remaining animals from the millions that once thundered across the plains. In December 1916, Goodnight invited another group of Indians to return to the canyon for what he billed as the Last Buffalo Hunt. For the occasion, he started his own film company. He wanted to chronicle the Old West, as he remembered it, for the first generation that would know it only from the movies.

In the silent film, Goodnight's herd is seen galloping over the rim of the canyon into a narrow defile, followed by a group of Kiowa braves in feathered headdresses—old men, plump from the idle confinement of the reservation. A single buffalo is cut away from the herd and quickly surrounded by circling braves who lean toward the animal as they discharge their arrows. The buffalo's knees buckle as he takes a few final steps. Then the film cuts to the Indians dancing around the dead animal, drinking cups of warm blood as its hide is being cut away. It was the last buffalo they would ever kill.

Goodnight's film also chronicles the end of another era—his own. Like a number of other independent cattlemen, Goodnight had assembled his first herd by rounding up stray longhorns, feral descendants of the animals brought by the Spanish conquistadors. In the economic desperation following the Civil War, longhorn cattle were selling for about two dollars a head in Texas, but they would bring as much as forty dollars in the stockyards of Chicago. The cowboy heyday began in 1867, when a herd of 2,400 steers was driven from San Antonio to the railhead in Abilene, Kansas, along what became known as the Chisholm Trail. Goodnight and his friend Oliver Loving pioneered another trail to Denver. (Their relationship was the model for Larry McMurtry's classic bromance, **Lonesome Dove**.) The cowboy era essentially came to an end in 1885, when barbed wire fenced off the plains. In that meager span of eighteen years, five million cattle and a million mustangs, along with uncounted numbers of hogs and other livestock, were taken to market; great fortunes sprang up in a state that had, until then, relied upon little more than subsistence farming; but most enduringly, a myth was born that continues to define Texas in the minds of people all over the world, and especially in the state itself.

Style is the most obvious legacy of the cowboy legend: the boots, which kept the cowboy's legs from chafing; the denim jeans that provided some protection against the constant brush of sharp grasses and thorny mesquite; and the broad-brimmed hat to shield against the sun—modest working clothes that made perfect sense for a man riding the range in 1875, but that continue to be the ensemble of choice for so many Texans whose lives are largely lived indoors. Press the jeans and add a crisp white shirt with pearl snap buttons, and you've got an Austin real-estate developer.

The cowboy style is an implicit pledge of allegiance to the mentality the myth embodies, which can be denominated as rugged individualism. The world is full of danger, and the cowboy has to be ready to defend himself and his family. In place of the law, the cowboy lives by a code of fairness and rough justice. He doesn't impose his will on others, and he bridles at the suggestion that anyone—especially government—has a right to tell him what to do. God and nature are forceful presences in the cowboy's life, although his stark and unforgiving circumstances, combined with endless spans of boredom, give rise to stoic bouts of existential despair. Willie Nelson and Waylon Jennings sang a memorable duet, "Mammas Don't Let Your Babies Grow Up to Be Cowboys," which speaks to the solitary blankness of such a life:

Cowboys ain't easy to love and they're harder to hold
They'd rather give you a song than diamonds or gold
Lonestar belt buckles and old faded Levi's and each night begins a new day

**If you don't understand him and he don't die
young
He'll probably just ride away.**

✶

IN 1948, George H. W. Bush—a decorated naval aviator during the Second World War, a graduate of Yale, son of a future U.S. senator from Connecticut, and an aspiring young oilman— moved his family to a little duplex on a dirt road in Odessa. It was hot, dry, flat as a tortilla, and 350 miles from the nearest airport, in Dallas. They shared a bathroom with two prostitutes—a mother-daughter combo—and often got locked out of the toilet by thoughtless clients. In 1950, the Bushes and their two children at the time, George W. and Robin, moved to Midland, a larger city twenty miles down the road, which was the headquarters of nearly every independent oilman in Texas. It is called Midland because it is half-way between Fort Worth and El Paso. The Bushes purchased a three-bedroom frame house on West Ohio Avenue. "We like to say that we're the only presidential house that was home to two presidents, two governors, and a first lady," my guide, Melissa Hagins, said as she took me through the house.

Midland in the fifties was an unpolished, hard-drinking boomtown. The Bushes arrived as a powerful civilizing force. They raised money to build a theater, a YMCA, and a symphony. Barbara was the den mother for the Cub Scouts. George taught Sunday school and coached Little League. There were enough other Ivy Leaguers also seeking their fortunes in West Texas that Bush started a branch of the Yale Club. In 1953, together with the brothers Hugh and Bill Liedtke, he formed an oil exploration company that he called Zapata after Marlon Brando's movie **Viva Zapata!** came out. They drilled 127 wells in West Texas without a single dry hole.

The walls of the Bush house are knotty pine, giving it the feel of a lake cottage. The tiny living room has a built-in seat in the bay window and a television of the era, with a rabbit-ears antenna. There is a fireplace in the dining room. George W.'s room has a foldout desk attached to a bookcase, built to replicate the one that had been there when he was a boy. There is a train set, a Cub Scout uniform draped across the bed, and a picture of little George riding a jackalope. Above the bed is a poster of Roy Rogers, "King of the Cowboys," atop his gorgeous palomino mount, Trigger. My guide told me that George and his friends carried a copy of "The Roy Rogers Riders Club Rules" in their wallets. "Be neat and clean," Roy advises. "Protect the weak and help them. Eat all your food and never waste any." There are ten altogether. Roy was prim and modest, with a smooth tenor voice, the kind of role model parents adore; but there was another force stirring the universe at the same time, darker and sexier, not at all wholesome. For boys our age, Roy Rogers was the anti-Elvis. I'm a year younger than George W., and Roy Rogers was a big figure in my life as well. I had a Roy Rogers cap gun, which I recently saw listed on eBay for a thousand bucks.

There is a single bathroom, with a tub, no shower, and a master bedroom in the corner, with a view of the large fenced backyard and doghouse. The kitchen has a window over the sink, a gas stove, and what would have been an extravagance at the time, a washer and dryer. A small sunroom with clapboard walls became Jeb's nursery when he was born in 1953.

The third bedroom has no door on it. The Bushes took it off when their daughter, Robin, was diagnosed with leukemia in 1954. It took her seven months to die. "That's when Mrs. Bush's hair turned white," Melissa told me. "She colored it for many years and then finally gave up." Barbara Bush was twenty-eight years old. She later recounted that the only thing that pulled her out of her prolonged depression was hearing George W.

tell a friend that he couldn't play because "I have to take care of my mother."

Like many Texans, I harbor a fondness for the Bush family that has nothing to do with their politics. Numberless people in the state can testify to their kindness and decency. Laura Bush was a librarian at a public school in Austin; as first lady of the state, she started the Texas Book Festival, which has been a boon to the state's libraries. (Later, she also began the National Book Festival in Washington, D.C.) Our daughter, Caroline, went to Austin High School with George and Laura's twins, Jenna and Barbara, when their father was governor. We used to go to the Christmas party at the Governor's Mansion each year, and the governor always asked Caroline to dance. He really liked to boogie; his shirt would get so sweaty you could see his body hair. "I don't drink or do drugs," he told me, "so I gotta do something to get it out of my system."

Texas was still in transition from its days of being overwhelmingly Democratic to being solidly Republican—two eras bookended by LBJ and George W. In each case, the metamorphosis of Texas politics would profoundly change the nation.

When Bush was governor, between 1995 and 2000, a cordial détente existed between the parties. The lieutenant governor, Bob Bullock, and

Pete Laney, the Speaker of the House, were both Democrats, and they became exhibits in Bush's argument that he would be a bipartisan president. Bullock was a titanic figure, whose ruinous personal life—alcoholism, cancer, chronic depression, five marriages—only added to his legend. He reminded me of Lyndon Johnson, with the same huge, battered face and an unbridled love of Texas that allowed him to see over the barriers of party loyalties. At Bush's fiftieth birthday party at the Governor's Mansion, in July 1996, Bullock offered a toast to the governor as "the next president of the United States." As far as I know, that was the first time such a statement had been made in public, and it was made by the highest Democratic official in the state.

That same year, Bush launched a new statewide reading initiative at the school where Roberta was teaching, Travis Heights Elementary, and the principal chose to stage the press event in Roberta's classroom. Roberta taught a mixed kindergarten, first-grade, and second-grade class, and she agreed reluctantly, since the event was scheduled to take place at naptime. She picked out some of her best readers to sit on the governor's lap, but when the news crews and reporters trooped in, one of her troublemakers, Ricky Hernandez, impish and adorable, crept through the crowd and caught Bush's eye. "Hey, padnah, hop on up," Bush said, and Ricky, who couldn't read a lick, crawled into the governor's lap. Bush read **There's a Ghost in the Boys' Bathroom**, as Ricky beamed, and of course that was the picture on the front pages of the newspapers the next morning. What wasn't reported was that later that afternoon Roberta had to send Ricky home because he had head lice.

In 1998, I was asked to read at a fundraising event for literacy that the former first lady Barbara Bush puts on in Houston each year. A well-known writer, Stephen Ambrose, had fallen ill, and they needed a substitute—tomorrow! Would I mind flying down with the governor? I wouldn't mind. I went over to the mansion the next afternoon and found the governor noshing pound cake in the kitchen. He was cheery and familiar. He always seemed a much more natural politician than his father, and totally at ease, like a gifted athlete who didn't feel the need to train. "Has Dad left yet?" the governor asked his mother on the phone before we left. "I need a hat. Tell him to bring several."

We flew on George W.'s personal plane, a King Air turboprop that Laura described as "perfect for Texas." By now, I and everyone else were sizing him up as a future president. He seemed unfazed by the challenge ahead of him. He picked up **The Dallas Morning News** from the pile of newspapers on the seat in front of him, glanced at it, then set it down. We chatted a bit about the Middle East. I had just been in Jerusalem, and I told him about the rift between American Jews and the Orthodox rabbinate in Israel, which had declared that the Reform and Conservative branches of the faith were not true Jews. Bush was unaware of the issue, but observed, "They better be careful they don't cut off their money base." I was struck by how little he knew about the region, or anyplace, really, outside of Texas. I often wondered how the son of a former president—who had also been ambassador to the United Nations and envoy to China, as well as director of the CIA—could be so unacquainted with the wider world. I inquired about a recent visit the governor had with a Russian strongman, Alexander Lebed. Bush had been amused by the Russian's fierce demeanor, which he said quickly melted away. "I always ask them about their families," which apparently did the trick. George W.'s complacency and his absence of curiosity, traits that would come to define him, and doom him, were already apparent on that airplane ride.

At the fundraiser, I was wedged into the program among writers who were household names, and because I didn't have a recent book to promote, I read an article I had written about Caroline's doll, whom she named Nephew. He was a ratty little cloth doll of a type called Monchhichis, made to look like some kind of diabolical lower primate. Nephew came into Caroline's possession when she was four. She was always telling me stories of his travels, to China or Dallas, and his many wives. I felt like the sultan Shahryar listening to the tales of Scheherazade. But then Caroline would throw Nephew over a balcony and imitate his screams as he fell to the street. When Caroline turned five, Barbie came into her life, and Nephew got sidelined. Finally, she gave the doll to me. "You're the only one who loves him now," she said.

A few days after the reading, I got a letter from the former president, which I suspect was typical of the thousands he wrote every year. He had typed it himself with several emendations scribbled in the margins. "Last night Barbara and I . . . got to talking about Nephew, engaging fellow that he obviously is.

"But did you know that George and Laura's daughter Barbara has a Nephew-like icon named 'Spikey'? Once Spikey got lost in the V.P. house—a crisis, much like the tanks rolling through the streets of Budapest, narrowly averted when Spikey was found hidden under a living room couch.

"Just ten days ago Spikey, still in tow, went to Italy with the twins and Barbara. Too bad Nephew couldn't make it."

A year later, as the presidential primaries were

about to begin, I ran into Laura at Antone's, the Austin blues club. Marcia Ball was playing. Laura was in the company of friends, drinking and smoking, which you never saw her do. It was a sweet moment, but I immediately thought how this intimate little community we all lived in was about to end. Soon the cameras would roll into town, reporters would be knocking over gravestones, and everything in our culture would be scrutinized and dissected. I had been a part of that process many times. Like it or not, we would be onstage, we would be reviewed, some of us would become famous beyond our circle, and others would be indicted.

★

BUSH FATHER AND SON provide a riveting field of study for anyone interested in Oedipal dramas. George W. went to the same schools, first Andover and then Yale, where the father had become a Phi Beta Kappa and the son became president of his fraternity. George W. did, however, go to Harvard Business School. Like his father, the son was a naval pilot, but whereas the father earned a Distinguished Flying Cross while serving in the Pacific theater during the Second World War, the son served in the Texas Air National Guard, which was a well-known refuge from the Vietnam War for privileged sons of prominent men and players for the Dallas Cowboys. Both Bushes became oilmen in Midland, where the father was a legend and the son broke even. George H.W. was a graceful athlete; he had been scouted by major-league teams when he played first base for Yale, and in Midland he used to dazzle the boys he coached by catching fly balls behind his back. George W. was a gym rat who would boast that in his first term as president, he had actually gained muscle mass. By becoming a partial owner of the Texas Rangers, the son eclipsed his father's baseball career, as he did as president when he was reelected to a second term in office. Both men would invade Iraq, the first time for good reasons and the second time for a lie sold to the American people, which would cause enduring damage to our country and set fire to the Middle East.

Neither man was the least bit self-reflective, a quality they seemed to think weak and pointless. "I don't brood," George W. said dismissively. Despite their Ivy League educations, each of them had a tendency to wander off into linguistic labyrinths that generated much discussion in psychiatric literature. When he was running for president the first time, George H.W. boasted about his close relationship to Ronald Reagan. "I have worked alongside him, and I am proud to be his partner. We have had triumphs. We have made mistakes. We have had sex." There was a startled gasp in the audience as Bush regrouped. "We have had setbacks," he corrected. When he was running for reelection, he remarked: "Somebody said . . . 'We pray for you over there.' That was not just because I threw up on the prime minister of Japan, either. Where was he when I needed him? But I said, 'Let me tell you something.' And I say this—I don't know whether any ministers from the Episcopal Church are here. I hope so. But I said to him this. 'You're on to something here. You cannot be President of the United States if you don't have faith. Remember Lincoln, going to his knees in times of trial in the Civil War and all that stuff. You can't be. And we are blessed. So don't feel sorry for— don't cry for me, Argentina.'" **Newsweek** began calling him the "Mysterious Easterner."

Bush-speak, as it became known, was taken to a new level by the son, who sometimes seemed to be totally unaware of the words marching out of his mouth. "More and more of our imports come from overseas," he observed. On education: "Rarely is the question asked, 'Is our children learning?'" On the eve of the election, he remarked, "They misunderestimated me."

W. actually made fun of his predilection for nonsensical utterance. "Now, most people would say, in speaking of the economy, we ought to make the pie bigger," he confessed at the annual Radio and Television Correspondents Association dinner in Washington soon after he took office. "I, however, am on record saying, 'We ought to make the pie higher.' It was a very complicated economic point I was trying to make." He was so easy to like in the early days.

Bush was a good governor, not corrupt, a centrist by Texas standards. He had even tried to raise taxes on business in order to meet the growing social needs of the state. That was heresy in the Republican Party and went nowhere, but at least he acknowledged the disparities that made Texas so coldhearted to its less fortunate citizens. He might have waited through another election cycle before he ran, to gain more experience, but he told his friends he felt like a cork in a river, and he simply surrendered to the flow. Part of his drive seemed to be a deep dislike of the eventual Democratic candidate, Al Gore—"the kind of guy you always wanted to punch out in high school," Bush told me at a Christmas gathering in 1998, before running off to church. "I'll pray for you," he said, as he playfully grabbed me by the neck. "I'll pray for myself, too."

Everything nearly came to an ignominious end for Bush in November 1999, as the presidential race was under way. The governor was jogging around Lady Bird Lake, trailed by his bodyguard, Roscoe Hughey, a state trooper, on a bicycle. Suddenly, a waste-disposal truck, which was carrying a trailer full of construction debris, careened out of control. Bush saw the trailer just as it began to tip over. He instinctively dove under a bridge culvert, getting scraped and bruised, as the trailer dumped debris on top of his bodyguard.

I later asked Bush about the incident, wondering if he'd done something to piss off the garbage workers. He laughed, but it really was a close call. "Roscoe's eyes were rolling back in his head," he told me. "I said, 'Roscoe, what's my name? What's my name?' Fortunately, he got it right the first time."

In the 2000 primaries, W. lost to John McCain in New Hampshire by 17 points, nearly torpedoing his campaign. Twelve years before, in the same Republican primaries, George H.W. had carried the entire East Coast. "My father is not a Texan," the governor explained. He said that, immediately after New Hampshire, he had been talking to his chief strategist, Karl Rove, about how to recover, and then, when Rove left, Laura said that she had two points she wanted to make. "One, Texans don't win in the East." The second point was about McCain. "You let him talk down to you." Bush seemed amazed by her insight. "This was a librarian from Midland, Texas, telling me this!"

On Election Day, I watched returns with friends in Dallas. During cocktails, Florida was declared for Democratic nominee Al Gore, and we went to dinner, certain that the election was over. By the time I got to my hotel room, Florida had flipped to Bush. I awakened at five in the morning and turned on the TV. Gore was now winning both the popular vote and the electoral vote, with Florida and Oregon still outstanding. This was only a couple of hours after the networks had declared Florida for Bush, and Gore had called him to concede, then called back twenty minutes later to withdraw his concession.

Bush began that morning with 246 electoral votes compared to 259 for Gore. Florida's 25 electoral votes would decide the issue. Bush was 1,784 votes ahead in the state, out of 5.8 million that had been cast. Rich Oppel, the editor of the **Austin American-Statesman,** told me he had stopped the presses twice during the night, before finally going with the headline "History on Hold."

The night after the election, I was the master of ceremonies at the Texas Book Festival gala, and there was a reception at the Governor's Mansion. Laura greeted us at the door and seemed relieved to have the opportunity to just chat about our children. Condoleezza Rice, the future national security adviser and secretary of state, was there, and I took the opportunity to ask if she thought the election stalemate posed a security problem. "Not at this point," she said. "Right now, I think most other countries are just looking at us with amusement." Dick Cheney, who was then still scouting potential vice presidents (other than himself), sat alone in an anteroom, gripping a drink and looking bewildered. Rick Perry, the recently elected lieutenant governor, stood in the foyer, obviously wondering which new office he was going to hold.

The governor finally arrived, agitated and exhausted. He had a bandage on his right temple where a boil had been lanced that afternoon. His nerves were showing, a side of him I had never seen. I asked him if he actually got elected, how he would govern with such a divided mandate. He said he would have to have Democrats in his cabinet (the only one, Norman Mineta, became secretary of transportation). As for the Florida recount then under way, "The sons of bitches are trying to steal the election. If they try it, there are a lot of other states we could contest." He added: "We could explode the entire electoral process if we wanted to. But we're not going to let that happen to this country." As for a possible reconciliation with Gore: "I don't want to talk to the man. He's no gentleman. He took back his word. He called me in the middle of the night to concede, then he calls me back ten, twenty minutes later to unconcede." He stared at the floor, eyes wide in disbelief.

The next day, I was on a panel at the festival,

and afterward, as I was walking out of the capitol to the book-signing tent, I came upon several hundred Gore supporters facing off with an equivalent number of Bush supporters only a few feet away, separated by several dozen state troopers. Both sides were waving signs and shouting slogans. It was very ritualized. "Bush has won, the people have spoken!" one side chanted, and the other responded, "Recount the vote!" There was a kabuki quality to the demonstration, at once theatrical and safe, representing the sharp division of the country but also its democratic restraints. Somehow it made me feel especially patriotic. I remarked to one of the troopers, "Isn't this great?" He grinned and said, "It's just wonderful."

Gore demanded a recount in precincts where he had done well. An immediate recount of all the ballots cast in the state via voting machines lowered Bush's lead to 327, with absentee ballots yet to be tabulated and a mass of ballots that were difficult to decipher. For thirty-six days the country was hypnotized by the intense partisan struggle under way in Florida, having to do with "undercounts," "butterfly" ballots, and "hanging," "pregnant," or "dimpled" chads—the bits of paper that hadn't been cleanly punched out. Nearly 3 percent of Florida voters—174,000 of them—had bungled their vote. At one point, Bush's lead dropped to 286 votes. Cheney had a heart attack.

Under the Constitution, the issue had to be resolved before December 12, when the electors would meet, or the election would be thrown into the House of Representatives. On December 11, the U.S. Supreme Court met to hear arguments by both sides, and at 10:00 p.m., in a 5–4 decision, the Court brought the recount to an end. Bush would be the nation's forty-third president.

Many Democrats still believe that the Court overturned the will of the people, arguing that Gore won the popular vote nationally, and might have won Florida if the recount he had sought had been allowed to proceed. Later, a consortium of newspapers did recount all the ballots. Paradoxically, under the restrictions that Gore had requested, Bush would have won by an even wider margin, and if the recount had followed the procedure demanded by Bush's team, Gore would have won. If every vote in Florida had been counted, Gore would have won under some scenarios (all dimpled or hanging chads were accepted) and Bush under others (a vote counted only when cleanly punched, or when the chad was detached on at least two corners). The ambiguity was maddening. We entertained friends from Massachusetts who were horrified that we would even speak to the Bushes after what they had done. "Rather, you should spit on their shoes and say, 'Sir, how dare you!'" the red-faced husband said. I admitted that we actually liked the family. "Surely not the mother!" he cried.

The mood at the annual Christmas party at the mansion was completely different from that of the party only a month before, during the book festival. I had a chat with Bush, who had met with President Clinton and Vice President Gore earlier that day. He said he had told Clinton that Gore made a mistake by not enlisting the president more in the campaign. "Yeah, we're still trying to figure Al out," Clinton said. Bush thought there wasn't much allegiance or affection between the two men. Clinton, he said, "didn't seem to mind my being president." As for his meeting with Gore, he acknowledged it was brief. "Yeah, sixteen minutes," he said. "What could you say? The man's not much of a conversationalist."

Bush was cheerful and relaxed, bouncing on his toes. A mutual friend of ours, Grant Thomas, who had been at Harvard the same time as Bush, walked in, and the president-elect grabbed him by the back of his neck and cried, "Grant! Can you believe this? I'm the president of the whole fucking United States!"

# SIX

# Turn the Radio On

One can drive across Texas and be in two different states at the same time: AM Texas and FM Texas. FM Texas is the silky voice of city dwellers in the kingdom of NPR. It is progressive, blue, reasonable, secular, and smug—almost like California. AM Texas speaks to the suburbs and the rural areas—Trumpland. It's endless bluster and endless ads. Paranoia and piety are the main items on the menu.

Alex Jones is Texas's main contribution to this indignant conversation. In addition to his radio program, **The Alex Jones Show,** he runs an influential website, InfoWars.com, a progenitor of the fake news phenomenon. **Rolling Stone** called Jones "the most paranoid man in America." In his hyperbolic imagination, the U.S. government has been behind nearly every disaster imaginable, including 9/11 ("an inside job"), the Oklahoma City bombing (a "false flag" operation), and the Sandy Hook massacre ("a giant hoax"). As for Hillary Clinton ("one of the most powerful criminal kingpins in history"), Jones alleges that she has "personally murdered and chopped up" children.

I met Jones in 2009, when filmmaker Richard Linklater invited me to a screening of **American Prince,** a documentary by Tommy Pallotta. Rick has always been drawn to alternative ways of thinking, like an anthropologist studying vision quests among Plains Indians. He cast Jones as a street-corner prophet with a bullhorn in **A Scanner Darkly,** a rotoscoped realization of Philip K. Dick's dystopian novel. Jones played a similar role in a previous Linklater film, **Waking Life.** I had only a dim idea who Jones was at the time. He had grown up in a suburb outside Dallas and moved to Austin. His defining moment was the siege by the U.S. government of the Branch Davidian compound in Waco, in 1993. After that, he became an apostle of the extreme libertarian antigovernment movement.

Rick impishly introduced us, and then stood back with his arms crossed and a delighted expression on his face. Jones has a chunky build and a graveled voice and probing eyes. He knew about my book on al-Qaeda, **The Looming Tower,** although I didn't have the impression that he had read it, or anything much on the subject. He ventured the opinion that American forces were sending "assassination squads" into Middle Eastern countries, "to take out the top guys" in al-Qaeda. I responded that a good source of mine, Jamal Khalifa, who was Osama bin Laden's brother-in-law, had been murdered in Madagascar, I believe by American Special Forces. At that point, I suppose we were in agreement. I found him pleasant and curious—playful, in a way.

And yet, Jones's bizarre assertions about 9/11 were already shouldering their way into the popular culture. He claims credit for founding the "9/11 Truth" movement, which in its most robust version goes like this: The U.S. government, in league with Israel, knew that al-Qaeda was going to strike America, but the terrorist group wasn't capable of pulling off such an ambitious plan by itself. To ensure the success of the attack, American operatives placed high explosives in the towers, which detonated after the planes struck, creating a "controlled bombing" to bring the buildings down. Moreover, the Pentagon wasn't actually struck by American Airlines Flight 77; it was hit by an American missile. As for the heroic actions of the passengers on the last of the hijacked planes, United Flight 93, who thwarted the attack on the White House, the Truthers assert that the plane was either shot down by a U.S. military jet or secretly landed safely. All this was done to provide an excuse to invade Iraq and steal the oil.

There is something mesmerizing about Jones's ability to rant. He reminds me of the televangelist Jimmy Swaggart, whom I once interviewed. Like Swaggart, Jones lives in a world of revelation, convincing himself of the truth of whatever comes out of his mouth. He may also be a "performance artist," as Jones's lawyer recently claimed in a custody battle with his former wife, but that suggests he doesn't really believe what he's saying—that he's only talking for effect. Rick later told me that about a week after 9/11, when he and Jones were walking to a screening of **Waking Life,** Jones admitted that the U.S. government wasn't actually responsible for 9/11, "but they're going to use this for all kinds of horrible stuff." "He was right about that," Rick observed, "but that kind of insight isn't easily monetized."

Jones claims a long history in Texas, saying that his "great-great-great-great-great-grandfather" was at Gonzales, the site of the famous cannon that inspired the "Come and Take It" flag. Jones made a speech in front of the Alamo in 2013, with the Gonzales flag flying behind him and a semiautomatic weapon slung over his shoulder. According to Jones, the central message his great-great-great-great-great-grandfather wanted to deliver to the

Mexican forces was "We're not turning our guns in and we're not running and we're not backing down. If you want 'em, come and take 'em!"

After the speech, he and the camera crew wandered over to sport with a small counterdemonstration in favor of gun control. There's a video of an older woman asking Jones to leave. She says that she wasn't trying to take his guns away from him. "Santa Anna wanted the guns!" Jones says as the woman starts to walk off. But then the woman's husband, an older, bald man in a sweater vest, steps in front of Jones. "A gun grab is something nobody in this country wants," he says.

"Well, sir, all I can say is, you're really getting in my space," Jones responds. They are actually standing very close together.

"Why don't you back up," the man says.

"No, I'm not gonna back up." Jones moves in closer, chest to chest. "Listen, I don't want to beat an old guy up, so don't touch me."

"This guy could take you out in a heartbeat, dear," the wife warns Jones.

Jones wisely steps back.

While the husband continues to engage with Jones, his exasperated wife tells him, "Sweetheart, you're giving them what they want." There's obviously something deeper going on between the couple. The husband clings to her wrist, but he can't tear himself away from Jones.

"Do you know that assault rifles are only used in two percent of crimes?" Jones asks.

"I know that an assault rifle was used to murder my daughter in Aurora," the husband says.

Jones jumps back. "I didn't touch your daughter!" he cries.

Jones had called the 2012 **Batman** shooting, in which twelve people were killed and seventy injured in a movie theater in the Denver suburb of Aurora, "a false flag, mind-control event." He contends that the movie itself was "a weaponized, propaganda warfare system" with subliminal messages designed to make people frightened of terrorism, so that "Bloomberg, Chuckie Schumer, Nancy Pelosi, and the usual suspects" could push for gun control. Similar Jones rants about mass tragedies being staged by the government have generated death threats for parents of the children murdered at Sandy Hook Elementary School. Another Jones acolyte walked into Comet Ping Pong, a family-oriented pizza parlor in Washington, D.C., in December 2016, and fired a semiautomatic weapon, saying he was there to investigate the claims, made by Jones, that the restaurant was the center of a child pornography ring, led by John Podesta, Hillary Clinton's campaign chairman. Jones eventually apologized for that incident, apparently under legal pressure, but he rarely accepts responsibility for the damage done to the reputations and lives of people he has slandered.

In the summer of 2015, when the U.S. Army announced its intention to conduct a massive, eight-week training exercise called Jade Helm, ranging across seven states, Jones floated the "news" that the federal government was planning to occupy Texas and impose martial law. Walmarts were being converted into concentration camps. Blue Bell Ice Cream trucks would become mobile morgues. "This is an invasion," he claimed, "in preparation for the financial collapse and maybe even Obama not leaving office." Instead of switching stations, Governor Greg Abbott hurriedly called out the Texas State Guard to "monitor" the exercise. (Yes, we have our own state militia, just in case.)

Jones's fantasies caught the ear of Donald Trump when he started suggesting that Hillary Clinton belonged in prison. That became a mantra in the Trump presidential campaign, as did Jones's allegation that President Obama and Hillary Clinton founded ISIS and that she was being kept alive only by drugs. "It is surreal to talk about issues here on air and then word for word hear Trump say it two days later," Jones marveled. On another occasion he remarked, "We're like synced—there isn't any wires in our ears—literally, to each other." Trump himself told Jones on his show, "Your reputation is amazing. I will not let you down. You will be very, very impressed, I hope. And I think we will be speaking a lot."

✦

THE AM POLITICAL AGENDA completed its takeover of Texas politics in 2014, when Dan Patrick, a drive-time radio talk show host from Houston, was elected lieutenant governor. He had a knack for shameless self-promotion—getting a vasectomy on the air, for instance. My friend Mimi Swartz, a journalist in Houston, wrote in **Texas Monthly** about being on a panel with Patrick in 2003 to interview candidates to be mayor of Houston. "He could not have been more polite or solicitous," Mimi wrote of Patrick. "Just as the program started, he turned to me and casually suggested the following: 'Let me see your questions to make sure we don't duplicate each other.'" He then proceeded to ask all her questions himself—"leaving me to scramble," Mimi recalled, "dumbfounded, in search of new ones as I simultaneously tried to figure out what kind of person was sitting next to me."

Patrick was first elected to the Texas Senate in 2006, running as an outsider. "It was as if Rush Limbaugh were running," Bill Miller, a prominent lobbyist in Austin, told me. Patrick crushed three well-known candidates in the Republican primary, and won the general election with nearly 70 percent of the vote.

Talented and relentless, Patrick brought with him the expected AM platform of anti-abortion absolutism and hostility to same-sex marriage and illegal immigration. "When he was first elected, he was treated as a pariah in the Senate," Miller said. "Everyone thought he was going to be a crazy man." But he won respect through his service on the education committee, eventually serving as its chairman. "He was recognized for his artfulness," says Miller. In 2014, Patrick beat the incumbent lieutenant governor, David Dewhurst, in the primary, and then rolled into office atop another Republican tidal wave. Evan Smith, the cofounder of **The Texas Tribune**, an online journal of state politics, said of Patrick, "He's the most conservative person ever elected to statewide office in the history of Texas."

FM and AM Texas rarely talk to each other, but in September 2015, after the shooting of a police officer in Houston by a former mental patient, Patrick appeared on an NPR station in Austin. Patrick had urged Texans to be always respectful of peace officers and to thoughtfully pick up their tabs when they see them in restaurants. David Brown, the urbane host of **Texas Standard**, gently pointed out that there had been a substantial backlash online to Patrick's statement. Videos of police abuse and the shooting of unarmed citizens were generating national concern about police behavior. "Even people who don't engage in reckless rhetoric have said things like 'Look, respect has to be earned,'" Brown said. "There's a lot of skepticism out there. How do you convince those people?"

"You know, your type of interview has to stop," Patrick abruptly replied. "When I was asked to do an interview on NPR, I asked myself, 'Do I really want to do this? They're not in the police officers' corner.' And you've proven that by your interview."

(Patrick declined several opportunities to speak with me.)

Patrick's signature accomplishment has been the passage of laws allowing certified license holders to openly carry weapons and also to carry concealed weapons on public college campuses. He told Chuck Todd on **Meet the Press** that the fear that guns in public places would create undue alarm was "just propaganda by those who either don't like guns or who are afraid of guns."

The lieutenant governor's statement made me recall an incident on May 11, 2013, when Steve Harrigan and I were in Dallas for a literary event, along with our wives and Steve's daughter Charlotte. We decided to visit the George W. Bush Library on the campus of Southern Methodist University. It was less than a month after the Boston Marathon bombing and the day before a mass shooting at a Mother's Day parade in New Orleans. We were lined up with a large crowd in the vast marble atrium, called Freedom Hall, waiting to enter the exhibitions, when someone cried out, "Active shooter!"

Everyone in the room did exactly the wrong thing: we all hit the deck. An old man near me fell; I saw his head bounce on the marble floor. We were trapped inside a stone box, totally exposed. The library was locked down. Out of nowhere two campus cops appeared with automatic weapons. A private security guard crept behind the ticket booth with his unholstered pistol. People were openly weeping. Roberta was hunched between two evangelical women who whispered urgent prayers into her ears. "I knew this would happen," Steve's daughter said, giving voice to the lack of surprise we felt to be caught in yet another tragedy of the sort that we've all read about and watched on TV.

As it turned out, the event in Dallas was "nothing." A black child had been playing outside with a toy gun, which his parents had purchased earlier at the Texas Ranger museum. Like all toy weapons these days, it had an orange tip to clearly distinguish it from the real thing. The boy needed to go inside to the bathroom, so he gave his toy to his father, who was on a park bench smoking. Suddenly there was a black man with a gun. The cops put him on the ground and handcuffed him, then questioned him for two hours before letting him go. The panic that we experienced that day was unwarranted, but it underscored the fact that the open display of weapons is unnerving, even in Texas, and perhaps especially on college campuses.

The age of mass shootings in public spaces actually began on a campus in Texas—on August 1, 1966, when Charles Whitman, a twenty-five-year-old engineering student, Eagle Scout, and former marine, murdered his mother and his wife, then barricaded himself in the top of the landmark tower in the heart of the University of Texas in Austin. He had a duffel bag full of weapons and a clear view of the entire low-slung town. He could see the narrow lake that divides Austin into north and south. To the west was the Balcones Fault, where the Hill Country begins, and to the east the flat coastal plain. When Whitman pulled the trigger and changed America, the giant clock above him showed that it was 11:48 a.m.

For the next ninety-six minutes, Whitman fired on the campus and the adjacent shops along Guadalupe Street. The first person he shot was Claire Wilson James, a classmate of mine from Woodrow Wilson High School in Dallas. Claire was in summer school. She was eight months pregnant, and Whitman apparently aimed at her unborn child, who was the first to die. Claire lay on the blistering pavement, her abdomen ripped open, pretending to be dead. Her boyfriend, Thomas Eckman, fell dead beside her, shot through the neck. Whitman would shoot forty-three people from the tower that day, killing fourteen (a fifteenth victim eventually succumbed in 2001 from complications from the injury to his kidney).

The plaza in front of the tower where Claire lay with her dead boyfriend was about half the size of a football field, totally exposed. You can't imagine how hot the pavement is in August. As she lay there, believing that this was how her life would end, a redheaded coed named Rita Jones (later, Rita Starpattern, a visual artist) suddenly ran out to her and asked how she might help. Claire told her to run or she'd get shot. Instead, Rita lay beside her on the blistering concrete, peppering Claire with personal questions about what classes she was taking and where she grew up, keeping her from sinking into unconsciousness. Finally, about an hour into the siege, two daring seventeen-year-old boys raced out and dragged Claire to safety behind a statue of Jefferson Davis.

Within minutes of Whitman's sniper attack, students and citizens began firing back. There were deer rifles in the dormitories, and pistols in purses and glove compartments. Armed vigilantes crouched behind statues of Confederate heroes or took aim behind the narrow shelter of a telephone pole. "There was a mood of insanity, of wildness, of craziness in the air," one of the students later recalled.

There were no SWAT teams back then, although the improvisatory police response to the tower shooting would immediately make the case for them. Nor did the university even have a police force of its own. An Austin cop named Houston McCoy, one of the first responders, had a shotgun, which was useless at a distance, so he drove a student to his apartment to pick up his rifle, and then stopped at a hardware store to buy ammunition. There was practically no direction from police headquarters; this kind of thing was completely new. An innovative police sharpshooter tried to shoot Whitman from a private plane. Meantime, three police officers, and a civilian deputized on the spot, climbed to the top of the tower, stepping over the bodies of people Whitman had slain on his way up.

AM Texas and FM Texas drew opposing lessons from the UT shooting. Claire James would later testify before the Texas legislature that the return fire impeded her rescue and prevented police from taking effective action. The courageous Austin police officers who ascended to the top of the tower did have to dodge the incoming fusillade, which showered them with dust and bits of limestone as they crept along the observation deck. On the other hand, gun proponents argued that by keeping Whitman pinned down, the vigilantes reduced the number of casualties by forcing him to shoot through rainwater spouts. "Before anybody fired at him, he had the run of the place. He could shoot over the walls and he could find targets," Ray Martinez, one of the cops who finally shot Whitman to death, recalled. "But of course I was concerned I was going to get killed by friendly fire when we were up there."

The law didn't change after that. It remained illegal for Texans to carry guns outside their home or vehicle. Then, in 1991, George Hennard, who was thirty-five and unemployed, drove his blue Ford pickup through the plate-glass window of the Luby's cafeteria in Killeen. There were about 150 people having lunch. At first, they thought it was a freakish accident. A veterinarian in the room rushed to assist Hennard, who shot him, and then cried, "It's payback time, Bell County! I hope y'all enjoy this!"

Suzanna Hupp, a chiropractor, was having lunch with her parents. "My father and I got down on the floor and we put the table in front of us," she later testified before the U.S. Congress. "It took me a good forty-five seconds to realize this man wasn't there to commit a robbery, he wasn't there for a 'hit.' He was there to shoot as many people as he possibly could." She reached for her purse, where she kept her pistol, then realized that she had left her gun in her car, fearing that she might lose her chiropractor's license if she were caught carrying a concealed weapon.

Her father bravely rushed the shooter, but he was quickly shot down. Hupp told her mother that they needed to make a break for it, and then she raced to the back of the building and jumped out a window. When she looked back, she realized her mother had gone to comfort her dying husband. Hennard put a bullet in her head. "All women of Killeen and Belton are vipers!" he cried. He shot fifty people, killing twenty-three of them, most of them women, before killing himself.

"I'm not really mad at the guy who did this," Hupp told lawmakers in Washington. "That's like being mad at a rabid dog." She continued: "I'm mad at my legislators for legislating me out of the right to protect me and my family." In 1996, Hupp got elected to the Texas House of Representatives, and subsequently passed a law allowing concealed weapons. It was signed by then governor George W. Bush.

That wasn't sufficient for the gun lobby, however. They wanted Texans to have the right to openly carry their handguns—as was already legal in forty-four other states. When framed that way, it did seem odd that Texas gun laws were more restrictive than those in most other places, but did we really want gunslingers in our restaurants and theaters? Gun advocates in Texas set people on edge by parading down Congress Avenue in front of the state capitol, carrying their long guns, as was legal, or walking into Target stores, which they selected for symbolic purposes. Polls showed that two-thirds of Texans opposed the measure, as did a large majority of the police chiefs in the state, but their complaints didn't register. Open carry became legal on January 1, 2016. It's rare to see anyone in public strapping a sidearm, but everywhere you look on public buildings you see signs in English and Spanish barring weapons, both openly carried and concealed. Punitive lawmakers required the font of the lengthy texts be an inch high. Scientific measurements were taken, showing that, when stacked on top of each other, the two signs were the height of a pony.

The statistics on crime and guns are often confounding. Nationally, guns account for 60 percent of all homicides; and yet gun violence has been declining for the last decade. The murder rate in Texas has dropped from 16.9 per 100,000 in 1980 to 4.8 in 2015—an astonishing decline. In California, the most restrictive state in the country for gun ownership, the murder rate is exactly the same as in Texas. The states with the lowest homicide rates are North Dakota and Wyoming, which have very permissive gun laws; and lowest of all, at 1.6 per 100,000, is Vermont, which has "constitutional carry"—i.e., anyone over the age of sixteen can carry a gun. (Vermont is one of thirteen states where permits to carry concealed weapons are not required.) Chicago, which has highly restrictive gun laws, also has one of the highest rates of gun homicides in the country, but it doesn't compare with the District of Columbia, which tops the charts in both restrictive gun laws and gun homicides. When President Obama said, "States with the most gun laws tend to have the fewest gun deaths," he was including suicides, which account for nearly two-thirds of gun deaths nationally.

Still, the rate of murder by gun in the United States is far above that of any other developed Western country, and has been increasing since 2015. The rate of gun murders in the United States is six times higher than in Canada, and more than twenty times higher than in Australia.

Although I appreciate the efforts of the anti-gun lobby, I doubt there is room for anything other than modest reforms. The NRA has permanently changed America. There are now more than 300 million guns in the country—42 percent of the total of civilian firearms in the whole world. Other countries with a high rate of gun ownership (though nowhere near as high as the United States), such as Switzerland, Sweden, and France, have lower rates of gun deaths, largely because of more stringent licensing rules and an emphasis on gun safety. Universal background checks that keep guns away from violent offenders, people on the terrorist watch list, and the mentally ill are the most important steps we could take to limit the damage that guns do to our society.

In November 2017, twenty-six people were shot to death at the First Baptist Church in Sutherland Springs, Texas. Another twenty were injured. Eight of those killed were children. It was (at this writing) the deadliest mass shooting in Texas history. These days, it seems that the killers are always aiming for the record books. In this case, the killer had once escaped from a psychiatric hospital. He had been court-martialed for domestic abuse by the air force, which then failed to put his name in the FBI's database, which might have prevented him from buying weapons over the counter. He was flagged again and again for abusive behavior and death threats. It's hard to imagine a more glaring example of the failure of our national gun laws to prevent a dangerous man from breaking the hearts of so many innocent people.

However, we now live inside the logic that the NRA has created for us: in a world where so many bad people have guns, good people must arm themselves. When the killer came out of the church, leaving behind a lake of blood, a neighbor, Stephen Willeford, who happened to have been a former firearms instructor for the NRA, ran barefoot out of his house, carrying a similar assault-style weapon. He shot the killer twice, and then pursued him in a high-speed chase that ended with the killer's suicide.

President Trump, who was in South Korea at the time, was asked whether the "extreme vetting" he demanded for visa applicants should also be applied to gun purchases. He replied that it would have made "no difference" in the murders in Sutherland Springs, except that stricter laws might have prevented Willeford from having the means to respond. "Instead of having twenty-six dead, he would've had hundreds more dead," the president said. Shortly after the killings, Texas attorney general Ken Paxton said on Fox News that the best solution to future church killings was to arm the parishioners.

Even if stricter gun laws in Texas were clearly shown to make us safer, Texas politicians are so enchanted by guns that there's no chance of that happening. There's a locker-room lust for weaponry that belies the noble-sounding proclamations about self-protection and Second Amendment rights. In 2010, Governor Rick Perry boasted of killing a coyote that was menacing his daughter's Labrador. Perry was jogging at the time, but naturally he was packing heat—a Ruger .380—and he dispatched the coyote with a single shot. The gun's manufacturer promptly issued a Coyote Special edition of the gun, which comes in a box labeled For Sale to Texans Only.

The idea of jogging with a gun may sound uncomfortable and a little bizarre, but in this category Perry is not as goofy as Ted Cruz. In the midst of his presidential campaign, Cruz posted a YouTube video titled **Making Machine-Gun Bacon with Ted Cruz**. "There are few things I enjoy more than on weekends cooking breakfast with the family," he informs us, as he stands at a firing range. "Of course, in Texas, we cook bacon a little differently than most folks." He wraps a strip of bacon around the muzzle of a semiautomatic AR-15 (not an actual machine gun), and around that, a piece of foil. Then he fires away. Soon, grease is spattering among the shell casings. "Mmmm! Machine-gun bacon!" the senator says, as he snacks on the finished product. The object of the video apparently was to show a jollier and more human side of the candidate.

With more than a million Texans licensed to carry handguns, the state is actually far behind Florida, with 1.7 million. "I'm EMBARRASSED," Governor Greg Abbott tweeted in 2015; "Texas #2 in nation for new gun purchases, behind

CALIFORNIA. Let's pick up the pace Texans. @ NRA."

On June 13, 2015, a gunman assaulted police headquarters in Dallas in an armored van that he had purchased on eBay. It was billed as a "Zombie Apocalypse Assault Vehicle," and came equipped with gun ports and bulletproof windows. Police were finally able to disable the vehicle and kill the shooter with a .50-caliber sniper rifle (also available on the Internet). Governor Abbott discounted the event as an "isolated incident by someone who had serious mental challenges, as well as a possible criminal background," without remarking that those alarming deficiencies had not prevented the shooter from purchasing powerful weapons. That same day, Governor Abbott went to a gun range in Pflugerville, outside Austin, and signed into law the bill requiring public universities and colleges to allow handguns on campus and in dorms. He did this despite the vehement opposition from the chancellor of the University of Texas system, William McRaven, the former navy admiral who as head of the United States Special Operations Command had overseen the operation that killed Osama bin Laden. The bill went into effect on August 1, 2016, exactly fifty years after the Whitman shooting.

When the students returned for the fall semester, a protest group called Cocks Not Glocks handed out more than 4,500 dildos. Some of them were huge and I think possibly lethal. There was a dildo-juggling contest and T-shirts emblazoned with the slogan Take It and Come. Although there is a policy at the university forbidding the public display of any image that is obscene, the administration sagely chose to let this issue reside in the domain of free speech. Supporters of the protest were tying the sex toys onto their back-packs, and others were planting them in the shade of the campus live oaks, where they looked like a forest of mushrooms after a heavy rain.

★

AN ECCENTRIC FEATURE of the new gun laws is that people entering the state capitol can skip the long lines of tourists waiting to pass through the metal detectors if they show the guards a license-to-carry permit. In other words, the people most likely to bring weapons into the building aren't scanned at all. Many of the people who breeze through are lawmakers or staffers who actually do tote concealed weapons into the offices and onto the floor of the legislature. But some lobbyists and reporters have also obtained gun licenses just to skirt the lines.

I'm one of those people.

In the spring of 2016, I signed up to take a class at Central Texas Gun Works that would qualify me to carry a weapon. There were about thirty people in the class, including six women. Most of the day was spent learning the Texas general firearms laws, which are more nuanced and confusing than I expected. One can't carry a gun in amusement parks, hospitals, sporting events, school buses, bars, a polling place, a court, a correctional facility, or "within 1000 feet of a correctional facility designated as a place of execution on a day of execution if proper notice is posted." Private businesses, such as supermarkets, can ban guns from their premises; Whole Foods has done so, but Kroger has not.

One of the surprises is that if you have a handgun in your car and you're drunk, it doesn't matter if you're unlicensed; but if you are licensed, you are liable to be charged with a Class A misdemeanor, which can mean a year in jail and a $4,000 fine. "A lot of my students decide not to get the license because of that," our instructor, Michael Cargill, told us. He showed some cautionary real-life videos. A convenience-store security camera recorded a customer who happened upon a robbery in progress; the customer frantically pulls out his concealed weapon and plugs the clerk, not the robber. Another video shows a target shooter plunking cans off a log with a rifle; one bullet misfires and the shooter peeks down the barrel to see what's going on, when suddenly his gimme cap is blown off his head. People do a lot of stupid things with guns, which is one reason I've always been wary of owning one.

Much of the law portion of this class was taken up with the consequences of shooting another person, which is what handguns are for, coyotes notwithstanding. It's lawful to pull the trigger if someone has broken into your home or business or vehicle, or to prevent the commission of a serious crime. Like many states, Texas also has a "stand your ground" provision, which says that a person who is present in a place where he has a right to be also has the right to use deadly force if he reasonably believes it is necessary to protect himself or others. That was the defense in the acquittal of George Zimmerman in Florida after he killed the unarmed black high school student Trayvon Martin in 2012.

"Your life will change the moment you pull the trigger," Cargill warned us. For one thing, you'll be under arrest while the cops sort out whether or not to charge you, a process that can take several days. And there are personal consequences that are difficult to calculate. One of Cargill's previous students did shoot an intruder in his home, a seventeen-year-old boy whose last words were "Would you call my mother?"

After we took a written exam, an ex-cop came into the class to sell us insurance for legal expenses in case we shot anybody. Several people signed up (I did not). Then we drove out to the firing range, an open pit behind the airport surrounded by mesquite trees and pin oaks. There was another class in the range next to us practicing some kind of tactical exercise, which consisted of loping along with a pistol and firing at metal targets— **Ping! Ping! Ping!**—then performing a barrel roll and grabbing a shotgun and blowing away a Bernie Sanders yard sign. That seemed politically off to me. Sanders was far more liberal on gun laws than any of his Democratic opponents in the presidential primary. All of my classmates arrived with their own weapons; I was the only one who had to rent one. Even the middle-aged women in the class brought along their Colts and Berettas and Smith & Wessons. When my turn to shoot came, Cargill handed me a 9mm Glock.

I hadn't fired a handgun in fifty years, since I was in high school. For a while, there was a snub-nosed .38 in our house; it was the gun my uncle used to kill himself. I don't know why my father brought it home. I took it out in the country with some friends and we tried shooting bottles off a fence post, but it was not made for target practice. After a while, the gun disappeared from the house. I never knew what happened to it.

I chatted with some of my fellow students at the firing range, curious as to what had brought them here. The mixed group included an old bearded hippie, an ex-cop, a physical therapist. One woman with a SIG Sauer P226, the kind of pistol that U.S. Navy SEAL teams use, said she "just wanted to get out of my comfort zone." There was an Asian man in a button-down shirt who was continually checking his email as he waited to shoot. He said that he had bought his semiautomatic pistol several years ago but never really used it. "So why'd you buy it?" I asked him. "That was back when Obama was going to take away our guns," he said, as he briefly glanced up from his phone. "I thought I'd better go ahead and get one while I could." (Obama termed the notion that he was planning to take away Americans' guns a conspiracy theory.)

There was one guy I was especially curious about. He was burly and bearded and had tattoos spilling down his right arm. He wore a black T-shirt that said Stop Terrorism—Shoot Back. The fear of domestic terrorism is overblown, but it has certainly empowered gun advocates. "Innocents like us will continue to be slaughtered in concert halls, sports stadiums, restaurants and airplanes," Wayne LaPierre, the leader of the National Rifle Association, said shortly after the Paris terror attacks in 2015. "But when evil comes knocking on our door, Americans have a power no other people on the planet share"—i.e., the Second Amendment. Such fearmongering has been extremely effective. Whenever there's another mass shooting in Whitman's America, gun sales invariably rise. In the decade between 2005 and 2015, more than 300,000 Americans were killed by guns compared with 94 who died in domestic terror attacks.

The man in the Stop Terrorism T-shirt was hanging around with a young couple; it turned out they had all moved down from Chicago together. I asked them what made them choose Texas. "The weather," they said unanimously. They told me they had been classmates at Northern Illinois University in 2008, when a graduate student named Steven Kazmierczak burst into Cole Hall. An oceanography class was under way in the auditorium. Like Whitman, Kazmierczak was toting an armory of weapons, and he had the students trapped. Police later recovered fifty-four bullet casings and shotgun shells. Twenty-one people were shot, and six died, including Kazmierczak, who killed himself before the police arrived. As it happened, the shooter was wearing a black T-shirt that said Terrorist.

I asked the three of them if the Texas gun laws were one of the reasons they had chosen my state. "Not entirely, but it was a plus," one of them said.

I knew from the few times I went hunting as a boy with my dad that I was a good shot. I liked the feel of the gun in my hand and the little kick when it fired, like a horse cocking its head when you give him your heels. We were shooting at a blue silhouette with the bull's-eye at mid-sternum. I scored 246 out of 250. I began to think about what it would be like to own my own handgun.

According to a study published by Injury Prevention, about 35 percent of Texans own guns, close to the national average. I still have my old Remington .22 from my Boy Scout days on the top shelf in the hall closet, so I guess I'm included in that number. Despite the controversy that rages on this issue now, the incidence of gun ownership in the United States has declined from more than half of all households in 1982 to a little more than a third currently—the lowest it has been in almost forty years. And yet the United States still has the highest rate of gun ownership in the world—88.8 guns per 100 residents—and gun purchases are also at historic highs. The statistics are skewed by the fact that gun owners are acquiring significant personal arsenals. My Stop Terrorism—Shoot Back informant told me he has nine guns; that's one more than the average gun owner possesses, according to **The Washington Post**. Our instructor, Michael Cargill, told us he was carrying three concealed weapons while he was teaching class. I couldn't spot any of them.

I was at a book club recently in Austin where

one of the members recalled being in a restaurant in Houston when President George H. W. Bush and the first lady entered. The Secret Service set up a metal detector that the other diners had to pass through. "They had a big bowl for people to drop their guns in," the woman recalled, "and there were all these big-haired Houston women pulling pistols out of their purses." I've never seen anything similar in Texas, but the reputation for a high rate of gun possession does affect behavior; in my experience, Texans drive far more courteously than New Yorkers or, my God, Bostonians, where the consequences of being a jerk may not be fatal. Part of me longs to live in a place where people are assumed to be disarmed, like England, which has very few guns and also hardly any snakes. The English don't even have poison ivy. In Texas, it sometimes seems that every living thing can bite or poke or sting or shoot you. You always have to be a little bit on guard.

Speaking of snakes, I was down at the capitol one wintry day and ran into a group of Jaycees from Sweetwater, a West Texas town famed for its annual rattlesnake roundup. To promote the event, the Jaycees had brought a dozen rattlers and dumped them out on the chilly outdoor rotunda. The Jaycees were striding around in Kevlar boots. They would prod the lethargic creatures with hooked poles every once in a while to stir them to life, and the snakes would hiss and rattle and then return to their somnolent state. "They get a little lazy," one of the Jaycees said disparagingly. A few tourists and staffers ventured out onto the patio, but most people were standing at the windows with their mouths open.

The spokesman of the Jaycees was Rob McCann. "We've been doing the roundup for fifty-eight years," he told me. They find about four to five thousand pounds of snakes a year; one year, they gathered fifteen thousand pounds, and yet the number of snakes in Sweetwater never seems to diminish. "We hunt the same dens year after year," the first man said. "You want to hold one?"

"Not especially."

That evening I called our daughter, Caroline, who was in Chicago finishing her MFA at the Art Institute. I asked her how she was getting along. She was living near a country-and-western bar so she wouldn't feel so far from home, but it wasn't the same. "People here can't dance," she complained.

I mentioned that I'd just been to the capitol and visited the snake handlers. "Oh, I love Texas!" she said with a lack of irony that is hard to convey.

★

A GOOD FRIEND OF MINE, John Burnett, is a reporter for NPR. He and Hawk Mendenhall, the station manager for KUT, our local NPR affiliate, literally embody FM Texas. They have been cycling across the state to raise money for charity. In 2015, they rode from Brownsville, at the very bottom of the horn-shaped tip of the state, to the Red River on the border of Oklahoma, logging 734 miles. That's farther than from Charlotte, North Carolina, to New York. A year later, they pedaled from Sunland Park, New Mexico, just west of El Paso, to Merryville, Louisiana, just across the Sabine River, a total of 1,113 miles over seventeen days, mostly on two-lane back roads through the small towns of the state. West Texas was one long stretch of headwinds and road-killed jackrabbits, through counties that are larger than some New England states. Once they passed Navasota, the South began. "Suddenly, the waitresses began calling us 'honey' and 'sweetheart.' We saw a lot of Confederate flags," John said. "The state hasn't changed so much as it has become more like 'Texas'—the stereotype—than it's ever been. There are so many more barbecue joints, more gun shops and target ranges. But one thing that hasn't changed is the deep, abiding friendliness."

John and Hawk stopped to eat at the J and P Bar & Grill in Comstock, near the Mexican border. "A couple of cowboys walked in," John recalled. He stiffened a bit when he saw them. "I could feel the cultural distance immediately." The cowboys still had their spurs on. Their hair was matted in the shape of their hats, and they had the vivid tan lines of men who live outdoors. They were drinking Coors Light and shooting pool, but they obviously took note of John and Hawk, two gray-haired men in garish Spandex outfits like aging Spider-Men. One of the cowboys finally demanded to know what they were up to.

"We're riding across Texas on our bikes," John said.

"Why the hell would you do that?"

John explained that they were raising money to buy bicycles and books for schoolchildren in Kenya.

The cowboys returned to the pool table, but as John and Hawk were leaving, one of them stuffed two $20 bills in John's pocket. "Give this to them kids in Africa," he said.

Friendliness is a sort of mandate in the state. The state motto is Friendship. Highway signs enjoin us to Drive Friendly. And indeed, if you are traveling on a two-lane road and see a vehicle coming from the opposite direction, the protocol is to raise an index finger about an inch off the rim of the steering wheel in a laconic salute. Steve's brother-in-law says he decided to move to Texas when he saw people thanking the bus driver as they disembarked.

Texas advertises itself in travel magazines as "a whole other country"—an echo of its decade of independence as a republic—and it still loves to think of itself as an independent entity. It is certainly big enough to stand alone. "Texas is more than five times the size of New York state," John Bainbridge marveled in 1961, and "bigger than any country in Europe except Russia." I still recall the gloom that settled over Texas in January 1959, when Alaska joined the Union. We had to change the lyrics of our kitschy state song:

> **Texas, Our Texas! All hail the mighty State!**
> **Texas, Our Texas! So wonderful so great!**
> **Largest and grandest, withstanding ev'ry test**
> **O Empire wide and glorious, you stand**
> **supremely blest!**

Suddenly, we weren't the "largest" anymore, we were the "boldest."

The Republic of Texas was far larger than the present entity, taking in half of New Mexico, portions of Oklahoma, Kansas, Colorado, and southern Wyoming. We have stopped mourning the loss of all those mountains and trout streams, but the imaginative lure of a distant Texan Camelot seems only to get stronger. "When we came into the nation in 1845, we were a republic," Rick Perry informed a group of visitors when he was still governor. "And one of the deals was, we can leave any time we want. So, we're kind of thinking about that again." Every schoolchild learns in the seventh grade, while taking the mandatory Texas history class, that when Texas entered the Union it came with a prenuptial agreement: the possibility of splitting itself into five states—with ten senators!—any time it chooses. It does not have the right to secede, however.

Texas isn't actually alone in its longing to break free of the federal grip. A 2014 Reuters poll found that nearly a fourth of all Americans would like to see their own state leave the Union, about the same as the number of Texans who feel that way. After the Trump victory, secession fever suddenly jumped to California. We recently learned that a lot of secessionist fever was being fanned by Russian trolls on Facebook. The largest secessionist page, "Heart of Texas," was among the Russian propaganda sites that Facebook shut down; it had more followers than the official Texas Democrat and Texas Republican party Facebook pages combined.

And yet, it's a strange, dysfunctional marriage between Texas and the United States. Texas is at once the most super-American of states and the most indigestible. A 2011 MyLife.com poll found that five of the ten most patriotic cities in America—measured by the percentage of the population in the armed forces, veteran spending, community and social service workers, and

fireworks popularity on the Fourth of July—
were in Texas. At the same time, there is a defiant sense of apartness and a grudging feeling of
being bossed around. When our current governor, Greg Abbott, was the Texas attorney general,
he described his job this way: "I go into the office
in the morning, I sue Barack Obama, and then I
go home." As governor, under Trump, with even
less to do, he advocates a constitutional convention to consider various amendments that would
transfer power from the federal government to
the states, which his predecessor Rick Perry once
called the "lavatories of democracy." A recent law
would create the Texas Bullion Depository—"the
first state-level facility of its kind in the nation,"
Governor Abbott tweeted when he signed the bill,
adding, "California may be the golden state, but
Texans deserve to keep their gold in-state!"

The depository was seen as a step toward putting
Texas on a gold standard if and when we divorce
ourselves from the United States. Actually, most
of the billion dollars in gold that the state believes
belongs in Texas is owned by the University of
Texas Investment Management Company ($861
million!), which has no interest in taking that out
of an HSBC bank vault in New York City.

Sanford Levinson, a distinguished law professor
at UT, compares Texas to Scotland—another formerly independent nation that has never entirely

accepted the loss of its independence. The difference is that Scotland actually can secede, if its voters choose to; for Texas, that battle has long since been lost. The only way Texit might work is through a constitutional amendment that would allow American voters to say: Just go.

## SEVEN

# Big D

On July 7, 2016, hundreds of marchers on a hot summer night in Dallas were protesting the police slayings of black men in Minnesota and Louisiana. Two days before, a video had surfaced that showed two white cops in Baton Rouge shooting Alton Sterling, 37, who was already pinned to the ground when one of the officers cried out, "He's got a gun!" They shot him six times. Sterling did have a loaded .38 in his pocket. Another video appeared the next day, streaming on Facebook Live. When the video begins, Philando Castile, 32, has already been shot. He had been pulled over by police in a suburb of St. Paul for a broken taillight. When he voluntarily disclosed, as required by law, that he had a license to carry a gun, and then reached for his wallet, one of the officers shot him four times.

Castile's girlfriend, Diamond Reynolds, narrates the video as Castile, moaning and covered in blood, slumps against her. "He just shot his arm off," she says of the cop, who is still pointing his weapon at the dying man. "I told him not to reach for it!" the officer cries in an agitated voice. "I told him to get his hand open!"

"You told him to get his ID, sir, his driver's license," she says.

Castile falls silent. "Please don't tell me that my boyfriend went just like that," Reynolds says. Her four-year-old daughter is in the backseat.

"Keep your hands where you are!" the cop says huskily.

"Yes, I will, sir, I'll keep my hands where they are. Please don't tell me this, Lord. Please, Jesus, don't tell me that he's gone."

By now, a number of cops have raced to the scene. They are all holding weapons on Reynolds. They order her to get out of the car and walk backward toward them, then drop to her knees. They take the phone out of her hands and toss it on the ground, but it's still recording, pointed at the sky and the electrical lines overhead, as she is handcuffed. "They threw my phone, Facebook," Reynolds says, as an ambulance siren sounds in the background. A cop repeatedly screams, "Fuck! Fuck!" (The policeman who shot Castile, Jeronimo Yanez, was later acquitted of all charges against him.)

These two killings shook the country. A movement, Black Lives Matter, had sprung up in 2013, after the acquittal of George Zimmerman, the neighborhood watch captain who killed Trayvon Martin, an unarmed black teenager, in a gated community in Central Florida. Other police shootings caused the movement to spread and passions to rise.

There were protests against the killings all over the country, but Dallas was an inappropriate target for such a demonstration; in the last few years, under the leadership of its black police chief, David O. Brown, the murder rate was lower than it had been since 1930, and police shootings had dropped sharply, along with complaints about improper use of force. Although the police were undermanned and underpaid, the Dallas department had developed a national reputation for fair and nonviolent action. Indeed, during the march, some officers tweeted photographs of themselves standing with the marchers.

One could believe that if there was a way of healing the rift between police and African American communities, it was to be found in Dallas. More than anyone in the city, perhaps in the country, David Brown understood the pain that both the police and the black community were experiencing. On Father's Day 2010, a few weeks after he had been sworn in as police chief, his own son, David Brown Jr., shot and killed two men, one of them a cop.

But perhaps Dallas is destined to shoulder the burden of certain tragedies that mark our path as a country. When the killer, Micah Johnson, opened fire during the Black Lives Matter march, he was only two blocks from Dealey Plaza, the site of Kennedy's assassination. The echoes were unnerving. The wounded and slain were taken to Parkland Hospital, where the president had been pronounced dead. Lee Harvey Oswald and Micah Johnson were both military veterans with undistinguished records. Discontented with their inconsequential lives and angry at America, Oswald had turned to Marxism and Johnson to a black separatist movement called the New Black Panther Party, which is headquartered in Dallas. They were opportunists, trying to murder their way into history. Before killing Kennedy, Oswald had taken a shot at General Edwin Walker, a right-wing racist. Johnson had filled his house with bomb-making materials and must have been planning a bloody spectacle, but he hadn't settled on a target. The month before he killed the police officers, Johnson had asked permission from organizers to bring guns to a protest rally against Donald Trump.

⋆

THE LAST TIME I had been in Dallas was in 2013, to give a speech on the fiftieth anniversary of the Kennedy assassination. Dallas has always had a divided opinion about acknowledging that tragedy. An argument raged for years about whether to tear down the Texas School Book Depository, where Oswald worked and made the fatal shot, or turn it into the museum that it is today. The shame and humiliation that Dallasites of that era felt, when Dallas was called the City of Hate, still lingered; even half a century later there was a reluctance to revisit the tragedy—indeed, this would be the first official commemoration of the event. Dallas's mayor, Mike Rawlings, saw the fiftieth anniversary as an opportunity to provide catharsis for a wound that has never entirely healed.

Oddly, the symposium was held in a country-western nightclub in the old warehouse district. Behind the large stage was a photograph of the president and the first lady in the open convertible on that fateful day. Our handsome, lantern-jawed governor John Connally and his wife, Nellie, were in the seat in front of the Kennedys, waving to the friendly crowd. Kennedy had come to Texas in order to heal the political rift between the conservative faction of the Democratic Party in the state, represented by Connally, and the liberal wing, led by Senator Ralph Yarborough.

In my speech, I said that I saw Dallas as a city of paradoxes. When two contradictory propositions appear to be equally true, they may contain an inner truth, a mystery that holds opposing realities together in a strange and powerful dynamic. For instance, in 1963, when I was a junior in high school, I was governed by two such unreconcilable convictions: nothing would ever happen in Dallas, and the world as we knew it would soon come to an end. We were living in the shadow of nuclear annihilation, which infused the overheated religious atmosphere of the city with a giddy sense of apocalypse. The city was experiencing all the usual turbulence of a boomtown, including high rates of suicide, murder, and divorce, along with a right-wing political culture that had run off the rails. And yet, to a sixteen-year-old virgin, Dallas seemed frozen, unchangeable, and stultifying. Everybody dressed alike and thought alike and voted alike, which added to the sense of cultural paralysis. The only black person I knew was our weekly maid. In such a racially segregated environment, the main dividing line in the white community was between the Methodists (which we were) and the Baptists. I scarcely knew any Episcopalians. The first man I knew to sport a beard, other than Santa Claus, was Stanley Marcus—the city's great merchant—whose decision to grow one caused an uproar.

Political violence was already a feature of the city before Kennedy came to town. In November 1960, during the presidential campaign, Lyndon Johnson was making a speech at the Adolphus Hotel downtown. He and Lady Bird were greeted by a group of wealthy white women, later termed the Mink Coat Mob. This was a time in American politics when civility was still a part of public life, so the assault by these enraged women—spitting, cursing—was a shock. Bill Moyers, Johnson's former press secretary, later told me that he actually believed these cosseted society ladies were going to tear him to pieces right there in the lobby of the hotel. The extreme partisanship that would eventually overwhelm American politics was beginning to come of age—here, in my own city.

Then, in October 1963, Adlai Stevenson, at that time the U.S. ambassador to the United Nations, appeared in Dallas to speak on United Nations Day. The United Nations was seen as a communist front in Texas. There were billboards and bumper stickers all over the state demanding Get the U.S. Out of the U.N. Earlier that same year, the state legislature had passed a law criminalizing the display of the United Nations flag.

Stevenson had split the Texas Democratic Party when he ran for president in 1952 against Dwight

Eisenhower. The main issue in Texas at the time was whether the state's boundary extended from the shore at low tide to three marine leagues—about nine miles—into the Gulf of Mexico, an area called the tidelands. For a hundred years, Texas's claim to the tidelands was uncontested. Then oil was discovered in the Gulf, and the federal government asserted ownership.

Other states had similar claims, but Texas had a stronger case: it had entered the Union as an independent country, with its seaward boundary clearly accepted. The tidelands issue became the greatest conflict between the states and the federal government since the Civil War. Stevenson opposed ceding the tidelands to Texas, but Eisenhower, who was born in the state, supported the claim of Texas and other coastal states to their submerged lands. He signed a bill to that effect, but the dispute wasn't resolved until 1960, when the U.S. Supreme Court ruled in Texas's favor, and the 2,440,650 underwater acres finally belonged to the state, free and clear. So much wealth has come into Texas as a result. Our public schools were built in part by oil leases from the Gulf.

In Texas, Stevenson embodied the egg-headed intellectuals of the Eastern Establishment. Governor Allan Shivers's wife, Marialice, observed of the Democratic candidate, "No man who wears white shoes will ever be elected president of the

United States." Governor Shivers then led a faction of Democrats supporting Eisenhower, called Shivercrats. It was a foreshadowing of the great political pivot that would turn Texas red.

Stanley Marcus had urged Stevenson not to come to Dallas, but he didn't want to appear craven to the daring New Frontiersmen of the Kennedy administration. Heckled off the stage, Stevenson left the auditorium, guarded by a cordon of police officers, who pushed through a crowd of a hundred protestors. For whatever reason, Stevenson decided to step outside his zone of protection, attempting to reason with a woman, the wife of a prominent insurance executive. She was carrying a sign that read If You Seek Peace, Ask Jesus, which she brought down on the ambassador's head, a spectacular expression of the Dallas paradox.

One month later, on November 22, my father was waiting for Kennedy at the Trade Mart along with other city leaders, who were expecting the president for lunch. Meanwhile, Kennedy's motorcade was driving past our church, First United Methodist, at the corner of Ross Avenue and North Harwood Street, where our pastor and staff were standing on the sidewalk. The motorcade turned onto Main Street, where thousands of Dallasites were waving and cheering. It was a lovely fall day. As they entered Dealey Plaza,

Nellie Connally turned and remarked, "You can't say Dallas doesn't love you, Mr. President." They were the last words he heard in life. The Dallas paradox.

In my speech, I said that if John F. Kennedy was fated to be murdered somewhere, I was glad it happened in Dallas. Yes, the city was wrongly held responsible for the president's death. Nearly everyone in the country, and certainly everyone in Dallas, immediately believed that Kennedy's killer must have been a right-wing fanatic. How confounding it was to learn that Oswald was a Marxist—this in a city where there were scarcely any Democrats. And yet the city was taken down, humiliated, in a way that few places in our country have ever been, made to take the blame for a tragedy caused by someone who was, if anything, the opposite of the Dallas mentality, the Anti-Dallas.

But humiliation was exactly what Dallas needed. The city's extreme partisanship, its militarism, isolationism, and America-firstness, were taking us into a dark place. Dallas was becoming the headquarters of a new kind of corporate fascism, which suppressed democratic checks and balances while bullying its opponents into silence. **The Dallas Morning News**, the most important paper in the state and one of the leading papers in the country, gave voice to the extremism and justified it. There seemed to be no force strong enough to resist this dangerous trend; as it turned out, though, one terrible deed changed everything. Dallas became more open and tolerant, more progressive, more "vigorous," to use a favorite Kennedy word. Dallas is a far better city because Kennedy died there.

Now, I look out at the country and wonder if America is turning into Dallas 1963. That would be the greatest paradox of all.

★

THE BLACK LIVES MATTER MARCH had been assembled overnight. Although the march itself was peaceful, Jeff Hood, a white Baptist minister and co-organizer of the protest, had given voice to sentiments similar to those that Micah Johnson had expressed, calling police the enemy. "God damn white America!" Hood shouted through a bullhorn. "White America is a fucking lie!" The minister later explained, "We were interested in creating a space where anger could be let out." Soon after Hood spoke, the killer began his assault. "Immediately when I heard the shots, I looked up and saw what I believed were two police officers that went down," Hood said. "I grabbed my shirt. I felt like I might have been shot so I was feeling around. The sergeant [standing next to me] ran toward the shooting. I ran in the opposite direction. I was concerned about the seven or eight hundred people behind me. I was screaming, 'Run! Run! Active shooter! Active shooter! Run! Run!'"

Chief Brown would note that within the Black Lives Matter march, there were about twenty or thirty people carrying rifles and ammo gear, some wearing gas masks and bulletproof vests. There's no telling how many were carrying concealed weapons. They scattered like everyone else when the shots rang out. Lieutenant Governor Dan Patrick, the prime mover in the liberalization of Texas gun laws, called those people "hypocrites." Imagine what would have happened had they actually started firing. Many of the marchers believed that they were being targeted by the police; that was, after all, the reason they were protesting in the first place. There is raw footage from one of the television stations showing marchers screaming at the police during the siege. No doubt, in the confusion those armed protestors would have been aiming at the cops. While the Dallas assault was going on, cops had to track down each of the marchers who was openly carrying a weapon to make sure he or she wasn't the shooter. It's amazing that only five people were killed, all of them police officers, and nine other cops injured, along with two civilians.

Once again, the city was grieving, angry, and

on edge. How would the world view Dallas now? At a candlelight vigil a few days after the killings, a detective next to me remarked, "One crazed person doesn't represent the entire community," although of course the lesson of Dallas in 1963 was that a single armed assassin could frame the reputation of a city for decades.

"We can choose to let the anger fester inside us," said Senior Corporal Marie St. John, the partner of Michael Smith, one of those killed, "or we can take our agony and anguish and direct it toward good, toward fostering an environment of hope." Officer Patrick Zamarripa was a navy veteran who had joined the police department in 2011 after three tours in Iraq. His fellow officer Josh Rodriguez recalled that the day his friend died, he had bought a meal for a homeless man who complained that his potato chips had been stolen. Zamarripa had sat with him while he ate and made sure he felt safe. "He wanted to be a hero to everyone," his friend said.

★

THE DALLAS—FORT WORTH AREA, known as the Metroplex, serves as the corporate headquarters for many of the most important publicly traded companies in the country, including ExxonMobil, one of the most profitable companies in the world. Other giants—Toyota, Liberty

Mutual, JPMorgan Chase—are joining the flock. Dallas is the hottest market in the country for commercial construction. Even at the height of the oil crash in 2015, Dallas alone added nearly a hundred thousand jobs. And Dallas likes to spend its wealth. It has more shopping centers per capita than any other city in the country.

But if Dallas provides a model for the Trumpian economy, there is a dark side to it as well. Although income inequality in the Metroplex is below that of America's other largest cities—New York, Los Angeles, and Chicago—when measured by neighborhoods, the greater Dallas area is the most unequal big city in America, divided by pockets of concentrated poverty and extreme affluence. One cannot miss the racial division that is at the heart of this disparity. Nationally, on average, black people make up 40 percent of the homeless population, but in Dallas, according to a census of the homeless in January 2017, that figure is 63 percent.

The morning after the candlelight vigil at Dallas City Hall, Cindy Crain, the director of the Metro Dallas Homeless Alliance, escorted me to a couple of the tent cities under the highway overpasses. "There's a lot of pressure to get the homeless out of town," Crain told me, as we parked on Coombs Street under the I-45 flyway. A few months earlier, there would have been three hundred tents, but the city had ordered the encampment to be closed. When we visited, there were about 120 people remaining. Churches in the area had once provided food and tents, but their congregations had decided that they were contributing to the homeless problem by supporting the lifestyle. Crain was checking to see if the people under the flyway had found another spot to live. All of them had to be gone within a week, and yet the shelters around town were brimming. "I only have housing for four people," she said. "I don't know what the others are going to do."

"This spot is ninety percent black," Crain said as she hobbled across the rubbled ground. She had recently undergone a hip operation and was walking with a cane, which she mainly used as a pointer. "This is the drug section, this is the elderly section," she said. "The average resident is an African American male, about fifty years old, touching the criminal justice system. Many of them are disabled." I could see a few wheelchairs among the battered bikes and shopping carts scattered about. There were piles of trash and empty quart bottles of cheap beer. Traffic rumbled overhead. A woman squatted beside a small wood fire brewing camp coffee next to the railroad track.

Everyone I met was from Texas and most from the Dallas area. A man introduced himself as Cowboy, the only white person I saw in this camp.

He said he'd been here the longest, four years.
He had a **Playboy** tattoo on his arm and lived in
a kind of fort made of plywood and cardboard.
There was a woman named Tammy, who wore a
sports bra and black slacks. She came from Plano,
an affluent community north of Dallas, and she
complained of liver problems. I asked her what
brought her to this place. "I was in the Terrell
State Hospital," she said, mentioning a psychiatric facility. She was also in prison. "I finally got
burned out in Dallas," she said. Harold Dixon is a
former high school athlete who has been homeless
"a long time." He's sixty years old and has a bad
knee. "I used to work for Toyota, in the car wash,"
he said. That was his last job. Many of the older
people among the homeless have never qualified
for Social Security benefits because they were
incarcerated, either in prison or in mental facilities. "Almost all these people have lived institu-
tional lives," Crain said. Unless they have family
willing to take them in, or can find a temporary
shelter with space, they have few alternatives to
living on the street.

Crain dropped me off at CitySquare, a social
services consortium housed in clean, utilitarian
offices on Malcolm X Boulevard in South Dallas. There were kids playing ball in the yard. The
facility offered a food pantry, a health clinic, job
training, financial coaching, a literacy center, and

a legal adviser. "This is a collective impact center," Larry M. James, the director of CitySquare, told me. "Our mission is to help working families survive and move them toward thriving." In the past year, the organization served fifty-five thousand people. In the distance was the city's striking skyline, a beacon of opportunity that seems out of reach for so many.

"I grew up in a very different Texas," James said, as we headed downtown to the Morton H. Meyerson Symphony Center, where President Obama was going to speak. Now, he observed, "the things that draw people here are the same things that make people poor." The low tax base entices industry but chokes off social services. The state's refusal to expand Medicaid is an especially galling example, James believes. "It's such low-hanging fruit and it could relieve so much misery."

Later, I talked to Congresswoman Eddie Bernice Johnson, from Dallas, who expressed her frustration. The city has passed bonds to create what she calls "a model program" for housing the homeless. "But that doesn't take care of the people who don't want to live in shelters," she said. "It tells me about the inadequacy of mental health care in Texas. Sometimes, I think we're going backwards as a state. We are the leading state in technology. We're the leading state in trade. Certainly, Dallas has the lowest unemployment of any big city in the country. Where we're lacking is in mental health care and public education."

★

AS I WAS STANDING in line to go through security for the president's speech, I ran into Andy Stoker, the pastor of my old church, First United Methodist. The last time I was in that church, I stood in the pulpit and gave a eulogy for my father. For him, First Church had been a spiritual home. He had left a bequest to the church to create a meal service for the homeless. But for me, the church was a source of disillusionment and anger. It was in that very church that another tragedy had taken place that would shake the city of Dallas, a tragedy that also touched my family's life.

Walker Railey was one of the great stars of Methodism when he took over the pulpit of First Church in 1980. I was living in Austin by then, but I sometimes saw him preach when I came back to the city. Railey was bald, with a bulbous forehead and intense blue eyes, which scanned his congregation like searchlights. I experienced what so many would later remark on—Railey's gift for seeming to speak directly to me.

Dallas at the time had more churches per capita than any other city in America. The preachers were compensated like business executives, which allowed them entrée into the uppermost social circles. The piety that the city was known for hid another Dallas, however—one that had the highest rate of overall crime and the highest divorce rate in the country. Railey quickly became seen as a progressive leader, championing causes that were often unpopular within such a conservative milieu—gay rights, racial justice, opposition to the death penalty, equal rights for women—issues that brought younger people into the congregation. His social activism was just what Dallas needed. In his very first sermon, he had blown into the microphone on the pulpit, indicating that he was breathing life back into the church.

On Easter Sunday 1987, Railey preached what would be his last sermon in First Church. For the past several weeks he had been receiving threatening letters, including one that very morning. "Easter is when Christ arose, but you are going down," the message said.

Railey approached the pulpit wearing a bulletproof vest under the pastoral stole that his wife, Peggy, had sewed for him. She was an organist in the church and the mother of their two young children. Uniformed police officers guarded the entryways. The odd topic Railey had chosen to speak on this Easter was drawn from a book titled **The Passover Plot**, which airs the theory that Jesus faked his Crucifixion.

Three days later, Railey came home to find Peggy lying on the floor of the garage, her face blue, her body heaving. She had been strangled. Police would later say that Railey's three-year-old son had been partially strangled as well. "Wife of Anti-Racist Cleric Is Attacked," read the headline in **The New York Times**. Railey was viewed as a martyr for racial justice; it was as if the threats against him and the attempted murder of his wife were attacks on Dallas as well. His friend Rabbi Sheldon Zimmerman of Temple Emanu-El, who had lunch with Railey the very day of the attack, said that he had been "singled out because of his almost prophetic stance in regard to injustice in any form." Peggy had fallen into a coma.

Nine days after the attack, Railey himself was in a coma, having swallowed three bottles of anti-depressants and tranquilizers. He left behind a suicide note, calling himself "the lowest of the low," and saying that he was besieged by demons. By that time, the police had discovered inconsistencies in his story. They learned that he himself had written the threatening letters he received. They also discovered that he had been having an affair with a psychotherapist who called herself Lucy Papillon. Her family name was actually Goodrich. She was the daughter of the minister of the church when I was growing up. Dr. Robert E. Goodrich Jr. and his wife, Thelma, were close friends of my parents, and Lucy played the piano in the adult Sunday school class my father had taught for many years. Her brother, Bob, was an all-American split end on my high school team.

Railey recovered. He was the only suspect in the case, but the evidence against him was entirely circumstantial, despite his semi-confession. In my interview with him, in 1987, I confronted him with the lies he had told, but he evaded, trying to keep the conversation on a theological level, repeatedly turning to my own quarrels with the church, which he had heard about through the grapevine. I was certain he was guilty and told him so.

Soon after my interview, Railey went off to California to be with Lucy. Eventually, he began working in another church. In 1993, he was tried for Peggy's attempted murder and acquitted. He did not contest a civil suit filed by Peggy's parents, however, which found him responsible for the attack, and which demanded an $18 million judgment. Railey declared bankruptcy, voiding the judgment, but agreed to pay alimony of $337 a month in return for a divorce from Peggy. He married a wealthy widow two months later. She also died, reportedly of liver failure, in 2005. The last I heard, Railey had been fired from the homeless ministry in Los Angeles, where he served as the director of fundraising and community relations, after officials learned from a reporter that Lucy was volunteering at the same mission. On the ministry's website, Railey described himself as a global peacemaker involved in monitoring elections in Third World countries, freeing hostages in Bolivia, and fighting poverty in Haiti. There is no evidence for any of this. Peggy Railey finally died in 2011, twenty-four years after the attack, never having regained consciousness.

In the security line for the president's speech, I asked Pastor Stoker how the church was doing. "We're still in the healing stage," he told me. "Next Easter, it will be the thirtieth anniversary."

★

"DO YOU FEEL NERVOUS every time a president comes to Dallas?" I asked Robert Wilonsky, a city columnist for **The Dallas Morning News.** We were sitting in the press section of the symphony hall. Robert rolled his eyes. "My mother was the X-ray technician on duty in Parkland when Kennedy was killed," he said.

Wilonsky is a third-generation Dallasite. He harks back to a generation of reporters from another era, the kind who used to be called "hard-boiled" but who also carried the emotional weight of the city in their soft hearts. He would have been at home with Studs Terkel or Jimmy Breslin. During the Black Lives Matter shoot-out, he had been downtown, and close enough to the robot bomb that killed the shooter to feel the concussion go through his body. His nerves were still jangled.

Below us, the auditorium was filled with blue uniforms. The injured officers who were able to leave the hospital sat together, in their bandages and slings. On the stage were an interfaith choir and a police choir. The cops in the choir were visibly exhausted, and some of them kept nodding off, despite the presence on the stage of both Texas senators, John Cornyn and Ted Cruz; former president George W. Bush and Laura; President Barack Obama and Michelle; Vice President Joe Biden and Jill; Mayor Mike Rawlings; police chief David Brown; and James Spiller, the chief of the transit police, which had also lost an officer.

"The past few days have been some of the darkest in our city's history," Mayor Rawlings said. "I've searched hard in my soul to discover what mistakes we made. I've asked, 'Why us?'" He boldly added, "There is a reason this happened here, in this place, this time in American history. This is our chance to lead, and to build a new model for a community, for a city, and for our country."

After seven years of near seclusion, George W. got a standing ovation in his adopted hometown when he approached the podium. He looked much older, his hairline receding, his face deeply lined. He still had that way of squinting when he makes a point. "At times, it seems like the forces pulling us apart are stronger than the forces binding us together," he said. "Too often, we judge other groups by their worst examples, while judging ourselves by our best intentions." As he spoke, I wished for the millionth time that he hadn't invaded Iraq.

"Another community torn apart," Obama said. "More hearts broken. More questions about what caused, and what might prevent another such tragedy . . . The deepest fault lines of our democracy have suddenly been exposed, perhaps even widened." He was preaching in his familiar deliberate cadence, making sure every phrase sank in. "Faced with this violence, we wonder if the divides of race in America can ever be bridged. We wonder if an African American community that feels unfairly targeted by police, and police departments that feel unfairly maligned for doing their jobs, can ever understand each other's experience." Then he said, "We are not as divided as we seem." Those who use violent rhetoric against the police "not only make the jobs of police officers even more dangerous, but they do a disservice to the very cause of justice that they claim to promote."

I glanced down to the section below me, where

Lieutenant Governor Dan Patrick was intently watching the president speak. Patrick applauded when Obama praised the police department, but otherwise seemed to study him like the political adversary he is.

The division between these two men, and what they represent, really does seem unbridgeable. The America that Obama evoked in his speech was a community drawn together by common ideals while acknowledging the burdens of segregation and racial hatred. The Texas that Patrick seeks to create is one of exclusion. On his first day in the Texas Senate, he walked out when an imam gave the invocation. He opposed gay marriage, managed to strengthen anti-abortion laws, and crafted the gun laws that make it possible for Texans to carry weapons in public. There are two competing visions of the future, and of the two, Dan Patrick's may be the more enduring one.

"Can we do this?" Obama asked, near the end of his speech. "I don't know. I confess that sometimes I, too, experience doubt. I've been to too many of these things. I've seen too many families go through this. But then I am reminded of what the Lord tells Ezekiel: 'I will give you a new heart,' the Lord says, 'and put a new spirit in you. I will remove your heart of stone and give you a heart of flesh.'"

After the speech, I joined Robert Wilonsky for

dinner. He brought along his colleague Dr. Seema Yasmin, whom he introduced as "the new Dallas." Seema, a British Muslim of Indian extraction, was teaching public health at the University of Texas at Dallas while also writing for the newspaper. That morning she had profiled a surgeon at Parkland Hospital, Dr. Brian Williams, who had treated the wounded the night of the shooting. "I want Dallas police also to see me, a black man, and understand that I will support you, I will defend you, and I will care for you," Williams had said. "That doesn't mean that I do not fear you." When the shooting began, Seema's husband, who is black, had offered to drive her downtown. She immediately rejected the idea, fearing that the police would mistake him for an assailant.

Everywhere you saw blue ribbons on trees and people embracing cops. There were two police cruisers parked in front of police headquarters, buried under flowers and balloons and children's drawings. It was immensely touching, but transitory. "Three weeks from now, after all the funerals are over, it will all be forgotten, and we'll be fucked," Robert said. He asked me, as a former Dallasite who had written a book that was very critical of the city during the era of the Kennedy assassination, what I thought of Dallas now.

"I think it is a noble city," I said.

"Noble?" he said, with an edge of disbelief in his voice.

I said that Dallas was a far more tolerant city than the one I grew up in. It's still neurotic, pious, and materialistic, but in part because of the assassination and the humiliation it was made to endure, Dallas has become more open and diverse, more interesting and introspective in a way that it had never been in the past. "Dallas has shown it has the ability to transform suffering into social change," I said.

Robert was quiet, and I saw him wipe away a tear. It had been an emotional week.

When a police officer dies, there's an eerie send-off. As the flag is taken from his coffin and folded into a triangle, a "last call" comes over the police band. "Foxtrot 415, are you by the radio?" the dispatcher said, as Patrick Zamarripa was buried in the Dallas–Fort Worth National Cemetery.

"Five thirty-one," comes the response, "please put Foxtrot 415 on a double six."

"Received, Foxtrot 415 is double six. All elements, all elements, Foxtrot 415, Police officer Patrick Zamarripa, badge 10112, is out of service. End of watch: July 7, 2016. Godspeed, Patrick."

# EIGHT

# Sausage Makers

When Frederick Law Olmsted passed through Texas in 1853, he became besotted with the majesty of the Texas legislature. "I have seen several similar bodies at the North; the Federal Congress; and the Parliament of Great Britain, in both its branches, on occasions of great moment; but none of them commanded my involuntary respect for their simple manly dignity and trustworthiness for the duties that engaged them, more than the General Assembly of Texas," he wrote. This passage is possibly unique in the political chronicles of the state. Fairly considered, the Texas legislature is more functional than the U.S. Congress, and more genteel than the House of Commons, but a recurrent crop of crackpots and ideologues has fed the state's reputation for aggressive know-nothingism and proudly retrograde politics.

Texas has always had a burlesque side to its

politics. Molly Ivins made a national reputation as a humor writer by lampooning the people we elect to office. One of my favorites in this category was Mike Martin, a state representative from Longview. In 1981, someone shotgunned the trailer he lived in during his months in Austin. Martin, who was inside, was slightly injured. He declared that the shooting was in reprisal for an investigation he was pursuing that involved a satanic cult. Later, his cousin admitted that he had fired the weapon at Martin's behest, ostensibly to gain Martin sympathy votes in his reelection campaign. Martin fled Austin, but as Molly noted, the police "tracked him to earth at his momma's house, where he was found hiding in the stereo cabinet." She added, "He always did want to be the Speaker."

Molly, who died in 2007, would have loved writing about Mary Lou Bruner, a seventy-year-old retired schoolteacher from Mineola, who in 2016 ran as a Republican for an open seat on the Texas State Board of Education. Because 10 percent of the public school students in the nation live in Texas, the state exerts a great influence on the textbook-publishing industry. During her campaign, Bruner posted on Facebook that Barack Obama had worked as a male prostitute in his twenties. "That is how he paid for his drugs," she reasoned. Bruner went on to assert that climate change is a "ridiculous hoax," school shootings are caused by students being taught evolution, and dinosaurs are extinct because the ones on Noah's Ark were too young to reproduce. Somehow, she lost a runoff.

For several years, like many reporters, I had been receiving emails from a man named Rob Morrow. He claimed that George H. W. Bush was "a seriously addicted homosexual pedophile," who also was involved with a CIA drug-smuggling ring with the Clintons. In 2011, Morrow took out a full-page ad in a local newspaper:

HAVE YOU EVER HAD SEX WITH RICK PERRY?
**Are you a stripper, an escort, or just a "young hottie" impressed by an arrogant, entitled governor of Texas?**

I never heard that anyone came forward because of the ad, which Morrow said was designed to expose "a Christian-buzzwords-spouting, 'family values' hypocrite and fraud."

Morrow, 53, a Princeton graduate with an MBA from the University of Texas, describes himself as an independent investor. In 2015, he wrote a book with the political provocateur and Donald Trump adviser Roger Stone, called **The Clintons' War on Women. The Austin American-Statesman** noted that it "appears to be serving as a playbook for Trump" in his attacks on the Clintons. (Upon its publication, Trump tweeted, "The latest book on Hillary—Wow, a really tough one!")

In March 2016, Morrow was elected the Republican Party chairman in Travis County. He tweeted, "Top priority for Travis GOP: beautiful Big Titty women!!" Morrow began popping up everywhere, wearing the tricorne motley fool hat that he started sporting after his victory. Mainstream party officials were mortified. They promised to "explore every single option that exists" to remove Morrow from power. Morrow responded, "They can go fuck themselves."

My friend Steve Harrigan was part of a history panel that was discussing his latest novel, **A Friend of Mr. Lincoln,** when the newly elected GOP chairman showed up. In the middle of a sober discussion about the Lincoln administration, Morrow asked, "How many of you would agree with me that Lyndon Johnson was responsible for the assassination of John F. Kennedy?" One of the startled historians asked if Morrow had any proof. He didn't, but he claimed that there were numerous other murders that the Bushes and the Clintons had committed or covered up.

Texas Republicans were already having an unhappy time of it in 2016. Perry, now an ex-governor, was KO'd early in the presidential primaries, and Senator Cruz—"Lyin' Ted"—was overmatched by Donald Trump. Compounding the humiliation, Rob Morrow announced that he was running for president himself. That turned out to be against the rules for the Travis County chairman. In August, Morrow was deposed.

That month, Trump campaigned in Austin. Morrow protested his party's nominee by carrying a giant red sign saying:

TRUMP

IS A

CHILD RAPIST

Roger Stone, who was present at Trump's campaign event, claimed that he had the police escort his coauthor away from the rally. To add to the insult, Stone tweeted that Morrow was a "Clinton quisling."

★

I ONCE WROTE a play that was set in the Texas House of Representatives, my favorite political body. The hero was a rancher from West Texas who represented House District 74, which in real life stretches across thirty-seven thousand square miles—making it larger than the state of Indiana. While I was researching the subject, I met in Austin with Pete Laney, a Democrat and a cotton farmer from Hale County, who was Speaker of the House at the time. Laney was known as a scrupulously fair and honest leader who inspired a bipartisan spirit among the members. The grateful representatives called him Dicknose.

We sat down in the Speaker's office, and I explained to Laney that I was having a plot problem: My hero, Sonny Lamb, was in a war with the biggest lobbyist in the state over an ethics reform bill. How could the lobbyist retaliate? Laney rubbed his hands together and said, "Well, you could put a toxic waste dump in Sonny's district, and that would mess him up right and left."

Laney was inspired by an actual law passed in 1991, allowing sewage sludge from New York City to be shipped by train to Sierra Blanca, a little desert town in District 74, ninety miles southeast of El Paso. The train became known as the Poo-Poo Choo-Choo.

"Another thing," I said. "I'd like my lobbyist to take some legislators on a hunting trip. What would they likely be hunting?"

"Pigs," said Laney.

"Pigs?"

"Wild pigs. They're taking over the whole state!" Laney said. "You ever seen one? Huge. They got these tusks out to here."

"How do you hunt them?"

"Well, I don't hunt 'em myself, but I got a friend

who does." He punched an intercom button on his phone. "Honey, get Sharp on the phone," he said.

In a moment, John Sharp, the state comptroller of public accounts (now chancellor of the Texas A&M system), was on the speaker. "Sharp," said Laney, "I got a young man here wants to know how you hunt pigs."

"Oh!" Sharp cried. "Well, we do it at night, with pistols. Everybody wearing cutoffs and tennis shoes. We'll set the dogs loose, and when they start baying we come running. Now, the dogs will go after the pig's nuts, so the pig will back up against a tree to protect himself. So then you just take your pistol and pop him in the eye."

And these were progressive Democrats. More or less.

★

IN JANUARY 2003, the Republicans took over the Texas legislature, for the first time in 130 years, and Laney lost the Speakership—to Tom Craddick, a Midland Republican. More than anyone, Craddick was responsible for gaining a Republican majority in the House. "There were eight Republicans in the House when I got elected, in 1969, and one in the Senate," Craddick told me. "The first time I tried to introduce a bill, they told me I couldn't, because I was a Republican."

He was also, at twenty-five, the youngest member of the House. "Back then, most of the other members were retired, and they ran for office as a civic duty," he said. Now, at seventy-three, he is the longest-serving legislator in Texas history.

I once lobbied Craddick, when he was Speaker, to make Camp Mabry—a Texas State Guard facility in the heart of Austin, eight hundred acres of poorly used and superfluous training ground—into our version of Central Park. Craddick was going to make it a Speaker's bill, but then he lost the gavel to Joe Straus, who has shown no interest in my park idea. It's still a project of mine.

Craddick is slight and white-haired, wry and friendly, with a bit of slur in his speech and a shuffle in his step. He's easy to miss in the crowd of vigorous young legislators, few of whom were in office when Craddick turned the House into a Republican domain. His crusade started in the late 1980s. The party had practically no infrastructure, so Craddick helped to organize campaigns for the candidates, requiring them to report to him how many doors they had knocked on and how many mailers had been sent out. In 2002, Republicans finally got control, and the coup was complete. Craddick became the first Republican Speaker since Reconstruction. "But it wasn't just about winning elections," he told me. "We had a redistricting plan."

In those same 2002 elections, 56 percent of Texans who voted for a U.S. representative chose a Republican, but Democrats nevertheless held more seats—seventeen to fifteen—in the U.S. House. Craddick worked with Tom DeLay, from Sugar Land, near Houston, who was then the majority whip, to put into motion a sweeping plan to create a permanent Republican majority in the U.S. House.

Under Craddick's leadership, the Texas legislature began carving historic congressional districts into new fiefdoms. Taking care not to violate Supreme Court guidelines on minority representation, lawmakers jigsawed Texas into shapes that would decisively capture the state for the right.

In May 2003, the redistricting plan came up for a vote in the Texas House. Unable to block it, more than fifty Democratic members of the Texas House fled to Oklahoma. The next morning, when Craddick gaveled the House to order, he realized he didn't have a quorum. He locked down the capitol chamber to prevent any more defections and called out the state troopers to hunt down the missing members, who became known as the Killer Ds.

In the midst of this hubbub, Pete Laney, the deposed Speaker, flew his Piper turboprop from the Panhandle to Ardmore, Oklahoma, where he joined his colleagues at the Holiday Inn. Someone in DeLay's office got Laney's flight plan from the Department of Homeland Security by claiming that Laney's plane was "overdue" and might have crashed or been seized by terrorists. Soon, Texas troopers and national reporters were swarming into Ardmore, but the defiant Democrats stayed put until the session ended without a vote on redistricting. Governor Rick Perry called a special session for late June, whereupon eleven state senators fled to New Mexico. It took two more special sessions to ram the vote through.

The fruits of Craddick and DeLay's Republican revolution can be seen in the current Texas delegation to the U.S. House of Representatives: twenty-five Republicans and eleven Democrats, a far more conservative profile than the actual political demography of the state. The Austin metro area, the heart of liberal Texas, was divvied up into six congressional districts, and only one elected representative is a Democrat. I'm now represented by Roger Williams, an automobile dealer from Weatherford, two hundred miles north of Austin. Another congressman, Lamar Smith, lives in San Antonio, but his new district sweeps in the University of Texas in Austin. Smith, a member of the Tea Party caucus who denies that human activity affects global warming, heads the House Committee on Science, Space, and Technology, which oversees NASA, the Department of Energy, and the Environmental Protection Agency. (In November 2017, Smith announced he would not run again.) Lloyd Doggett is the only Democrat representing the Austin area, and his district runs along I-35, from East Austin to East San Antonio, scooping up as many Democrats in one basket as possible.

The redistricting process that took place in Texas has since been replicated in statehouses around the country, creating districts that are practically immune to challenge and giving Republicans an impregnable edge. "Texas became a model for how to get control," Craddick told me.

In 2005, DeLay was prosecuted for money laundering and conspiracy in connection with the illegal use of corporate funds related to financing Republican candidates in Texas. Craddick was also questioned, but he was never indicted. DeLay's conviction was overturned on appeal, in 2013, but by then he had resigned from Congress and made an unexpected appearance on **Dancing with the Stars.** The show has become a pathway for redemption for disgraced Texas politicos. Rick Perry, who was also indicted—in 2014, for abusing his power as governor—was also cleared, and also celebrated his comeback on **Dancing with the Stars.** Now he heads the Department of Energy. I wonder if Ted Cruz can dance.

⭐

THE MAJESTIC TEXAS CAPITOL, in Austin, was constructed in 1888 of pink granite, for which the state, destitute at the time, paid with three million acres of public land in the Panhandle—about the size of Connecticut. The capitol was said to be the seventh-largest building in the world, and as one would expect, it is somewhat taller than its uncle in Washington, D.C. During the summer, nighthawks swirl around the crowning statue on the dome: the Goddess of Liberty, holding aloft a golden star.

The legislature meets every other year for 140 days, reflecting the state's native aversion to government. The sessions begin on the second Tuesday in January and end on Memorial Day. The legislature's only mandated task is to produce a two-year balanced budget, which was about $100 billion per year in the 2015 session. Two years later, the lower price of oil and a rise in population augured substantial cutbacks and a struggle to meet the expanding health, education, and safety needs of the state's citizens.

When I visited the capitol in January 2017, a group of high school girls stood on a terrazzo mosaic in the middle of the rotunda. In the center was the seal of the Republic of Texas, a lone star wreathed by branches of olive and live oak. "It's two hundred and eighteen feet from this star to the one above," a guide told them, gesturing to its mate on the ceiling of the dome high above the girls. "You could fit the Statue of Liberty in here." Around the Republic of Texas seal are those of the five other nations that Texas has been part of—Spain, France, Mexico, the United States, and the Confederacy.

The walls of the rotunda are ringed with portraits of our former governors. When Greg Abbott, our current governor, leaves office, his portrait will go where Perry's is now, and those of all the previous governors will take one step to the left. When a portrait gets to the end of the ground-floor circle, it rises to the wall of the floor above, and then higher and higher and further into obscurity.

The next portrait to make the ascent from the lobby floor is that of W. Lee "Pappy" O'Daniel. In some respects, O'Daniel, a Democrat, was a precursor of Donald Trump. He was a political naïf who had never even cast a ballot when he ran for governor in 1938, and he wasn't even eligible to vote for himself because he hadn't paid his poll tax. He passed himself off as a rube, but he was actually a savvy operator. He was a flour salesman who made a fortune in Fort Worth real estate, but he found his true métier when he began hosting a radio show with his band, the Light Crust Doughboys. It became the most popular show in

the state. Radio was his Twitter. When his opponents staged a rally, sometimes hundreds might
attend, but O'Daniel spoke to tens of thousands.
Nothing like that had ever happened in Texas
before. In his first race, he defeated eleven contenders without a runoff.

As governor, he reneged on the promises he
had made to abolish the death penalty, block the
sales tax, and raise pensions. His only real political platform was to stir things up. He was a scaremonger, railing against "Communistic labor-leader
racketeers" and politically controlled newspapers.
He was terribly ineffectual, but such a wonderful
showman that, in 1941, voters elected him to the
U.S. Senate over the young Lyndon Johnson. The
portrait of O'Daniel in the rotunda shows a handsome, full-faced man with slicked-back hair and a
"Who, me?" look in his eye.

Next to him is Coke Stevenson, whose steadfast demeanor was so much appreciated that he
served longer than any other governor until Rick
Perry. He was succeeded by Beauford Jester, whom
I once described as "the last happy man to govern
Texas." He died in the arms of his mistress on the
midnight sleeper to Houston.

Of all the governors on the rotunda wall, Ann
Richards, who served from 1991 to 1995, is the
most memorable, at least in my lifetime. She was
incredibly vivid, with that stark white hair swept

and sprayed into a blinding pompadour—Molly Ivins called it "hard hair"—and a switchblade sense of humor that was honed on the primitive male chauvinism she had grown up with. She became a national figure when she gave the keynote address at the 1988 Democratic convention. "Poor George," she said of the Republican nominee, George H. W. Bush, "he can't help it. He was born with a silver foot in his mouth." She wasn't nice, but she had a wonderful smile and batted those icy blue eyes when she stuck the knife in.

She was a recovering alcoholic and a single mother of four, so her rise to governor was a near miracle. Although she had been a successful state treasurer, her wealthy opponent, West Texas rancher and oilman Clayton Williams Jr., won the Republican primary in a landslide and was ahead by 30 points when the general election began. He blew that lead with a series of character-revealing gaffes. He told reporters that rape was like inclement weather: "If it's inevitable, just relax and enjoy it." He had to fight off persistent rumors that he had invited his ranch hands and clients to join in "honey hunts," which involved scattering prostitutes on his property like Easter eggs. But Williams still held a commanding lead in the polls when he met Richards at a forum in Dallas. She stuck out her hand and said, "Hello, Claytie." He declined the gesture, violating the cowboy code that is deeply ingrained in every Texan. In that instant, Williams lost the election.

Richards wore designer suits but picked her teeth, and she cleaned her fingernails with a Swiss Army knife. I think she was always a little amazed, after storming the ramparts, to find herself in the seat of power, but she cherished the comedy of the situation. Molly once told me that when the ACLU filed suit against a manger scene in the capitol, she called Governor Richards and asked, "Annie, is it really necessary to remove the crèche?"

"I'm afraid so," Richards replied, "and it's a shame because it's about the only time we ever had three wise men in the capitol."

Richards had the most amazing drawl—a weapon that could be devastatingly comic, but with a cut-the-crap edge to it. She was a flirt and she loved dirty jokes. Once we had a fundraiser for a mutual friend in the ballroom of the Four Seasons. The writer Kinky Friedman, who is also the lead singer of Kinky Friedman and the Texas Jewboys, seized the opportunity to tell the story of going to the beach with a family friend who wore a swimsuit that was so tight it squeezed one of his balls into view. It's not so funny when I tell it, but Richards was laughing so hard she could barely stay in her chair.

Despite the state's super-religious reputation,

there has always been a tolerance for sexual misdemeanors on the part of elected officials. Charlie Wilson, the U.S. representative from the Second District, in East Texas, one of the most conservative parts of the state, was a drunk, a drug user, and the most energetic playboy on Capitol Hill, who enjoyed lounging in hot tubs with showgirls and cocaine. He was elected to twelve terms.

The tolerance for sexual liberty didn't extend to Richards, however. She had surrounded herself with a coterie of very powerful women, which led to countless innuendos and slurs about her sexual orientation. She complained to a lobbyist I know, "I could be fucking Charlie Wilson on Sam Houston's bed, and they'd still call me a lesbian."

Richards's loss, in 1994, after a single term, to George W. Bush, marked the end of the Democratic Party as a force of any consequence in the state.

★

ON THE WINTER DAY in 2017 that I was going through security at the capitol—waving my new concealed-weapon permit to escape any actual scrutiny—the current governor whizzed by in his wheelchair. Greg Abbott was a great track star in high school, having never lost a race, but in 1984 a tree fell on him while he was jogging through the wealthy enclave of Houston's River Oaks, leaving him paralyzed from the waist down. He had just graduated from law school and had no health insurance. Fortunately, he won a $9 million judgment from the homeowner whose tree had fallen, and from the tree company that had inspected the tree and failed to recommend its removal. Later, as a member of the Texas Supreme Court, and then as attorney general, Abbott supported measures that capped pain-and-suffering damages in medical malpractice cases at $250,000.

Abbott's pet issue is fending off the malevolent influence of California. "Texas is being Californiaized, and you might not even be noticing it," he declared in 2015. "It's being done at the city level with bag bans, fracking bans, tree-cutting bans. We're forming a patchwork quilt of bans and rules and regulations that is eroding the Texas model." He warned that the "Texas miracle" could become a "California nightmare."

This obsession with California really puzzles me. I play keyboards in a blues band, WhoDo, and our drummer has a sticker on his kit saying Stop Californication of Texas Music. The mayor of Austin, Steve Adler, a Democrat, warned that if our city stays on its current path, "we'll end up like San Francisco," with out-of-control housing costs. The newspapers often feature gloating stories about how many Californians are fleeing to Texas (eight per day to Austin alone), as an indication of the vast superiority of the Texas way of life; but if Texas could snatch away Hollywood, San Francisco, Silicon Valley, the California university system, the climate, the mountains, and the celebrities, I think the state would put up with a few more plastic-bag bans.

I love being in California for many reasons, but as a Texan I sometimes bridle at the elite disdain and raw contempt that Californians express toward my state. They reverse the sentiments you hear in Texas, like Greg Abbott speaking into a mirror. Historically, the two states act as a political seesaw. Texas was as blue as the cloudless sky in the first half of the twentieth century, when California was as red as a beet. The defining political figures of our time—Lyndon Johnson and Ronald Reagan—emerged from these opposing political climates, shaping the country and changing the world. The fact that America can contain two such assertive, contrary forces as Texas and California is a testament to our political dynamism, but more and more I feel that America is being compelled to make a choice between the models these states embody. Under the Trump administration, Texas is clearly the winning archetype. The wave of conservatism that has rolled through so many statehouses and the three branches of the federal government makes the entire country look a lot more like Texas.

It's not just the politics; the mentality and life-styles of Texas and California are foreign to each other. They are alike, however, in their conformity. I had a liberal friend who moved from Texas to California. A few years later, I asked her what living there was like. "It's confusing," she said. "I've never lived in a place where everybody agrees with me."

In 2013, I had a play, **Fallaci,** produced at the Berkeley Repertory Theatre. Berkeley and Austin are often thought to be political cognates—Austin being the "Berkeley of Texas." I think this is a stretch. Once, while I was walking to rehearsals in Berkeley, I passed a woman who had an energetic Chihuahua on a leash. The dog's paws were skittering all over the pavement as it strained to race ahead. As I passed by, the woman was instructing the Chihuahua, "Moderation, moderation."

In Austin, we don't have such high expectations of Chihuahuas.

★

AT SIXTY, Greg Abbott is still a vigorous man; his aides were racing through the rotunda to keep up with him. Although he remains in the shadows of his predecessors Rick Perry and George Bush, I suspect he has similar ambitions. He latched on to a proposal, already adopted by ten other states, to call a constitutional convention, aimed at reining in the power of the federal government. Abbott rebranded it as the Texas Plan. It would require the federal government to balance its budget, as Texas does, and prohibit government agencies— such as the EPA and the Department of Labor— from issuing regulations that override state laws. As attorney general, Abbott was on the losing end of many lawsuits that he filed on behalf of the State of Texas against the U.S. government—he objected to the Affordable Care Act, and to many federal environmental controls. Under the Texas Plan, the Supreme Court would need a supermajority of seven justices to strike down a state law. Abbott designated the Texas Plan an emergency item, and it quickly passed the legislature and was signed into law, worrying mainstream Republican lawmakers in Washington, who fear that in the current political climate, such an effort could lead to a runaway assault on federal authority.

Another emergency item on the governor's list for the 2017 session was ethics reform, but his measure failed to address the most obvious ethical needs. "Some of the most egregious violations are in the governor's office," Lyle Larson, a state representative from San Antonio, told me. "It's well known that pay-for-play has been going on in that office for years. For you to be on the Parks and Wildlife board, for instance, or to be a regent at the university, you have to make significant contributions"—as much as $100,000 or more—to Abbott's campaign fund. "That's not in the governor's bill." (Abbott's press secretary assured me that "Governor Abbott selects and appoints individuals he believes are the most qualified and capable of bringing excellence to the organizations in which they serve." In any case, little came of ethics reform.)

For all of Abbott's initiatives, this session was dominated by Lieutenant Governor Patrick's priorities, which included capping property tax increases and addressing matters such as hailstorm-lawsuit reform (according to the Insurance Council of Texas, homeowners suffered $5 billion in losses from hailstorms in 2016, the highest in the nation, resulting in half a million insurance claims). The heart of Patrick's agenda consisted of the AM Texas platform of anti-abortion absolutism and hostility to same-sex marriage and undocumented workers. He proposed public subsidies—vouchers—for homeschooling and private school tuition. Despite the fact that a federal appeals court ruled in 2016 that the existing Texas voter ID law discriminates against minorities and the poor, Patrick sought to strengthen it. These bills would bend Texas further in the direction of the affluent and fortify the political strength of white evangelicals who feel threatened by rising minorities and changing social mores.

★

POLITICIANS SELDOM PAY a price for the damage that their legislation may do in the name of popular causes, such as declaring war or slashing taxes at the expense of vital social programs. Stiff-necked political philosophy is often mistaken for moral strength, as when Governor Rick Perry vetoed a bill in 2011 that would have banned texting while driving, saying that it was "a government effort to micromanage the behavior of adults." Texas is always above the national average in the number of highway fatalities. According to the Texas Department of Transportation, more than four hundred Texans are killed every year in crashes related to distracted driving, often because they are texting.

The sponsor of the bill that Perry vetoed was Tom Craddick, the ultraconservative former Speaker. He put the measure forward again in the 2017 session, for the fourth time. He compares it to the seat belt law, which, he notes, "is **very** unpopular" in his district. "But they say that ninety-five percent of the people obey the law."

On March 29, 2017, in the middle of the legislative session, a welder named Jody Kuchler called the sheriff's offices in Uvalde and Real Counties to say that a white truck was swerving all over a two-lane highway. "He's going to hit someone head-on or he's going to kill his own damn self," Kuchler told the cops. He then watched helplessly as the truck rammed into a bus carrying members of the First Baptist Church of New Braunfels. Thirteen people on the bus were killed. The driver of the errant truck was twenty-year-old Jack Dillon Young, who had taken a cocktail of drugs. He was largely unhurt. "He said, 'I'm sorry, I'm sorry. I was texting,'" Kuchler told reporters. "I said, 'Son, do you know what you just did?'"

That was just one of the accidents that might have been prevented if Rick Perry had signed the 2011 texting bill into law.

In that same session, the Republican state legislature turned its attention to defunding women's health programs. "This is a war on birth control and abortions," Wayne Christian, a state representative, Tea Party stalwart, and gospel singer, straightforwardly admitted. "That's what family planning is supposed to be about."

Texas has a long history with the abortion issue. In 1970, Norma McCorvey, under the name Jane Roe, brought suit against the legendary district attorney of Dallas, Henry Wade. McCorvey was a reform-school dropout who at the age of twenty-one was pregnant with her third child. At the time, abortion was prohibited in Texas unless the life of the mother was endangered. There were only six states in the country where abortion was legal. Two young Austin attorneys, Sarah Weddington and Linda Coffee, took up the case, and in 1973 the U.S. Supreme Court ruled, in **Roe v. Wade**, that the right to privacy under the due process clause of the Fourteenth Amendment included a woman's decision to seek an abortion. However, the court also specified that the state has an obligation to balance a woman's right to choose against the protection of her health and the potential viability of her fetus.

The decision came too late for McCorvey, who had the baby and gave it up for adoption. McCorvey was working in an abortion clinic in Dallas when she suddenly had a conversion experience and decided that abortion was wrong. She subsequently joined the anti-abortion group Operation Rescue, whose director, Flip Benham, baptized her in 1995 in a backyard swimming pool.

The long-term goals of cultural conservatives in Texas are to cut off access to abortion, end state subsidies for birth control, and gut state funding for Planned Parenthood—which, until 2011, served 60 percent of the health needs for low-income women in the state. The legislators slashed the family planning budget from $111.5 million to $37.9 million. Eighty-two family-planning clinics were shut down as a result. By defunding Planned

Parenthood, the legislature incidentally blocked many women from getting cancer scans and other vital health treatments.

In March 2012, Rick Perry, who had just dropped out of his first presidential race, signed a bill requiring all women seeking an abortion to have a sonogram twenty-four hours before the procedure. Carol Alvarado, a Democratic representative from Houston, pointed out on the House floor that, for a woman who is less than eight to ten weeks pregnant, such a procedure would require a "transvaginal sonogram." She actually displayed the required instrument to the discomfited lawmakers, a white plastic wand that resembled an elongated pistol, which would be inserted into the woman's vagina—"government intrusion at its best," she observed. Nonetheless, the bill passed, 107–42. "This is a great day for Texas," Dan Patrick, then a state senator, declared. "This is a great day for women's health."

Texas has the highest rate of uninsured people in the nation, and about 17 percent of Texan women and girls live in poverty. After the family-planning budget was cut, many women no longer had access to birth control, and there was a sharp rise in childbirths covered by Medicaid. Subsequently, maternal deaths in Texas have doubled, from 18.6 per 100,000 live births in 2010 to 35.8 in 2014—not only the worst in the nation but worse than the rate in countries such as Armenia, Egypt, and Romania; it's more than twice the rate of maternal deaths in Lebanon. Those figures represent six hundred dead Texas women.

Researchers say it's not entirely clear what accounts for the rise in maternal mortality, since the rate was already rising before the 2011 laws went into effect. Obesity, heart disease, drug overdoses, and lack of health insurance—all serious problems in the state—play a role. Misreporting may be a factor. "Still, in the absence of war, natural disaster, or severe economic upheaval, the doubling of a mortality rate within a two year period in a state with almost 400,000 annual births seems unlikely," an article in the September 2016 issue of **Obstetrics and Gynecology** reported.

The mystery might be cleared up if Governor Abbott would release records about the causes of death for these women. In 2011, when he was attorney general, he issued an opinion that information about the deceased would be withheld, supposedly to prevent fraud.

Fed up with the callous treatment of women, Jessica Farrar, a liberal state representative from Houston, filed House Bill 4260, the Man's Right to Know Act, using the same patronizing "we're doing this for your own good" language that characterizes the many bills directed at abortion and women's health—for instance, requiring a sonogram and a rectal exam before prescribing Viagra. Then there's this:

### SEC. 173.010. FINES RELATED TO MASTURBATORY EMISSIONS

Masturbatory emissions created in health or medical facilities will be stored for the purposes of conception for a current or future wife.

(a) Emissions outside of a woman's vagina, or created outside of a health or medical facility, will be charged a $100 civil penalty for each emission, and will be considered an act against an unborn child, and failing to preserve the sanctity of life.

The bill never made it to the House floor.

Children have also faced heartless treatment in Texas. In 2015, a federal judge, Janis Graham Jack, ruled that foster children "almost uniformly leave State custody more damaged than when they entered." The state, she said, was violating the children's constitutional rights by exposing them to unreasonable risks of harm. The judge declared that state oversight agencies adopted a policy of "deliberate indifference" toward the plight of the children in their care, even in the face of repeated abuse and, sometimes, homicide. "Rape, abuse, psychotropic medication, and instability are the norm," the judge stated.

Governor Abbott promised to overhaul the child-welfare system, but things have only gotten worse since he stepped in. In fiscal year 2016 alone, at least 200 children died of maltreatment in the state, compared with 173 the previous year, and that doesn't include more than 100 other deaths that are still being investigated. Child Protective Services, the state unit charged with investigating cases of abuse, is in chaos. Nevertheless, Attorney General Ken Paxton appealed the judge's decision to appoint a special master to oversee the foster-care system because it would amount to a "federal takeover."

Nearly a year after the judge's ruling, an investigation by **The Dallas Morning News** found that as of September 2016, more than 4,700 children at high risk of abuse or severe neglect had not yet been contacted by state agencies. In the meantime, hundreds of children have been sleeping on air mattresses in hotels, emergency shelters, and even in government offices because the state has nowhere else to put them. Hundreds of caseworkers have also quit, complaining that they were overworked, demoralized, poorly paid, and often in danger. Union officials have said that higher pay would help attract more applicants to the job, which offers a starting salary of about $37,000 a year, but state officials countered with a plan to lower the educational requirements for caseworkers. During the 2017 legislative session, while bills addressing the child-welfare crisis were being considered, a teenage girl who was being housed in a state office building fled in the middle of the night. She was hit by a van and killed.

Despite this shameful record, Texas ranks in the middle of various measures of child-welfare systems, according to the Foundation for Government Accountability, ahead of New York, California, and Massachusetts, which is the worst.

★

LOBBYISTS GET THEIR NAME because they stand in the lobby. When I returned to the capitol in February 2017, about fifty of them, almost all men in dark suits, stood outside the Senate chamber, forming a mosh pit for any actual senator who might appear. Although they pose as supplicants, lobbyists actually write much of the legislation and corral the votes.

Bill Miller, a friend and neighbor, has worked in the lobby for three decades. When he first arrived, he noticed that all the political leaders had animal heads mounted on their walls, so Bill had a papier-mâché sea lion head made up for his office.

"Wow, you killed a sea lion?" an impressed legislator asked.

"Yeah," said Bill. "With a surfboard."

Inside the Senate chamber, a crucial debate was under way concerning Senate Bill 4, known as the sanctuary cities bill—one of the governor's priorities. It essentially required Texas to join the Trump administration's crackdown on undocumented immigrants. There are about a million in Houston and Dallas alone.

A few days earlier, 450 people had lined up to testify before the Senate Committee on State Affairs in protest of S.B. 4, which they saw as a discriminatory measure that would codify racial profiling. The line snaked around the rotunda and up to the second level. The hearing lasted more than sixteen hours, breaking up well after midnight. The police chiefs from Austin and San Antonio testified that the bill would harm their ability to work with immigrant communities. A young woman spoke about attempting suicide after her father was deported. In the end, the bill passed out of committee, 7–2, on partisan lines. Clearly, no minds had been changed.

Federal immigration authorities often ask local law-enforcement officials to put a hold—called a detainer—on people in their custody until their citizenship status can be verified. Our sheriff in Travis County, Sally Hernandez, a political novice who had been in office for only a month when the legislature convened, had promoted Austin as

a "sanctuary city" in her campaign. She declared
that she would honor detainers solely for cases in
which individuals are charged with violent crime;
otherwise, people who posted bond would be
released.

It was as if Sheriff Hernandez had just opened the
door to a mob of flesh-eating zombies. Perhaps she
didn't fully appreciate what liberal Austin and Travis
County represent to the Republican—largely Tea
Party—establishment. Governor Abbott abruptly
cut off $1.5 million in state grants to the county. He
went on Bill O'Reilly's TV show and said of S.B.
4, "Today we introduced legislation that will put
the hammer down on Travis County as well as any
sanctuary city policy in the state of Texas."

"Is Miss Hernandez doing this for political
reasons?" O'Reilly asked. "I don't understand her
motivation."

"She is doing it to pander to the ideology of the
left, just like what you see in **California**," Abbott
responded.

S.B. 4 was quickly loaded up with punitive
amendments, all of which were endorsed by the
entirely white Republican majority. (Of the thirty-
one members of the Texas Senate, only eleven
are Democrats; seven of them are Latino.) Under
one amendment, Sheriff Hernandez—"Sanctuary
Sally," as the governor began calling her—could

be jailed for up to a year if she refused to grant a detainer.

✶

S.B. 4 WAS ALSO HIGH on Dan Patrick's agenda. As the bill was being debated in the Senate, he watched from the dais, occasionally conferring with the parliamentarian or a clerk. At sixty-seven, Patrick has a full head of brown hair that is graying at the temples. He is tall and assured, with an easy smile. It was hard to square this confident, popular public official with the turbulent life that had brought him to this point.

He was born Dannie Scott Goeb, in a blue-collar neighborhood in East Baltimore, where his father was the circulation manager for the **Baltimore Sun** and his mother was a bookkeeper. Dannie was the first in his family to go to college: he graduated from the University of Maryland, Baltimore County in 1972, with a BA in English. He had an early marriage to a high school sweetheart, which ended in 1973. At the time, Dannie Goeb was selling class rings and caps and gowns for the Carnation Company. He was a talented salesman, but that wasn't his dream. He wanted to host **The Tonight Show.**

He got his first job in television doing sports and weather on the weekends at WNEP in Scranton, Pennsylvania—the same station where Bill O'Reilly got his start. He adopted a new name, Dan Patrick. Along with the name, apparently, came an evolving new persona. Seven months after that first broadcasting job, Patrick was the sports director of a station in Washington, D.C. In October 1979, he moved to Houston, where he became the sports anchor at KHOU, a CBS affiliate. He had a genius for stirring up attention—getting two Houston Oilers cheerleaders to paint his body blue, for instance, or once reciting scores with a cougar in his lap. The funny hats and fake beards he sometimes wore failed to pull the station out of the gutter, though, and it was sold in 1984, to owners who wanted a more sober-minded anchor on the sports desk. "I couldn't be a phoney so I resigned," Patrick announced in a newspaper advertisement, in which he invited Houstonians to his latest venture, a sports bar near Rice University. He grew a beard and set a goal of becoming a millionaire in six years. After that, maybe politics. "I see no reason why I couldn't be president," he told **Texas Monthly** at the time.

Like so many Texans in the early 1980s, Patrick thought the boom would never end. "Within two years, I had become involved in five establishments," he wrote in a spiritual memoir, **The Second Most Important Book You Will Ever Read**, that he published in 2002. "I had hundreds of employees and a huge in-over-my-head nightmare." In 1986, when the bust hit with full force, he declared bankruptcy.

The psychic cost of that tragedy is not mentioned in **The Second Most Important Book You Will Ever Read**. In 1989, Patrick gave a deposition in a lawsuit that he had filed against **The Houston Post** and its gossip writer, Paul Harasim. Patrick asserted that Harasim had libeled him by writing a false story about a physical encounter at his nightclub. Harasim had written that Patrick had provoked a fight with Alvin "Boom Boom" Jackson, a six-foot-four, 250-pound former football player and hammer thrower at Penn State. Patrick denied that it was a fight or a "tussle," although it ended when he fell over a trash can behind the back door. Patrick objected to the statements in the article saying that he had lost his "cool" and had screamed insults at Jackson that people in the club had heard. Harasim quoted Boom Boom Jackson: "Maybe I could never have set a record for the hammer throw. But I could have thrown a manager out that night."

Patrick's suit was dismissed with prejudice in 1993.

In their questioning, the attorneys for Harasim and the **Post** elicited a portrait of a man who had numerous conflicts, both physical and professional. They also gained permission from Patrick to examine his medical records, which revealed his struggle with depression. He had been hospitalized for exhaustion and anxiety in 1982. Then, in 1986, he was hospitalized again. "Last night, I did a foolish thing," he told his physicians. "I attempted suicide. I took an overdose of medicine and cut my wrist. I was by myself and realized I did not want to die. I hailed a cab and took myself to the emergency room." It was the second time he had tried to kill himself. He told the doctors: "I have never experienced a state of happiness."

This was at the nadir of the oil economy. Bars and restaurants were among the most visible victims of the crash. The Saturday night before Patrick's suicide attempt, he'd had to shut down his nightclub. Three of his four restaurants would fail as well. The admitting physician's notes describe "feelings of worthlessness, helplessness, hopelessness and a marked decrease of self-esteem." Those were feelings that many in Texas experienced as their dreams came to a crashing end.

Later, in Patrick's first race for lieutenant governor, one of his opponents used the medical information against him, but it backfired. Patrick had taken a big risk—that was part of the Texas ethos—but he had also rebounded, and that fed his legend. In 1988, he rented time on a little AM station in Tomball, a bedroom community within the Houston broadcast area. When the shareholders of the station sued the owner, Patrick was able to negotiate a purchase for the debt. Six months later, he got a call from a then-unknown conservative talk-show host named Rush Limbaugh, who had been turned down by other Houston stations. Within a few months of Patrick's signing Limbaugh, the station had become a success. He bought another. In 1994, he sold controlling interest in his stations for nearly $27 million. That's a true Texas parable.

Now, as I looked at Patrick on the dais, at the pinnacle of Texas political power, I thought that Dannie Goeb had reinvented himself once again, this time as a happy man.

★

"WHAT PURPOSE, Senator Birdwell?" Patrick asked, as Brian Birdwell, a Republican from Granbury, southwest of Fort Worth, rose to speak in favor of the sanctuary cities bill. Birdwell is a retired army colonel who was badly burned in the attack on the Pentagon on 9/11. He has undergone thirty-nine operations and numerous skin grafts. He said he was worried about "a culture of insubordination" arising in Texas, adding that the next step would be outright insurrection. This was apparently a shot at Sheriff Hernandez. "What you tolerate today, you'll endorse tomorrow, and subsidize the day after."

Senator Juan "Chuy" Hinojosa, a Democrat from the fertile Rio Grande Valley, spoke against the bill. "I agree one hundred percent that we as a nation have the right to define our borders," he said. But he felt that the bill could become an excuse for wholesale expulsion of undocumented immigrants who have committed no crimes. "I was deported when I was five years old," he said. He and his father were American citizens, but his mother was undocumented. She was picking tomatoes in Hidalgo County, which abuts Mexico, when the Border Patrol arrived. "They put us in a paddy wagon and we didn't even have time to notify my father," he later told me. "We lived in Mexico for a year, while my father was looking for us."

Senator Hinojosa told me he thought Sheriff Hernandez was naive and inexperienced. "She talked about honoring detainers only in cases of violent crime, but suppose you've got somebody who smuggled in a hundred kilos of cocaine? If you got caught committing a burglary—hell, yeah, you ought to be detained."

Sheriff Hernandez defended herself in an op-ed: "Tasking our community police forces with the job of federal immigration agents creates a strain, which is why the detainer policy on non-violent criminals is optional."

As the debate raged, the Immigration and Customs Enforcement agency (ICE) began a national dragnet, targeting undocumented criminals and violent offenders, but also picking up undocumented bystanders. Fifty-one people were seized in Austin, fewer than half of whom were criminals—a lower proportion than in any other city in the country—leading residents to believe that the city had been singled out.

Many Mexican Americans in Texas support stricter enforcement of immigration laws. "As long as there is no profiling of Hispanics, we understand the process," Senator Hinojosa told me. "Since 9/11, the whole culture has changed." Under the current practice, however, undocumented migrants—especially those from Central America, who cross from Mexico—often simply surrender to the Border Patrol; if they are released into the interior, they are then given a court date, a year or two in the future. Hinojosa said it makes no sense to allow undocumented people into the country, let them go wherever they want, and then conduct raids to root them out. "It's a real broken system," he concluded.

In session after session, the Texas legislature has sought to impose strict rules on voter identification, with the putative goal of preventing election fraud. A 2011 law required voters to present a U.S. passport, a military identification card, a state driver's license, a concealed-weapon permit, or a Texas election identification certificate. The same law excluded federal and state government IDs, as well as student IDs, from being used at polling stations. A federal judge, Nelva Gonzales Ramos, in the Southern District of Texas, struck down the law, calling it "an unconstitutional poll tax." Texas appealed, but the appeal was rejected, in part because there was no actual evidence of voter fraud. (The U.S. Supreme Court refused to hear the case.) The appeals court sent the case back to Judge Ramos, asking her to determine if the law was intentionally discriminatory. If Ramos said yes, it could trigger federal monitoring of the state's election laws under the Voting Rights Act.

The question of voter fraud became a national issue after the 2016 presidential election. Gregg Phillips, a former official of the Texas Health and Human Services Commission, gave Donald Trump the false idea that he would have won the popular vote if illegal votes had been discounted. Phillips, the founder of a group called VoteStand, tweeted that three million unqualified voters cast ballots in the election. He refused to provide proof, though he told CNN that he had developed "algorithms" that could determine citizenship status. Trump demanded a widespread investigation into voter fraud.

In the midst of all this, Rosa Maria Ortega, a thirty-seven-year-old mother of four with a sixth-grade education, in Fort Worth, was found to have registered to vote illegally. She had lived in the United States since she was an infant and was a legal resident, entitled to serve in the military and required to pay taxes. She assumed she could also vote, and had done so previously, in 2012 and 2014. The local prosecutor decided to make an example of her. She was sentenced to eight years in prison. When she gets out, she may be deported to Mexico. I suppose it's an irony that she is a Republican, and actually voted for Ken Paxton, the Texas attorney general who has made voter fraud a signature issue.

In April, Judge Ramos ruled that the Texas voter ID law was intentionally designed to discriminate against minorities. Almost simultaneously, a panel of federal judges in San Antonio decreed that three of the state's thirty-six U.S. congressional districts were illegally drawn to disempower minorities.

Evan Smith, a cofounder of **The Texas Tribune**, has closely followed thirteen legislative sessions. He took note of the attack on sanctuary cities, the persistent unwillingness to adequately fund public education or to expand Medicaid (in a state with the most uninsured citizens in the country), and the $800 million of state funds allocated to expand border security. "White people are scared of change, believing that what they have is being taken away from them by people they consider unworthy," he told me. "But all they're doing is poking a bear with a stick. In 2004, the Anglo population in Texas became a minority. The reality is, it's all over for the Anglos."

★

THE MOST CONTENTIOUS ITEM on Dan Patrick's list of priorities for the 2017 session was the "bathroom bill," S.B. 6, which would bar transgender people in public schools and government buildings from using restroom or locker-room facilities that do not correspond to the sex listed on their birth certificates. It also overturns any local antidiscrimination ordinances that permit transgender citizens to choose which bathroom to use.

In 2016, a similar bill was signed into law in North Carolina. In response, musicians such as Bruce Springsteen and Pearl Jam canceled concerts, and sporting associations, including the NBA and the NCAA, dropped plans to hold events there. Governor Pat McCrory, who supported the law, lost his bid for reelection, in part because of the national outcry. Patrick contends that his bill will have no economic effect on Texas, and that the only people opposed to it are "the secular left" and the press. "They don't want prayer in public schools, they're not pro-life, they see nothing wrong with boys and girls showering together in the tenth grade, or a man being in a woman's bathroom," the lieutenant governor said at a prayer rally on the capitol steps. Attorney General Ken Paxton, who is under indictment for securities fraud, added, "This is a spiritual war."

The bathroom bill arose after the superintendent of schools in Fort Worth, following federal guidelines at the time, announced in 2016 that transgender students would be allowed to use the restroom or locker room that corresponded to their gender identity. He additionally suggested that teachers and administrators refer to students as "scholars" rather than "boys and girls." At the prayer rally, Patrick called for the superintendent's resignation, suggesting that these sorts of policies would be "the end of public education" and would ignite a mass revolt on the part of parents. "I believe it is the biggest issue facing families and schools in America since prayer was taken out of public school," Patrick concluded.

The business community in Texas went a little berserk over S.B. 6, and produced a report suggesting that passage could cost the state up to $8.5 billion (a figure discredited by PolitiFact). The Super Bowl was held in Houston a month after the legislature opened for business, and in response to the bathroom bill the National Football League intimated that, were S.B. 6 to pass, the championship might not visit Texas again. Governor Abbott, who had been keeping his head down, told the NFL to mind its own business.

Bathrooms have been an issue in the state before. At a Willie Nelson concert, in Austin, in the 1980s, I was in the men's room when a dozen desperate women barged in and laid siege to the stalls. It was actually a rather high-spirited interlude. It happened again on several occasions, until 1993, when Ann Richards was governor. She signed the "potty parity" bill, which mandated that new sports and entertainment facilities place two toilets in the women's restrooms for every one in the men's.

The bathroom bill was not unique to Texas— a dozen other states had similar bills pending—but it embodied the meanness and intolerance that people tend to associate with Texas. The bill was being sold as a way to protect women against sexual predators who might pose as transgender— a problem that scarcely exists. Laws already on the books protect women from being accosted or spied upon. The sponsors of the bill claimed that it was not meant to discriminate against transgender Texans, although the law would do just that. The only remedy for trans people would be to change their birth certificate, a costly and time-consuming procedure. The bill proposed fining schools or state agencies up to $10,500 per day for violations. "How are they going to enforce it?" Chuy Hinojosa asked me. "Would a woman have to raise her dress?" There was grumbling about the need to hire "pecker checkers."

We've talked about the bathroom bill at my regular Monday breakfast, which consists of Steve Harrigan, historian H. W. "Bill" Brands, and Gregory Curtis, the former editor of **Texas Monthly**. It seems inevitable that bathrooms of the future, at least in Texas, will devolve into unisex stalls, the way they already are in some restaurants. I said that I noticed a new bathroom in the Austin airport. The sign said, All Genders. Greg observed that would spell the end of urinals. We were all silent for a bit. That would be a loss.

Steve later reported a sign on a restroom door at an Austin restaurant that said:

WHATEVER

JUST WASH YOUR HANDS

★

ON MARCH 2, 2017, I returned to the capitol to have lunch with the Speaker of the House, Joe Straus, a laconic Republican from San Antonio. It was the hundred-and-eighty-first anniversary of the day Texas declared its independence from Mexico, and the beginning of the "high holy days" among Texas historians, climaxing on

March 6, the date of the fall of the Alamo. The capitol rotunda was filled with schoolchildren wearing coonskin hats and gingham dresses with frontier bonnets, getting ready to perform Marty Robbins's song "Ballad of the Alamo." Kids from the Texas School for the Deaf were there to sign as the other children sang. Four retirees representing Buffalo Soldiers—the black cavalrymen who made their mark in the Indian Wars—were getting ready to present the colors. A tall man wearing a top hat paced about, rehearsing Travis's letter from the Alamo. Meanwhile, on the floor of the House, resolutions were being offered to honor the "sacrifice of the heroes of the Alamo" and to commend notable citizens. A member advocated for the breakfast taco becoming the official state breakfast item.

I met Straus in his office. There was a bust of Sam Houston on the Speaker's desk. "You know, it's also his birthday," Straus said. He then switched on the closed-circuit television to watch a moment of the press conference for the Texas Freedom Caucus, a newly hatched group of a dozen cultural conservatives, led by Matt Schaefer, a state representative from Tyler, in East Texas. They model themselves on a similar body of House Republicans in Washington. They had formed in part because the term "Tea Party"—in Texas at least—had lost its meaning, since nearly every Republican in the legislature claimed to be unimpeachably conservative. The declared mission of the group was to "amplify the voice of liberty-minded grassroots Texans who want bold action to protect life, strengthen families, defend the Bill of Rights, restrain government, and revitalize personal and economic freedoms in Texas." What distinguished this group was that they were all vociferously anti-Straus.

Straus shot me a weary look.

"The thing that concerns me is the near-total loss of influence of the business community, which has allowed really bad ideas like the bathroom bill to fill the void," he said, as we sat down to some delicious crab cakes in the Speaker's private dining room. Audubon bird prints adorned the wall. "CEOs have stopped coming to the capitol to engage directly. They now work only through lobbyists, and it's just not the same."

Straus comes from a longtime Republican family in San Antonio. One of his ancestors founded the L. Frank Saddlery Co., which made saddles, harnesses, and whips. Teddy Roosevelt and the Rough Riders stopped in San Antonio to equip themselves with L. Frank gear on their way to the Spanish-American War. The company's slogan was: "The horse—next to woman, God's greatest gift to man."

When Straus is not in Austin, he is an executive in the insurance and investment business. He spent some time as a young man in Washington, where his wife, Julie Brink, worked in the Reagan White House and in the 1988 George H. W. Bush presidential campaign, while Joe served in the Commerce Department. **Texas Monthly** called him "the last moderating force in Texas politics."

Straus is trim and dapper, like an account executive out of **Mad Men**. He is certainly the most prominent Jewish politician in Texas history—a fact that has repeatedly been used against him in campaigns, to little effect. This is his fifth term as Speaker, which ties a record. He beat Tom Craddick for the post, one of the most dominating Speakers the House has ever had. Still, it's a surprise to many observers that the even-tempered Straus has persevered as long as he has. "All the things they said about him—'He'd show up at a gunfight with a butter knife,' 'He can't make a fist'—they were all wrong," Evan Smith told me. "Joe Straus is so much tougher than he appears."

His Speakership has concentrated on providing the workforce and infrastructure that Texas businesses need by protecting public education, building roads, establishing more top-tier universities, and expanding job training. Perhaps his biggest victory was passing the State Water Plan in 2013; when the state was in the middle of a devastating drought, Straus ushered through a $2 billion revolving loan fund for state water projects.

With each session, Straus has watched the Republican Party drift further away from the "compassionate conservatism" of the Governor Bush era to domination by social and religious ideologues, such as Patrick, for whom economic issues are secondary. Although both Democrats and non–Tea Party Republicans see Straus as a brake on the controversial cultural agenda being pushed by the lieutenant governor, Straus worries that his moderation is being used as a foil for the radicals. "I can only do so much to keep the focus on fiscal issues and away from the divisive stuff," he told me. "The confidence that people seem to have in the House to serve as a stopper only enables the Senate to run hotter than they ever have before."

Straus believed that most Republicans in the House didn't want to vote on the bathroom bill, but like their colleagues in Washington, they worry about being challenged from the right in the primaries. "If it gets to the floor it could be a close vote," Straus observed. "I can't imagine anyone really wanting to follow North Carolina's example, but I can't guarantee that's not going to happen." Meanwhile, he was pressing his own legislative agenda, which included additional funding for public schools, improving Child Protective

Services, and devoting more resources to mental health—all this in a session where the budget had been hit by the decline in oil and gas revenues.

Before the session began, Straus was issuing warnings against the bathroom bill. "I've become more blunt than ever," he told me. He frequently urges business leaders to stand up against such legislation. "I try to be diplomatic but clear: that if you give in on the bathroom bill to preserve a tax break, there's another equally awful idea right behind it."

The political story in Texas both reflects and influences the national scene. At a time when Democratic voices have been sidelined, the key struggle is within the Republican Party, between those who primarily align with business interests and those preoccupied with abortion, gay marriage, immigration, religion, and gun rights. The 2017 session in Austin would prove to be a bruising example of raw politics waged by two talented people, Straus and Patrick, both of whom fervently believe in their causes. There are crucial differences between Patrick's style of governance and Straus's, caused by the fact that the lieutenant governor is elected by the voters of the state, whereas the Speaker is chosen by House members. Unlike Patrick, who has total control over what bills come to the floor, Straus exercises influence by artfully appointing committee members who can pull the fangs from the most damaging legislation (or let bills languish until there's no time to consider them). "Dan Patrick rules by fear," Gene Wu, a Democratic state representative from Houston, told me. "Joe Straus rules by consensus."

★

A FEW WEEKS AFTER President Trump was inaugurated, he withdrew the protections that President Obama had instituted for transgender students in public schools. The U.S. Supreme Court now raised the stakes by refusing to hear the case of a transgender student from Virginia, Gavin Grimm, who had sued to be allowed to use the boys' bathroom at school. That left the issue up to individual states, at least for now. Dan Patrick said that the Texas bill would be a model for the rest of the nation.

The day after the Court's ruling, the Texas bill went to its first public hearing before the Senate Committee on State Affairs. A number of transgender Texans, along with their families, signed up to speak, as did preachers and business leaders and moral crusaders on both sides. More than four hundred names were on the list when the hearing finally began. The bill's author, Senator Lois Kolkhorst, a Republican from Brenham, said that it was designed to "find the balance of privacy, decency, respect, and dignity, to protect women, children, and all people."

Dana Hodges, the state director of a right-wing Christian organization called Concerned Women for America, was the first to testify. Like many supporters of the bill, she cast the issue as one of women's safety. "I myself was the victim of being videotaped by a hidden camera placed in a women's bathroom stall by a man," she said in a trembling voice. She held up a plastic coat hook that, she said, had a miniature camera embedded in it, like the one used to spy on her. Under questioning, she acknowledged that a non-transgender man had hidden the camera inside her stall, and that he had been punished under existing laws. Kolkhurst also conceded that she knew of no crimes that had been committed in Texas bathrooms by transgender persons. Her intent, she said, was to prevent nefarious people from taking advantage of inclusive bathroom policies. (Crimes against transgender people, meanwhile, are routine; according to **Texas Monthly,** a quarter of all transgender Texans have been physically assaulted.)

Dan Forest, the lieutenant governor of North Carolina, who had been a muscular advocate of that state's bathroom bill, came to Austin to testify that economic damage was minimal—affecting "less than one-tenth of one percent of the GDP." He asserted that no business had actually left the state because of the bill. (The Associated Press examined public records and interviewed only the business leaders who specifically said that they had canceled projects because of the bill. On the basis of that narrow data alone, the AP estimated that the potential loss on investment in the state would approach $4 billion over a dozen years.) On March 30, the North Carolina legislators, assailed on many fronts, partially repealed their bill.

In Austin, most of the witnesses spoke against the bathroom measure. One of them was Dr. Colt Keo-Meier, a transgender psychologist, who is currently enrolled in the medical school at the University of Texas Medical Branch in Galveston. He wore a white lab coat and a stethoscope around his neck. "If you pass this bill, I will not be able to continue attending medical school, because I will not be able to use the men's room," he said. "And look at me"—he has a full beard—"I certainly would not be able to go to the women's restroom safely." Concerns about voyeurism, he said, were misplaced: "I've used the women's restroom for twenty-three years and the men's for ten, and I've never seen any genitalia."

A woman in a short-sleeved black dress identified herself as Jess Herbst, the mayor of the tiny town of New Hope, north of Dallas, in a firmly Republican section of the state. A few weeks earlier, Mayor Herbst had written a letter to her constituents to tell them that she was taking hormone therapy and transitioning to female. She received what she said was overwhelming support. "It's not our responsibility to keep people from pretending to be us," she said. "I just want to be able to use the women's room and not have someone ask me at the door for my papers."

The testimony continued until nearly five in the morning, when the committee voted 8–1 to support the bill.

✴

AFTER DINNER on April 6, I went down to the capitol to watch the fight over the budget bill. As you enter the House chamber, you pass through large doors with glass panels etched with the state seal, the garlanded lone star, a motif repeated throughout the room, even in the skylights in the coffered ceiling above. During the day sunlight streams through the slatted shutters on either side of the upstairs gallery; at night, two star-shaped chandeliers illuminate the generous, open room. If you stand under them and look up, you'll see that the lights spell:

There is a schoolroom quality to the simple construction of the paired oaken desks, where the 150 members sit, two by two. Each desk has a small round panel of buttons for casting votes. The accompanying brown leather, high-back recliners also have the seal emblazoned on them. When you sit, there is an exhalation as the cushion adjusts; one lawmaker told me that a colleague taped over the vents on the back of the chair in front of him to keep the gust from mussing his hair.

In the center of the chamber is a wide aisle with a lectern and microphone at each end, where members present and question bills. The rostrum dominates the back of the chamber. There are three chairs on the platform; one for the Speaker in the center; one for the parliamentarian, and another for supplicants to come whisper in the Speaker's ear. Directly behind the rostrum is a shrine: two white columns, with velvet bunting draped between them, enclosing a silk flag that was carried in the Battle of San Jacinto. It features Lady Liberty holding a cutlass, which is draped with a banner saying LIBERTY OR DEATH. The original battle flag is only displayed while the legislature is in session; at other times, a reproduction takes its place. The room resonates with a sense of history and identity and pride.

The air-conditioning was merciless; one of the members showed me his long johns poking out from under his shirt cuffs. House members had been at it all day, and once again it would go on till early morning. I saw 5-Hour Energy shots arrayed on some desks.

Desperation suffuses the beautiful chamber on Budget Night—the last stand for bills that have not been funded. The trick is that in order to get the money for your legislation, you have to take it from somewhere else. The members were on guard, lest their own bills be raided. More than four hundred amendments to the budget were waiting their turn. One baffling amendment— offered by Valoree Swanson, a freshman Freedom Caucus member from a suburb of Houston— would prevent state funds from being used to renovate bathrooms in order to "allow or enable a man to enter a women's restroom facility."

There is a brass rail that circumscribes the chamber; only members, clerks, and pages can be inside it. Members of the press are supposed to sit at a table near the dais, but I like to hover around the rail, hoping to capture bored legislators. There are some wonderful people in the House. Senfronia Thompson is a seventy-eight-year-old former teacher from Houston. She's a Democrat in her twentieth term. Unlike a lot of other state legislatures, Texas still follows a tradition of awarding important posts to members of the minority party. This is true even in Dan Patrick's Senate.

Thompson, known as Ms. T, is the chair of the Local and Consent Calendars Committee, one of the gateways that many bills must pass through to reach the floor. She once told me that when she was a girl, African Americans were not welcome in the capitol. Now she is the longest-serving woman and black person in Texas legislative history. Among her accomplishments is a hate crimes act, passed in 2001, that includes protections for homosexuals. She has also fought against racial profiling and passed measures to help low-income Texans pay their utility bills.

Armando Martinez, a forty-two-year-old Democratic member from the Valley, is a firefighter and a paramedic. He showed up on the first day of the session with a bandage on his head; on New Year's Eve, he'd been hit by a stray celebratory bullet. Martinez filed a bill to prohibit the "reckless discharge of a firearm."

Dr. John Zerwas, an anesthesiologist from Richmond, Texas, is the chair of the House Appropriations Committee. A business-conservative Republican in the Straus mold, he is deeply respected in the legislature, and Straus selected him to craft the House version of the budget. The main difference between the House budget and the Senate budget is that Zerwas proposed dipping into the Rainy Day Fund—a spare $10 billion amassed from oil and gas taxes that the state has set aside for emergencies. The fund is projected to grow to $12 billion by the next legislative session, which is more than the actual budgets of a dozen other states. Patrick maintains that the fund should not be used for "ongoing expenses," but Zerwas proposed taking $2.5 billion out of the pot, in part to finance health care and public schools—Joe Straus priorities.

There was a telling incident in the afternoon, which would provide a glimpse of how the rest of the budget fight would play out. A freshman member, Briscoe Cain, presented an amendment to kill an advisory panel on palliative care. Normally, freshmen keep quiet, but Cain is an assertive member of the insurgent Freedom Caucus. He is thirty-two years old but looks much younger, and bratty, reminding me of Matthew Broderick in **Ferris Bueller's Day Off.** "This amendment seeks to get rid of what I've kinda nicknamed the 'advisory death panel,'" Cain said, using a term that is popular among the far right for end-of-life counseling.

Soon after he said those words, John Zerwas came to the front microphone and stood there, giving Cain what one reporter, Jonathan Tilove of the **Austin American-Statesman**, termed the **morem pellis hispidus distentione nervorum**—the hairy eyeball.

It's fascinating to watch the choreography of the

members when deep political chords are struck. The Freedom Caucus members gathered with Cain at the front of the chamber; the traditional Republicans, along with some Democrats, stood beside Zerwas at the microphone in the rear. It was a Texas version of the Montagues versus the Capulets.

"Would you please describe for me what a death panel is?" the mighty chairman of Appropriations demanded.

"A death panel is whereby a group of individuals unrelated to the person in the hospital decide whether or not that person will live or die," Cain replied.

"Have you ever understood, really, what palliative care is?" said Zerwas.

"Mr. Zerwas, being in your profession, I am sure you could inform this body better than I could," Cain replied, looking for help.

The old warhorses in the House knew, if Cain did not, that Zerwas had lost his first wife to brain cancer. He wore a ring on his right hand in her memory.

Zerwas said, "You could probably ask fifty, sixty, seventy, a **hundred** members in this House who have had somebody with a serious illness who has dealt with this particular issue."

Zerwas forced Cain, several times, to admit having made false or uninformed statements. "You know about this and I don't," Cain finally said. "My apologies." The amendment was withdrawn.

Cain later got a bit of redemption when he offered an amendment blocking any payment by the Texas Department of Criminal Justice for a "sex reassignment or gender transitioning" operation—something that has never actually happened. Cain's battle cry: "Don't California my Texas!"

I caught the eye of Pat Fallon, a Republican member from Frisco, a wealthy and intensely conservative bedroom community in the Dallas–Fort Worth Metroplex. Many young legislators, like Fallon, are not originally from Texas. I asked him how he came to the state. He said that after playing football for Notre Dame, he joined the Air Force and was stationed in Texas. "When they asked me my state of residence, I said, 'Massachusetts.' The payroll officer informed me that Massachusetts has a 5.6 percent income tax, but there's no income tax in Texas. I said, 'I'm a Texan!'"

This was his third term. So far, he's best known for coauthoring a bill in 2013 that reasserted the right of students and employees at public schools to say "Merry Christmas" rather than "Happy Holidays."

"Have you got an amendment?" I asked Fallon.

"Yeah, it's number one fifty-two, in which we defund the portion of the Travis County Public

Integrity Unit's investigation of insurance fraud and motor vehicle tax fraud." That unit has been under attack for years, because it also addresses crimes committed by state officials. Of course, anything attacking Austin and Travis County is reliably popular in the legislature. Austin is a spore of the California fungus that is destroying America.

"Who would do the investigating?" I asked.

"We'd give it to the attorney general," Fallon responded.

"But he's under indictment."

"I would prefer it not be that way," Fallon admitted. "But he hasn't been convicted."

Fallon ranks high on the conservative "report cards," compiled by watchdog groups, by which modern legislators live and die. The most feared is the Fiscal Responsibility Index, a powerful weapon against Republicans who are less than ultraradical. It is produced by Empower Texans, a group led by Michael Quinn Sullivan, a lobbyist who is known by his initials, MQS, which some members pronounce "Mucus."

Sullivan is tall and friendly. He likes to talk about Boy Scouts (he was an Eagle Scout), the Aggies (he was in the A&M Corps of Cadets), and his three children. He's a right-wing zealot, sometimes described as the most powerful non-elected political figure in Texas. Several years ago we had lunch, and Sullivan told me, "I'm not there to get a seat at the table. I'm there to get rid of the table." In other words, destroy the government.

Empower Texans is largely funded by a reclusive Midland oilman named Tim Dunn, an evangelical Christian who hopes to create in Texas a model of small government that could be replicated by other states and countries. Even people who hate Dunn's politics consider him the most effective moneyman in the state. His mission has been to push Republican lawmakers to the far right, eliminating the kind of middle-ground figures who support Joe Straus. Dunn has made it a mission to bring the Speaker down.

While Fallon and I were talking, Jonathan Stickland approached the front microphone. Stickland, a member of the Freedom Caucus, is a former pest-control operator from Bedford, near Arlington, who now lists himself as an oil-and-gas consultant. Stickland is heavyset, with a Falstaffian beard, narrow-set brown eyes, and an occasional broad smile, showing beautiful teeth. He made news last session by posting a sign outside his office:

REPRESENTATIVE
JONATHAN STICKLAND
FORMER FETUS
DISTRICT 92

Stickland's amendment was to defund the state's feral hog abatement program, which kills thousands of the rampaging beasts every year. Stickland called it a ridiculous waste of money. "It has not worked, and it will never work!" he cried, infuriating rural lawmakers, who consider wild hogs an existential menace. They converged on Stickland from all sides. Everything came to a dead stop. Faces were red. Fists were clenched.

While this was going on, Speaker Straus wandered over to say hello. He seemed totally at ease, smiling, hands in his pockets. He said, "I guess all the hogs are going to move to Arlington"—which is partly in Stickland's district. Straus was in no hurry to impose order. He looked at the scrum of impassioned lawmakers around Stickland. "And just think, these are the people responsible for spending $218 billion."

At the rear microphone stood Drew Springer Jr., a Republican from North Texas, whose district, twice the size of Maryland, is copiously supplied with wild pigs. He proposed attaching an amendment to Stickland's amendment. It would cut $900,000 in highway funds—the same amount as the hog abatement program—but only in Stickland's hometown. The measure immediately passed, with undisguised enthusiasm. Stickland pulled his amendment down, but then he charged toward Springer. They met in the middle of the chamber, nose to nose. Stickland is known to carry a concealed weapon, so I was a little worried. But other members separated the two men, and Straus reluctantly gaveled the House to order.

I left before the budget was finally passed, long after my bedtime. By dawn, it was clear that Dan Patrick and the Tea Party had suffered one defeat after another in Joe Straus's House. Earlier in the session, Patrick had demanded an up-or-down vote on subsidizing tuition for private schools, and it was crushed. A proposal to zero out money for the Texas Commission on the Arts was brushed aside. Governor Abbott's Texas Enterprise Fund, which he used to lure businesses to the state, would be emptied, and its budget of $43 million would be divided between Child Protective Services and therapy for disabled children. Ken Paxton, the attorney general, would lose more than $20 million from his budget for lawsuits; that money would be redirected to foster-care programs. None of these changes had become law yet; they had to be ratified by the Senate first.

At the end of the night, the exhausted Democrats and Republicans made a deal: the Dems would provide only nominal opposition to defunding Planned Parenthood, which was going to happen in any case; in return, the bathroom amendment was dropped. Other controversial amendments were placed in Article 11 of the budget, a kind of wish list of things to be debated one day. They call Article 11 "the graveyard."

But in the Texas legislature, the dead have been known to walk.

# NINE

# The City of the Violet Crown

When I tell people outside the state that I live in Texas, they often look at me uncomprehendingly. It's like saying that you cheat on your taxes. But if I say I live in Austin, the nearly universal response is, "Oh, Austin is cool." This from people who may have never even been here. For them, living in Austin is forgivable in a way that living in Texas is not.

The relationship between the capitol and the city of Austin is antagonistic. Austin has long been known as the blue dot on the red state. It sees itself as standing apart from the vulgar political culture of the rest of Texas, like Rome surrounded by the Goths. Republican politicians bridle at the disdain. "It's great to be out of the People's Republic of Austin," Governor Abbott declared recently at a Republican dinner in Bell County. "Once you cross the Travis County line, it starts smelling different. And you know what that fragrance is?

Freedom. It's the smell of freedom that does not exist in Austin, Texas."

This tirade was apparently triggered by a local ordinance that requires a permit to cut down a tree with a trunk diameter that exceeds nineteen inches. When Abbott was attorney general and living in Austin, he was infuriated when he had to compensate the city before cutting down a pecan tree that stood in the way of his future swimming pool.

Austin is a city of dogs and bars and food trucks, a pretty city with many quirky passions. At sunset, it is rimmed in refracted light, an atmospheric phenomenon known as the Belt of Venus. William Sydney Porter, a bank teller in Austin before he went to prison for embezzlement and adopted the pen name O. Henry, called Austin "the city of the violet crown." The hills that serve as a backdrop to the town are covered with junipers that bloom in January, emitting great puffs of red pollen, the source of what is locally called cedar fever. Someone described the citizens of Austin as "valedictorians on antihistamines."

When Roberta and I moved to Austin in 1980, we were folded into the bird-watching community. It began one day when a neighbor introduced himself; his name was Victor Emanuel, like the king of Italy. He was slender and bald, and strangely limber—he had a habit of crossing his arms behind his back. The neighbor kids were out playing in the front yard with our son, Gordon. Suddenly, Victor froze. "Do you hear that? It's a yellow-billed cuckoo. I bet it's up in a sycamore tree with a caterpillar in his mouth." Sure enough, there was the cuckoo with its dinner, surprised to be noticed. The bird took flight and Victor ran down the street after it, followed by the neighborhood children. Roberta and I looked at each other. It was our first encounter with this particular expression of genius.

Victor is known in the tribe of Texas birders as Hooded Warbler—his totemic bird name. The hooded warbler is a little yellow bird that darts around nervously, as Victor is known to do. The name was bestowed on him by Edgar Kincaid Jr., the father of the Texas birding community, a shy, mostly self-taught ornithologist. Although gentle and elaborately civil, Edgar was a misanthrope who hated to see the damage that humanity was inflicting on the natural world. The bird name he awarded himself was Cassowary, a flightless bird, native to Australia and New Guinea, that stands more than six feet tall and is sometimes labeled the most dangerous bird in the world. When provoked, it leaps up like Jackie Chan and plunges a five-inch talon into its adversary. It has been known to disembowel people.

Edgar lived by himself across the street from

the University of Texas in Austin (in a house that now serves as the office of the Michener Center for Writers). He had a terror of burglars, and instead of sleeping in a bed, he made a nest for himself of sleeping bags and bits of furniture. One night in 1985, someone really did break into his house and rob Edgar at gunpoint. Edgar died of a fever a few days later. In the birding community, people say that Cassowary died of fright.

Several years before Edgar passed away, I went birding with him and some of the most notable birders in the country, but not including Victor. We were headed down to Eagle Lake, a national wildlife refuge west of Houston. There are more than six hundred varieties of bird species in Texas, a greater number than in any other state, thanks to its biological diversity and the fact that it sits in the middle of the central migratory flyway. The goal of this expedition was to see the Ross's goose, which had been spotted among the mass of migratory snow geese that stop over in the rice fields during the winter. We saw pipits and shrikes and sandhill cranes, lots of hawks, and several bald eagles. Among the geese were the Canada goose, the white-fronted goose, and about four million of the aptly named snow geese that covered the field in a wintry carpet, but not a single Ross. "How do you tell the difference between a Ross and a snow goose?" I asked in frustration, after staring through my binoculars for an hour at the goose blizzard. "He's a little shorter," one of the birders replied. Edgar added, "And his bill is raspberry colored as opposed to pink." Those were damn small distinctions.

Another year, Roberta and I went with Victor to the same region to see the Attwater's prairie chicken do its mating dance. We went into the blinds, built on the grassy prairie, around four in the morning. A century ago, there were about a million of them along the Texas and Louisiana Gulf Coast, but the combination of grazing, drought, predators, and urbanization has reduced the wild population to fewer than a hundred individuals.

Just before six a.m., I heard a hollow, ghostly sound like someone blowing in a large bottle. It was the "booming" of the males. In the dimmest light of dawn, I began to discern their movement, ritually challenging one another as they staked out their territory. The rim of the sun appeared on the horizon, inflaming the colors of these splendid birds. The bodies of the males were the shade of brown sugar, with black stripes, the feathers turning maroon at the base of the throat. Bright golden air sacs on the neck ballooned as the males called, and their neck tufts stood up like antlers. Then the chickens began to dance.

One of the males stomped the earth, and the

other males—there were nine of them—followed along, in a kind of jig. Then two males charged each other, stumpy tails erect, fluttering into the air and nearly colliding, then retreating to their imagined property lines, staring each other down, beak to beak. During all this commotion, the females—such dowdy little critters to be the object of so much brilliant aggression—strolled by with a studied nonchalance.

After eight, with the sun fully up, the birds dispersed, and we emerged from the blind, dazed by the primitive magic of the performance. We had come to see every tuft of grass, every clod of dirt, as a vital landmark, invested with almost biblical significance, but in the full light of day it was difficult to even locate those signposts.

We spent the rest of the morning spotting eagles and shorebirds, and caracaras, the low-flying, black-and-white falcons you sometimes see in South Texas. As we passed the mass of snow geese, Victor casually noted, "Oh, look, y'all, a Ross's goose."

"Where?"

He pointed in the direction of about five hundred birds near a tree line a hundred yards away.

"How can you tell?"

"He's a little shorter," Victor said, "and his bill is raspberry colored as opposed to pink. There's another one."

★

TO MY ASTONISHMENT, Austin is now the second most popular tourist destination in the country, behind Las Vegas. One can already sniff the artifice and inauthenticity that transform previously charming environments into amusement parks for conventioneers. The very places that made Austin so hip are being demolished to make room for the hotels and office spaces needed to accommodate the flood of tourists and newcomers who have come to enjoy what no longer exists. **Forbes** magazine just determined that Austin is the best place to live in America, which will only take it further from the manageable town it was to the megacity it is destined to become. Another indication of Austin's growing international reputation is that Kim Jong Un placed the city on North Korea's nuclear strike list, right after New York, Washington, D.C., and Los Angeles. My band has a regular gig at a fabulous dive in East Austin, called the Skylark Lounge, which is tucked away behind an auto-body shop and not even visible from the street. If you sneezed, the whole place might turn a somersault. Recently, Yelp labeled it the best music venue in the nation, heralding its inevitable demise by the developers, if Kim Jong Un doesn't get it first.

Austin is divided, north and south, by the

Colorado River, which is dammed to make Lady Bird Lake. The riverbanks are lined with towering cypress trees, which fill up with cormorants and egrets in the winter months. There's a rusty train trestle spanning the water, covered with oddball graffiti, such as I'VE GOT NINJA STYLE KUNG-FUGRIP. I always feel an aesthetic release when the Southern Pacific freight train rumbles overhead while the rowing crews, like racing centipedes, pass underneath, and runners circle the path—a pleasing convergence of opposing motions. I'm reminded of Thomas Eakins's paintings of the oarsmen on the Schuylkill River, in Philadelphia, with the clouds mirrored in the rippled water like rumpled sheets.

Like the Seine in Paris, the Colorado serves as a cultural divide. On the north bank are downtown, the state capitol, and the University of Texas—anchors of a city historically made up of teachers and bureaucrats. The south bank has Tex-Mex restaurants and dance halls. Austin is on the tail end of the dance belt, which starts in Louisiana with New Orleans R&B, runs through Cajun zydeco, enters conjunto territory in South Texas, and then encounters the Czech waltzes and German polkas of Central Texas. The medium that the dance music travels through is Catholicism. In North Texas, the Southern Baptists and the Church of Christ hold sway. There's an old joke that the reason Baptists won't screw standing up is that somebody might think they were dancing.

When we arrived in Austin in 1980, there were drug dealers and prostitutes along South Congress Avenue. The women stationed themselves in front of the seed and feed store, where you could still buy dyed baby chicks for Easter. That's all been cleaned up now, but there's still a defiant residual funkiness that is pretty much all that remains of the city's unofficial slogan, Keep Austin Weird. We bought a duplex on the south side, in a neighborhood called Travis Heights. Most of the houses on the street, except one, were modest one-story affairs, although there was also a handsome brick semi-mansion belonging to William Broyles Jr., the editor of **Texas Monthly** and my boss at the time, who would later become a notable screenwriter. Molly Ivins lived several blocks away. Despite the celebrity of some of our neighbors, there was an appealing absence of pretense, which was part of the charm of South Austin. (The motto of our side of town, Molly once wrote, should be "South Austin! A Great Place to Buy Auto Parts!") Our next-door neighbor sold appliances, and next to him was Terrence Malick, the filmmaker, who occasionally walked our kids to school.

East and West Austin are divided by I-35, sometimes referred to as the Interracial Highway.

As black and Hispanic families have been pushed out of the east side through gentrification, Austin has become one of the most economically segregated cities in the country. The lack of affordable housing has taken an awful toll on the diversity that made the city so democratic in its youth.

Austin currently has one of the highest rates of start-up companies of any metro area in the country. From watching Austin transform itself into the city it is now, I've developed a very Texas theory of how cultures evolve. Mike Levy began **Texas Monthly** in 1973, and it became the seedbed for the literary community. Bill Wittliff, the screenwriter for the epic television series **Lonesome Dove** and a number of successful movies, decided not to move to Hollywood, and his intransigence made it plausible for filmmakers to stay in Austin. Now Richard Linklater, Robert Rodriguez, and many others have turned the city into a film capital of international stature. In the fall of 1980, John Mackey started the first certified organic grocery store in the United States. It was not much larger than a 7-Eleven. On Memorial Day 1981, we had the worst flood in seventy years, and the store was practically destroyed. Mackey had no insurance, but neighbors and customers helped clean it up and restock the shelves, courtesy of kindhearted creditors and vendors. By 2005, it had become a

Fortune 500 company, called Whole Foods. In 1983, Michael Dell, a freshman pre-med student at the University of Texas, started assembling computers in his dorm room. The following year he incorporated the Dell Computer Corporation, capitalizing the venture with a thousand dollars. What started as "three guys with screwdrivers" now employs 138,000 people. There are more than five thousand high-tech companies in Austin, and they all hark back to that freshman in room 2713 of the Dobie Center dormitory.

In each of these examples, a single individual with a unique vision started a company that became a hub for similar enterprises and in the process transformed the culture. These are stories Texans like to tell about themselves: how imaginative entrepreneurs—not government—conjure up entire industries and create opportunity in the form of good jobs and enlightened communities. Something similar is happening now in the city with the video game industry and national intelligence. There are so many ex-spooks moving to Austin it has become a kind of Texas Abbottabad.

The evolution of the Austin music scene is more organic and harder to explain. On the east side, there was Victory Grill, part of the Southern "Chitlin' Circuit," where Billie Holiday and Big Mama Thornton would perform. In the early

1950s, Bobby "Blue" Bland, then a soldier stationed at Fort Hood, would drive down to sing on amateur night. Rock and roll arrived, bringing Chuck Berry and James Brown and Ike and Tina Turner. On the south side of town was the headquarters for country music, the Broken Spoke, where Roy Acuff, Ernest Tubb, and Tex Ritter would play. There was a gas station on the north side, owned by Kenneth Threadgill, a country yodeler who also secured the first license to sell beer in Travis County. In the 1960s he began inviting hippies and folksingers to join his Wednesday-night singalongs. Janis Joplin would sing duets with him while she was studying art at the university. Clifford Antone, son of Lebanese immigrants in East Texas, came to UT in 1968, but he dropped out after his first arrest for smuggling pot. The blues club he started, Antone's, became an institution in the music world. The musicians he mentored, including Stevie Ray Vaughan and Gary Clark Jr., would rejuvenate the blues form, creating a distinctive Austin sound.

Then, in 1970, a local band manager named Eddie Wilson was looking for a venue in South Austin and stumbled across a decrepit National Guard armory. He transformed it into the Armadillo World Headquarters, a strange amalgamation of psychedelic, country, hippie, and rock and roll. There were only 250,000 people in Austin then, but 50,000 of them were students. Musicians began moving to town, as if some homing device were summoning them all at once. Jerry Jeff Walker came from New York, Guy Clark from Houston, Jimmie and Stevie Ray Vaughan from Dallas. Marcia Ball was on her way from Baton Rouge to San Francisco when her Austin-Healey Sprite broke down in Austin, and she never went farther. Austin already had a flourishing musical subculture, in other words, even before Willie Nelson played the Armadillo in August 1972.

All of these disparate cultural trends that were careening past each other in Austin like swirling electrons suddenly coalesced into a recognizable scene when Willie arrived. He occupies a place in Texas, and especially in Austin, that no one else can claim. He was a jazz-infused country singer with a gospel background, and a songwriter with some notable hits. When his house in Nashville burned down, he decided to return to his home state, hoping to find more creative freedom. He let his beard grow and put his hair in pigtails. You never saw a man looking like that in Texas, but Willie could get away with it.

Because he is so culturally confounding, and because his songs are so much a part of the land, everybody claims Willie. He's a leftist, a Bernie Sanders fan, but he's beloved even by Tea Party types like Ted Cruz and Rick Perry. For decades he has advocated legalization of marijuana in a state where the laws of possession are quite punitive. He has even been cultivating his own brand, Willie's Reserve. Every once in a while, some state trooper or deputy sheriff will pull Willie's bus over and "discover" his stash. Willie has gotten off with a free concert, but the arrests are universally seen as poor sportsmanship.

In 2016, I went to Willie's annual Fourth of July picnic. Mickey Raphael, Willie's harmonica player, invited me on the bus (there are actually three of them in Willie's entourage; this one was weed free). As Willie has gotten older and even more physically diminished, there's an existential quality to his performances. Nearly all of his contemporaries are gone. During performances, Willie stands alone in front, with Mickey a couple of steps behind his left shoulder, providing a kind of harmonic commentary. It's a conversation that has been going on a long time. "This is my forty-third picnic," Mickey told me.

As he was showing me around the bus, Mickey pulled back the drape on his closet. "You'll want to see this," he said, pulling out a gray guitar case. Inside was Trigger, the acoustic guitar that Willie named after Roy Rogers's beautiful horse. It is perhaps the most famous musical instrument in America, rivaled only by Lucille, B. B. King's black Gibson, although there have been many

Lucilles and only one Trigger. "Here," Mickey said, handing it to me.

Trigger is really light. It has a big hole near the bridge, worn through by Willie's pinky and ring fingers. Pick marks have scored the face paper thin. The entire instrument feels sheer, the frets worn down to nearly nothing. It's been signed many times—Leon Russell used a pocketknife—but the signatures are fading into the patina. If you saw this guitar at a garage sale, you would walk on by. And yet Trigger has somehow maintained its distinctive mellow voice, a sound Willie thought resembled that of his hero, Django Reinhardt, although to me it sounds like Willie himself, twangy and full of character.

I'm in a group that puts up statues in Austin, and our most recent work was a bronze Willie, holding Trigger, that now graces the entry to the **Austin City Limits** studio. I got to pose for that statue, holding a Martin guitar of the same model, N-20. Clete Shields, of Philadelphia, was our sculptor. In 2011, when the statue was cast and delivered to Austin, we covered it with a parachute and stored it in a movie studio until it could be installed. One night, Willie came by for a private unveiling. He was gracious but a little overwhelmed as he exchanged a long look with himself. Bill Wittliff, who is on our committee, explained that what we liked about this piece was its engagement with the audience. "People will come to you," he said. "Little children will touch your knee and seek your counsel."

"Do what I say and not what I do," Willie advised.

We kept the statue in the studio for months, but we couldn't seem to get Willie to agree on a date for the public unveiling. He was being modest or embarrassed or coy—we couldn't decide which. Finally, he allowed that he might be free on April 20, 2012. The date didn't mean anything to me, but Marcia Ball, another member of our committee, guffawed. "Four-twenty," she said. "You know what that is? It's National Marijuana Day."

So we unveiled the statue at 4:20 p.m. on April 20. Willie stood in front of his giant likeness and sang "Roll Me Up and Smoke Me When I Die."

★

WE NOW LIVE in a neighborhood called Tarrytown. Steve's house is just around the corner. We're in a forest of cedar elms, so it's shadier than most parts of town—always a consideration in Texas. When we first looked at the house, which is two stories and faced in yellow brick, it was late winter and the robins were churning through the berry bushes on the back fence, getting a little drunk. There was a lot of work to be done, but the house was sturdy, and I was sure I could feel at home here. I persuaded the bank I could afford the mortgage. I had sold a movie that Oliver Stone was going to direct. He had already cast Al Pacino in the lead role.

A week after we closed on the house, Oliver called me. "Larry, I had a bad dream last night," he said in his satanic whisper.

No movie.

I never learned exactly what happened. But I now owned a house way beyond my means. One lesson Hollywood teaches you is this: don't buy the house until you've eaten the popcorn. Still, I was trapped in one of those periodic episodes of lusting after wealth and fame.

When the lady across the street moved to New York, her house stayed vacant for three months, with a For Rent sign in front. One day, Roberta asked a neighbor to help jump-start our car. She had noticed that the rent sign was down, so she asked our neighbor if the house had been rented. "Yeah!" he said. "To a movie star!"

"Really? Who?"

"I think his name is Mark McDonald, or something like that. They say he's real handsome."

Roberta thought for a moment, then guessed, "Matthew McConaughey?"

"That's the one!"

She had seen some guy drive up in a big white van, wearing a cutoff sweatshirt. She almost took offense at the cheeky look he cast in her direction. Soon we began seeing him out in the yard, landscaping, usually with his shirt off, which attracted the attention of just about everybody. This was a few years before **People** magazine named him the "Sexiest Man Alive."

The house is a little gray one-story bungalow, the kind of place that, if it were suddenly torn down, you wouldn't remember what it looked like. Matthew labored to make it more attractive, putting in some sago palms and even some lights under the trees. He was certainly the world's best tenant. Within a few weeks, he knew everybody on the block. We understood that his presence among us was a kind of secret.

The world seemed out of balance. Matthew was by now a multimillionaire, his face was all over the newsstands—anything I might have envied in terms of money and fame he had in abundance. And yet there he was, mowing the yard of a modest little rent house in Tarrytown. He was from Uvalde, west of San Antonio, about an hour's drive from Mexico. He had gone to the University of Texas and was a big Longhorns fan. He got his break in the movie business in **Dazed and Confused**, by Austin filmmaker Richard Linklater. So there were many ties. But if he wanted to come back to Austin to live, there were much grander residences to consider—for instance, the house I couldn't afford.

It finally occurred to me that what Matthew wanted was what I already had: a quiet existence on a pretty street, with nice neighbors and a degree of anonymity that was hard to come by for a face as recognizable as his. He wanted to somehow return to ordinary life. And I wanted to escape it.

On a Saturday afternoon before the UT-Baylor football game, Matthew invited the neighbors over for a cookout. He and Roberta talked about the team. She is not a real sports fan, but she had gotten a bit of a crush on the UT quarterback, Major Applewhite, a scrappy, undersized redhead who led many memorable fourth-quarter comebacks (he's now the head coach at the University of Houston). Matthew was well known for hanging out with the players, so I teased Roberta by saying that he had met Major Applewhite. Roberta's jaw dropped. "You know **Major Applewhite?**" she exclaimed. Matthew burst into laughter. I think at that moment he must have felt that he had really done it; he had achieved ordinary life.

One autumn night in 1999, around three a.m., I was awakened by the sound of loud talking and dogs barking. I tried to go back to sleep, but I heard car doors shutting, more barking, and then the instantly recognizable sound of a police scan-

ner. I jumped up and pulled back the shade. There
were four police cruisers in front of our house.

"Roberta!" I said. "Something's going down!"

There was a cop standing in my yard when I
came out. "Sir, do you live here?" he asked.

I nodded. "What's going on?"

"We made an arrest at that house," he said,
indicating Matthew's bungalow. Then he asked if
I knew the person who lived there.

"Yes, it's Matthew McConaughey. Is that who
you arrested?"

The cop told me that Matthew was being
charged with being "disorderly" and having a
small amount of narcotics. I noticed Matthew
in the back of one of the cruisers. "Can I talk to
him?" I asked.

"No, he's in a stupor," the cop said.

He didn't look like he was in a stupor to me.
He was spitting mad.

"Someone in the neighborhood called in a
complaint," the cop said. "Actually, they called
twice. He was disturbing the peace."

"You're the ones who woke me up," I said.

The cop was clearly morose. "The females in
my family think he's the greatest guy," he said.
He added that the cop who made the arrest
hadn't known who Matthew was. That was
the reason for the squad-car convention. An
unmarked car pulled up and all the cops went

into a huddle. They wound up taking Matthew downtown. "We're going to low-profile it," the cop assured me.

"Yeah, good luck with that."

The news broke around noon. The story was that Matthew had been dancing around in the back of his house, naked, playing the bongos. Apparently he had left his back door open and annoyed a neighbor across the fence. When the cops arrived, they had spotted what they thought was a bong, so it turned into a drug bust. The cops burst into his den, and when Matthew yelled at them, they cuffed him. Then they swept up a bunch of his belongings in black trash bags—for "evidence." As it turned out, there were no drugs.

Everybody in town was on Matthew's side. Even Laura Bush confided at a party the next day that she was shocked at how the cops had behaved—entering a person's house without permission and no warrant.

By that time there were TV trucks stationed in front of our house. The tabloid press was all over the story. It was galling to see how the press behaves around celebrity news; that's one reason people hate reporters, even though this is exactly the kind of news they love to consume. The local paper committed the unpardonable sin of publishing Matthew's address, and after that our little street became a promenade of mothers pushing strollers and teenagers knocking on Matthew's door at all hours. Someone drove a nail into a tire on his van. The drug charges were dropped, but he paid a $50 fine for disturbing the peace. His fantasy of slipping back into ordinary life was punctured. The bongo incident "ruined it for me," he confided on the morning he packed his furniture in a moving van. He could never feel safe here again.

I talked to Steve about Matthew's broken dream of a normal existence. Steve was sympathetic, but he observed that movie stars like Matthew cultivate celebrity and can't expect to escape notoriety. In any case, "he's not a 'normal' person," Steve said. "He's a wild man living in Tarrytown."

★

DONALD TRUMP'S UNEXPECTED VICTORY marked a cultural turning point all over America. There were protests around the country, including in Austin, where on the Sunday after the election about 150 people gathered on the capitol steps and marched south down Congress Avenue. A small group of Trump supporters staged a counterprotest. According to the news reports, one man was especially conspicuous: Joseph Weidknecht, a laid-off sheet-metal worker, who stands six feet six and weighs 350 pounds. He was wearing a Make America Great Again gimme cap and carried a sign, "Proud to Be Deplorable"—a reference to Hillary Clinton's derogatory remark about Trump supporters. A number of the anti-Trump marchers, some wearing Guy Fawkes masks, began to mock him. They ripped the sign out of his hands and grabbed the hat off his head, then tried to set his shirt on fire. "I can handle myself in a brawl," Weidknecht later said, "but when they brought out the lighters, I was genuinely scared for my life."

Suddenly, a small woman wearing a hijab forced herself between Weidknecht and the people who were assaulting him. Amina Abdeen, a nineteen-year-old student at UT, had immigrated to the United States from Iraq when she was ten. "She stood there like a mountain, trying to stop the violence," Weidknecht said.

"I do not stand for what he stands for," Abdeen remarked after the police had arrived and arrested six of the protestors. "But I know his fears and concerns are valid. I love this country so much, and I don't like what I see coming."

As the new administration was attempting to block Muslims from entering the United States, anti-immigrant posters started appearing on campus buildings. "Imagine a Muslim-Free America," one said. A mosque was firebombed in Victoria in South Texas. Sid Miller, the boisterous agricultural commissioner, told the BBC that he worried about America becoming a Muslim country. (Muslims account for about one percent of the U.S. population.) He previously advocated dropping nuclear bombs on the Muslim world.

One of Roberta's close friends is a writer who is married to a professor. They are Jewish. They have a Black Lives Matter sign in their yard. As Senate Bill 4—targeting "sanctuary cities"—was being debated at the capitol, an unsigned letter was slipped under their front door, threatening the lives of their children, by name. "Is this Austin?" Roberta cried.

# TEN

# More Sausage

Texas is the nation's largest red state, with 38 electoral votes, which will likely increase to 41 or 42 after the next census. (California has 55 electoral votes, but it hasn't increased that number since 2003. New York has 29, but that number has been declining for decades.) If Texas went blue, there would be a Democratic electoral lock on the presidency. Republican margins of victory within the state have been shrinking for years, and the demographics suggest that Texas should already be in the blue column. It's a young, urban state with a majority of minority citizens. It should be as reliably blue as California; instead, it is the Red Planet in the political universe.

The only real election in Texas is the Republican primary, where normally about 1.5 million voters turn out. If you win 750,001 primary votes in a state of 27 million people, you can become governor or a U.S. senator. In 2012, Ted Cruz got the nomination with only 631,000 votes in a run-off. This happened despite the fact that he is such an un-Texan political figure—a Princeton and Harvard man, who in another era would have fit comfortably with British imperialists in their grand club rooms, perhaps sporting a moustache and a monocle. The fact that Cruz didn't cancel his Canadian passport until 2014 suggested to me that he was hedging his bets, culturally speaking.

There was hope for the Democrats, in 2014, that Wendy Davis—a glamorous blonde who captured national attention through her eleven-hour filibuster to block a bill banning abortions after twenty weeks of pregnancy—would be the champion that Texas Democrats needed if they were to regain the statehouse, but she lost in a landslide to Greg Abbott. She even lost the women's vote.

The 2016 presidential season promised to have a Texas stamp on it, with Perry and Cruz in the primary, along with Jeb Bush and Rand Paul, both of whom grew up in the state, and Carly Fiorina, who was born in Austin. They all washed out. Then, in early September, while the race between Trump and Clinton was tightening nationally, a **Washington Post**–SurveyMonkey poll showed Hillary Clinton ahead in Texas by one point. Other polls showed Trump very narrowly ahead.

This in a state that Mitt Romney carried in 2012 by 16 points.

Texans aren't used to being in play. We don't have the deluge of television ads and candidate forums that swing states experience during presidential election cycles, or the strife and anxiety that attend meaningful contests. For nearly four decades the outcome in Texas has been so clearly preordained that it was like watching the election from abroad. In May, Hillary Clinton excited expectations when she said in an interview with **New York** magazine, "If black and Latino voters come out and vote, we could win Texas," but her campaign director in Texas, Garry Mauro, quickly tried to douse unrealistic expectations. "We are not a battleground state," he insisted. Hope would not be quenched, however. The Democratic Party, which hasn't even got offices in many counties in the state, and had practically no identifiable candidates running for statewide office, stirred to life and began setting up operations in key cities. Senator Tim Kaine, the vice-presidential nominee, visited the state repeatedly, saying that he and Clinton "take Texas very seriously." **The Dallas Morning News** endorsed Clinton, the first Democrat the newspaper had chosen in seventy-five years. In October, the Clinton campaign began a modest media effort in the state's major cities, something that hadn't happened in decades. In Austin, 90 percent of qualified voters were registered, along with 80 percent of all qualified voters statewide.

Texans were wrought up. A mother in a Houston suburb kicked her seven-year-old son out of the house when he cast the wrong vote in a mock election at his school. She actually made a video of the scene. "Bye, Donald Trump lover," she says, as she forces the hysterical child out of the house with a suitcase and a sign: "My mom kicked me out because I voted for Donald Trump." The mother later claimed it was a joke, but the Texas Department of Family and Protective Services opened an investigation. There was a telling obituary in the **Houston Chronicle** that read: "Elene Meyer Davis was born in Yoakum, Texas on the 7th of October 1924, and died on the 7th of June 2016, of complications due to congestive heart failure and the 2016 Presidential campaign."

Despite the tumult and the expectations of a record turnout, only 42.62 percent of the registered voters actually went to the polls in Texas—again, one of the lowest in the nation. Young people, in the 18–24 range, vote at less than half the rate of those who are between 65 and 75. Only about 40 percent of those with a family income under $25,000 per year tend to vote, compared with about 75 percent of those whose income is above $75,000. Those with less than a high school education turn out to vote at a rate of 32 percent, a scale that rises to 82 percent for those with advanced degrees. The fact that turnout is chronically lower in Texas has less to do with race than it does with its disproportionate number of young, poor, and uneducated citizens. As Wendy Davis observed, "Texas is not a red state. It's a nonvoting blue state."

Trump carried Texas by 9 points, 52 percent to 43 percent, the same margin as Ohio. When I looked at the distribution of votes throughout the country, the blue cities against a blanket of red, it was hard to see where Texas ended and the rest of the country began. It is a red country with blue freckles.

Texas leads the nation in Latino population growth. Latinos account for more than half the 2.7 million new Texans since 2010. Every Democrat in Texas believes that if Hispanics voted at the same rate in Texas as they do in California, the state would already be blue. "The difference between Texas and California is the labor movement," Garnet Coleman, a Houston member of the Texas House of Representatives, told me. In the 1960s, Cesar Chavez began organizing the California farmworkers into a union, which didn't happen in Texas, a right-to-work state. "Labor unions create a culture of voting and political participation," Coleman observed. In Texas politics, Coleman believes, "everything is about race. It's veiled as public policy, but it encourages people to believe that their tax dollars are going to support lazy black and brown people." Political views have become more entrenched because of redistricting, and yet the demographic majority in Texas is far more progressive than its representatives. Coleman predicts a showdown. "This is the battle about the future of the country, based on a new majority, and we have to have this out."

★

AMONG REPUBLICANS who vote in Texas primaries, immigration is the hottest issue. Many state legislators who otherwise might not support S.B. 4 seemed intimidated by the political environment, and it was apparent that Speaker Straus and his team had no battle plan. One of Straus's chief lieutenants, Charlie Geren of Fort Worth, presented the bill in April 2017, which he offered up to "the will of the House." That was an invitation to Dan Patrick's frustrated counterparts to pile on.

Matt Schaefer, the leader of the Freedom Caucus, amended the bill to allow police officers to question a suspect's immigration status—a "show me your papers" provision that would place every Hispanic citizen in the state in a different class from Anglos. Law enforcement authorities in Texas's major cities had loudly opposed such an idea, saying that it would make immigrants less likely to report crimes. Art Acevedo, Houston's police chief, said that the number of Hispanics reporting rape in his city was already down 43 percent. Schaefer's amendment was similar to a 2010 Arizona law that had been partly struck down by the U.S. Supreme Court. "This is something that Texans in our district have been asking for," Schaefer said. "This is good policy."

Gene Wu, a House member from Houston who was born in China, spoke against the bill, tearfully comparing it to the 1882 Chinese Exclusion Act, America's first major anti-immigration law. "This topic is painful for me, because I'm an immigrant," he said. "My parents are immigrants. I represent a district filled with immigrants." As he spoke, supportive Democrats surrounded him. "Some are here as refugees," he continued. "Some are here as citizens. Some are here without papers. But they are **all** my people."

For Wu, the sanctuary cities bill was the natural culmination of the "bigoted, racist mentality" that has emerged in Texas, which he calls the epicenter of the Tea Party. "Trump is simply the most visible manifestation of that mentality," he told me. "It's been percolating up in the Republican Party for the past decade."

Another Democratic lawmaker, Ana Hernandez, of Houston, recalled coming to this country as a child: "I remember the constant fear my family lived with each day, the fear my parents experienced each day, as their two little girls went to school, not knowing if there would be an immigration raid that day."

Behind the scenes, the Republican and Democratic caucuses met for hours, trying to find a way to dodge Schaefer's amendment. "The Republicans came to us and said, 'Some of us are going to have a hard time voting against it,'" Wu told me. Knowing that the law would be challenged in court, the Republicans offered to shelve the amendment if the Democrats made some minor concessions. But the Democrats took too long to agree on terms, and the Republicans withdrew the offer.

After sixteen hours of emotional debate, ending at three in the morning, the House passed S.B. 4, with the "show me your papers" amendment. A week later, Governor Abbott signed it into law, on Facebook Live. "Citizens expect law-enforcement officers to enforce the law," he said. "Citizens deserve lawbreakers to face legal consequences."

As usual, the legislature passed a sweeping anti-abortion bill, one that bans the safest and most common procedure for second-trimester abortions—dilation and evacuation. The law also requires health-care facilities to bury or cremate aborted fetuses.

In addition, the legislature passed several bills to reform the agencies that oversee abused and endangered children—one of the governor's priorities. In the first seven months of the state's 2017 fiscal year, 314 foster children spent two or more nights in hotels or government offices. The new legislation gave raises to the underpaid caseworkers, but also stripped the state of some responsibility for its wards, handing that off to private contractors. Abbott said that Janis Graham Jack, the federal judge who ruled that Texas's foster-care system violated children's rights, should dismiss the case, because the new legislation "completely transforms the system in ways that will make it better." Abbott said that he expected that the state foster-care agencies would achieve "No. 1 ranking status in the United States of America." Child-welfare advocates worried that private groups might not have the expertise to take over case-management duties, particularly when dealing with troubled children.

The feral hog abatement program passed, despite Jonathan Stickland's opposition. And a new law allows hunting wild pigs from hot-air balloons. Texans could already shoot the pigs from helicopters, using actual machine guns, but balloons are more sporting. And who knew it was ever against the law to shoot pigs from balloons?

Speaker Straus continued to sideline the bathroom bill in the House. He remained certain that most of his members didn't really favor the measure, though they also didn't want to be seen as opposing it. He repeatedly called on the governor to stand with him. Until this session, Abbott had been known more as a business conservative, like Straus, than a cultural conservative, like Patrick, but he showed little interest in choosing sides. He was bound to lose favor in either case. Finally, Abbott blandly stated that he favored a bill "to protect privacy in bathrooms." He signaled that a bill then headed for a committee hearing in the House, H.B. 2899, was a "thoughtful proposal." It would not mandate bathroom use based on one's biological sex at birth, but it would overturn local antidiscrimination ordinances.

On May 21, the House began to debate the measure. Once again, hours of anguished testimony ensued. Half a dozen female members wandered into the men's bathroom just off the House floor. "We're feeling like making trouble today," one of the women, Gina Hinojosa, a Democrat from Austin, told reporters. "It's that kind of mood."

I wondered whether minds are ever actually changed in these kinds of hearings. This legislative session had already endured many late nights, even on this subject. The people had the opportunity to make themselves heard; that's their fundamental democratic right. By an outsized margin, they spoke against the bathroom bill. Among the many affecting facts that lawmakers had to consider was the vulnerability of the transgender population, which is already bullied and stigmatized. A study by the Williams Institute at the UCLA School of Law in 2014 found that more than 40 percent of transgender individuals attempt suicide, more than twice the rate among gay and bisexual adults, and nearly ten times higher than the U.S. average.

Shortly before dawn, the House committee members retired without a vote, effectively killing the measure. At the last minute, several members scrambled to sign on as cosponsors for a dead bill, the most desirable outcome imaginable.

There were still eight days left in the session.

★

ONE OF THE MOTIVE FORCES behind the bathroom bill, and a major supporter of Dan Patrick, is Dr. Steven Hotze, a Houston physician and longtime ultraconservative kingmaker. Starting in the 1990s, he made a fortune from alternative hormone-replacement therapies and the sale of controversial supplements, such as colloidal silver, which Dr. Hotze recommends for colds, flu, "and even pet health." Colloidal silver can cause argyria, a condition in which a patient's skin permanently turns the color of a blue jay.

Hotze is affiliated with an evangelical Christian group called the Coalition on Revival. He signed their manifesto in 1986, which endorses the idea that "the ultimate cause of all disease, deformity, disability, and death is the sin of Adam and Eve." As for government: "We deny that any final authority outside the Bible (e.g., reason, experience, majority opinion, elite opinion, nature, etc.) ought to be accepted as the standard of government for any individual, group, or jurisdiction."

Hotze has hosted a show on the talk-radio station that Patrick now owns in Houston. He has even released a couple of songs—or perhaps they should be called lamentations—such as "God Fearing Texans Stop Obamacare":

> **What would Sam Houston do?**
> **What would Davy Crockett do?**
> **I know what I'm going to do.**
> **I'm going to fight Obamacare,**
> **I'm going to defeat Obamacare.**

Hotze's main cause is attacking homosexuals, or "homofascists," as he calls them. "The homosexual political movement will force churches, schools, businesses, and individuals to accept, to affirm, and even celebrate those who participate in anal sex," he has said. Sodomy, he went on, "will be mandated to be taught to children in the schools at an early age, starting in kindergarten." It goes without saying that homosexuals "want to make Texas a clone of California."

"He is the LeBron James of hating on gays," Evan Smith, the CEO of the **Texas Tribune,** told me. "He's the MVP every year. There is no close second."

In 2014, when Dan Patrick first ran for lieutenant governor, Hotze became one of his chief fundraisers. In a video endorsement, he stands next to Patrick and says, "Dan Patrick's leadership will keep Texas the most conservative state in the country."

In the video, Patrick makes it clear what the stakes are in his election. "The Democrats understand that if they can take Texas, they'll never have a Republican in the White House again," he says. "They will control the country. There's not another Texas to move to, folks. This is it."

In 2015, Hotze became involved in defeating an antidiscrimination ordinance in Houston that was championed by the city's lesbian mayor, Annise Parker. Hotze passed out bumper stickers saying "No Men in Women's Bathrooms," the same formulation that Patrick and his colleagues would apply to S.B. 6, which they styled "The Women's Privacy Act."

Hotze runs a political action committee called Conservative Republicans of Texas, and he maintains that group's website. "There are Texas legislators," Hotze wrote on the site in May 2017, "who would allow perverted men and boys, who sexually fantasize that they are women, to enter women's and girls' bathrooms, showers, and locker rooms." He implored his readers to pray with him:

In the name of Jesus, I prophesy and declare: May all the individuals serving in the state Legislature, and their staff, who support, promote and practice sodomy and other perverted, sexually deviant lifestyles, who support the killing of unborn babies, and who hate God's Law and God's Word, receive just retribution from God for their evil actions . . . May they be consumed, collapse, rot and be blown away as dust from their current positions because of their wicked works, thoughts and deeds. May people scorn them and nations abhor them. May their punishment lead them to repentance and faith in Christ. May God's will be done in their lives.

In an email to me, Patrick's office described Hotze as a "longtime supporter," but added, "The Lieutenant Governor does not agree with everything that any of his supporters say or do."

Straus told me, "Steve Hotze exists on the fringes. Mainstream Republicans don't take him seriously."

Meanwhile, Hotze was campaigning to have Straus removed as Speaker.

★

IN THE MIDDLE of all this political chaos, Tom Mechler, chairman of the state Republican Party, resigned. He issued a letter pleading for unity and civility. "A party that is fractured by anger and backbiting is a party that will not succeed," he wrote in his resignation note. He also warned that Republicans had failed to attract voters beyond the shrinking Anglo electorate, and was destined for electoral extinction. "If we do not continue to make efforts to engage in the diverse communities across Texas, our state will turn blue," he warned. He urged that the next chairman reshape the party in the image of modern Texas.

Soon after Mechler's resignation, Rob Morrow—the former Travis County GOP chairman, with the motley fool hat—announced his candidacy for the statewide position. His priorities had not changed since he was drummed out of the county office: "I like big titties. I am a proponent of boobyliciousness. In the past several years I have shared on social media the pics of over 500 extremely hot, busty women." He concluded by saying, "I am for having bikini contests at the Alamo every 4th of July. Case closed."

✶

THE TWELVE MEMBERS of the ultraconservative Freedom Caucus were furious at Straus and his allies for keeping their bills off the floor, legislation that included yet more bills targeting abortion, and measures that would further loosen gun laws. They decided to get revenge.

It was called the Mother's Day Massacre.

Bills that are not considered controversial are often placed on the local and consent calendar. Included were 121 uncontested bills awaiting a pro forma vote in the House. However, if five or more members object to a bill, it must then go through the normal legislative process and be scheduled for discussion on the House floor. The clock for such discussions ran out at midnight on May 11, the Thursday before Mother's Day weekend. Hours before midnight, the Freedom Caucus objected to the entire slate of consent bills, making it impossible for them to be heard in the 2017 session. The doomed consent bills included two that addressed the sharp rise in maternal mortality in Texas. Shawn Thierry, a Democrat from Houston, begged Freedom Caucus members to spare her bill, which would have commissioned a study that focused on low-income black mothers. Thierry herself had nearly died giving birth four years before because of a severe reaction to an epidural. She was forty-two years old at the time, an age when pregnancy complications are more likely. "But I certainly didn't know that I was three times more likely to die by virtue of being African American," she said after reading a state-issued report. She argued that her bill was pro-life, because the mothers who died in childbirth had carried their babies to term. The Freedom Caucus members agreed with her on this point, but they refused her request, explaining that it wasn't personal. "It was like a drive-by shooting," Thierry later said.

Next, the Freedom Caucus chewed up time in leisurely debate, bringing the House to a standstill. An hour passed as they considered inconsequential amendments to a bill on industrial-workforce training. It was an old tactic, perfected by minority Democrats in the past.

Drew Springer, the representative from North Texas who killed Stickland's anti-hog-abatement amendment, pleaded for H.B. 810, which would fund experimental stem-cell treatments. He spoke on behalf of his wife, who was in a wheelchair. Such treatments "might give somebody like my wife a chance to walk," he said, between sobs, as supporters gathered around the microphone. "I'll trade every single bill I've ever passed, every single one, to get the chance to hear H.B. 810." The Freedom Caucus gave in on this one, and it passed.

Among the slain consent bills was H.B. 3302, a sunset safety-net bill. It had been crafted to preserve important state agencies that would otherwise be phased out under the automatic review policy, which takes place every twelve years. One of the five agencies up for review was the state medical board. If the medical board expired, there would be no one to license doctors. It wasn't clear if members of the Freedom Caucus had realized the far-reaching consequences of killing H.B. 3302.

Dan Patrick, however, recognized that an important lever had been handed to him. The only way to avoid the consequences of H.B. 3302 failing to pass was for a similar bill to be passed in the Senate—which had a later deadline—and then be sent back to the House. On the Monday after Mother's Day, Straus wrote a letter to Patrick, formally requesting that the Senate pass such a bill, along with the budget, so that the legislature could avoid a special session. In response, Patrick privately sent him the specific terms for such a deal. The House had to pass the bathroom bill and another of Patrick's priorities, a bill that intended to put a brake on local property taxes.

In return, the Senate would agree to pass its own version of the sunset safety net bill, as well as the budget and several other items, including one championed by Straus, which dealt with school finance reform. Over the years, the state's contribution to public schools has sharply diminished, with property taxes having to make up the difference. To restore the balance, Straus wanted to add $1.5 billion from the state to the public schools. However, Patrick's offer came with what Straus called a "poison pill"—a provision for vouchers for private schools, which the House had already firmly rejected; moreover, under Patrick's terms, the state's contribution would be a fraction of what Straus proposed.

Patrick felt that Texas schools had enough money. In an op-ed published in early June, he noted that total education spending, including universities, was already the largest item in the budget—"about fifty-two per cent of all state dollars." He added: "It is disingenuous to suggest that we are, somehow, holding back funding that we could spend on schools." (PolitiFact pointed out that education spending, as a percentage of the Texas budget, is lower than it has been in at least twenty years. It is among the lowest, per capita, in the country.)

By now, the ill will between Patrick and Straus had spilled over into the chambers they led. San

Antonio Republican Lyle Larson, who is close to
Straus, accused the Senate of "taking hostages"
when it promised to pass certain House bills only
if the House voted for Patrick's priorities. "I've got
six," Larson cried. "How many other bills were
held hostage by the Texas Senate?"

A roar went up in the House, which only increased in volume when Democrat Harold Dut-
ton, a black state representative from Houston,
took the microphone. "When the Senate won't **respect** us, they need to **expect** us," he said. "I don't
know if they can **see** us, but would you open the
door so they can **hear** us?" The House doors were
flung open as the frustrated representatives bayed
like wolves at the Senate chamber.

Governor Abbott had warned Straus that he
would demand action on the bathroom bill, even
if he had to call a special session to get it. With
the Speaker's blessing, a compromise was crafted
by Chris Paddie, a Republican representative from
Marshall. It was styled as an amendment to a bill
on school safety and would affect grade schools
and high schools but not universities or government buildings. It affirmed the right of all students to use the bathroom with "privacy, dignity,
and safety," but it did not explicitly bar students
from using particular bathrooms.

Across Texas, school districts and chambers of
commerce seemed resigned to accept the amend-

ment. In Straus's opinion, it codified a reasonable practice that many schools had already adopted. Still, there was bitter opposition in the House by members who saw it as appeasement. Rafael Anchia, a Democratic state representative from Dallas, reminded the other members that since January, when they began debating the bathroom issue, ten transgender people had been violently killed in the United States. He read their names aloud.

The amendment passed the House, but it didn't satisfy Patrick. Straus refused to go further. He declared that Patrick could take Paddie's amendment or leave it. "For many of us—and especially for me—this was a compromise. As far as I'm concerned, it was enough. We will go no further. This is the right thing to do in order to protect our economy from billions of dollars in losses and more importantly to protect the safety of some very vulnerable young Texans." He added that it was "absurd" that the bathroom bill had taken on more urgency than fixing the school finance system.

Patrick called a press conference shortly afterward. He said of Straus's remarks, "Instead of siding with the people of Texas—and, as a Republican, siding with Republicans of Texas—he has decided to support the policies of Barack Obama, who said, 'I want boys and girls in every shower in every school in the country.'" (Obama never said that.) Patrick then added a remark aimed directly at the reluctant Governor Abbott: "Tonight, I'm making it very clear, Governor. I want you to call us back on your own time."

The two chambers succeeded in passing a budget, but a special session seemed inevitable.

Abbott clearly hated the position he had been thrust into. He had said repeatedly that there was still time in the regular session to resolve these issues. But time had now run out. A special session devoted almost entirely to the bathroom bill would focus even more unwanted national attention on Texas.

To add to the pressure, on May 27, the CEOs of fourteen companies with a significant presence in Texas, including Apple, Amazon, Cisco, Google, and IBM, sent Abbott a letter. "We are gravely concerned that any such legislation would deeply tarnish Texas' reputation as open and friendly to businesses and families," it said. The bill would harm the companies' ability to recruit talent to the state, they asserted, adding: "Discrimination is wrong and it has no place in Texas." Ray Perryman, a respected economist in Waco, did his own study of the bathroom bill. He forecast that its passage would cost the state $3.3 billion in gross state product and the loss of 36,000 jobs, most of them in the tourist industry. Indeed, convention bookings in the state were already suffering cancellations while the measure was being discussed.

Reporters caught up with Abbott at a gun range, where he signed a bill lowering the cost of handgun licenses. "Texans' ability to bear arms is going to be even bolder today than it's ever been before," he said. He then shot a few rounds at a target sheet, which he proudly displayed to the reporters, who have generally been very kind to him. This was the day after Montana had held a special election and chosen as U.S. representative a candidate who had body-slammed a reporter, sending him to the hospital. It was also the same season in which Trump had declared the press to be the enemy. Abbott held up his bullet-riddled target and said, "I'm gonna carry this around in case I see any reporters."

On the Friday before the end of the regular session, Straus told me, the lieutenant governor sent two emissaries from the Senate to visit with the Speaker in his office. They seemed nervous. One of the senators carried an envelope, apparently containing the language of the bathroom bill that Patrick would accept. The senator, a lawyer whose name Straus would not disclose, told Straus that the language had been carefully crafted to ensure that the bill would override any local antidiscrimination ordinances. The senator started to open the envelope, but Straus said not to bother. "I'm not a lawyer, but I am a Texan," he said. "I'm disgusted by all this. Tell the lieutenant governor I don't want the suicide of a single Texan on my hands."

★

DURING THE REGULAR SESSION of the Eighty-fifth Texas Legislature, more than 6,600 bills were filed, and more than 1,200 were passed and sent to the governor to sign. The session was widely viewed as being dictated by Dan Patrick, but many of the signature items he sought— school vouchers, property-tax rollbacks, and the bathroom bill—failed to pass.

The major cities in Texas quickly joined in a lawsuit against S.B. 4—the sanctuary cities bill— saying that its provisions would lead to racial profiling, and that regulating immigration is a power reserved for the federal government. However, the U.S. attorney general, Jeff Sessions, announced that the Justice Department was on the side of S.B. 4. "President Trump has made a commitment to keep America safe," he said. "Texas has admirably followed his lead by mandating statewide cooperation with federal immigration laws that require the removal of illegal aliens who have committed crimes." Faced with the possibility of being incarcerated in her own jail if she disobeyed federal immigration detention requests,

Travis County Sheriff Sally Hernandez said that her office would comply with the new law.

The last day of the session, Memorial Day, is usually spent in presentations of proclamations, commendations to the staff, and good-byes among colleagues who have endured 140 of the most intense days of their lives together. Some of the members will retire; others may be defeated in the next election; those who endure will be back in eighteen months for another round.

Meanwhile, buses began arriving at the capitol. Hundreds of protestors, some from distant states, burst through the doors, filling all four levels of the rotunda and spilling into the House gallery. They blew whistles and unfurled banners ("See You in Court!") and chanted "S.B. 4 has got to go!" One of the leaders of the protest, Stephanie Gharakhanian, explained to reporters, "We wanted to make sure we gave them the send-off they deserve."

The House came to a halt amid the pandemonium. A few of the Democrats on the floor looked up at the chanting protestors and began to applaud. State troopers cleared the gallery and broke up the demonstration, but by that time the attempted bonhomie that usually characterizes the final day had blown up. Matt Rinaldi, a member of the Freedom Caucus from Dallas County, who is sometimes rated the most conservative member of the House, later told Fox Business Network that he noticed several banners bearing the message "I Am Undocumented and Here to Stay." He says he decided to summon Immigration and Customs Enforcement, and then bragged about it to his Hispanic colleagues.

A shoving match broke out on the House floor. Curses flew, along with spittle. Afterward, Rinaldi posted on Facebook that Alfonso "Poncho" Nevárez, a Democrat from the border town of Eagle Pass, had threatened his life. "Poncho told me he would 'get me on the way to my car,'" Rinaldi wrote. He said he made it clear that "I would shoot him in self-defense."

★

THE CAPITOL WAS SUBDUED the day after the session ended. In the House chamber, docents were leading school tours and explaining, in English and Spanish, the identities of the famous Texans in the portraits along the walls. I like the one of Stephen F. Austin with his musket, a spotted hound at his feet. In the rotunda, a high school orchestra was playing a piece for woodwinds. I went up on the second-floor tier, where the acoustics were better. The students were from Kountze, a little East Texas town that had the distinction, in 1991, of electing America's first Muslim mayor. The musicians were arrayed in the center of the rotunda atop the seals of the Republic and the five other nations that Texas had once been part of. I was moved by the thought that the long and bloody march of Texas history had paused at this moment, with small-town kids bringing all the diverse voices of our state into harmony.

Speaker Straus was waiting in his chambers, seated on his couch in his shirtsleeves, under a painting of Hereford cattle. He looked more relaxed than I thought was warranted, given that the governor was poised to call a special session that would likely focus on Patrick's two must-pass bills. But Straus seemed satisfied. He boasted that the priorities of the House—**his** priorities—had been mostly accomplished. "We did the Child Protective Services reforms, adding fourteen hundred new caseworkers," he said. "We made tremendous progress on mental health reforms." Texas's decrepit hospitals were going to be upgraded. A health-care plan for retired teachers was saved. Massive cuts to higher education were averted. "These were issues a little bit under the radar because they're not sensational, but they're issues that are going to make a big difference in Texas lives," Straus said. "What we didn't achieve was to begin fixing the school finance system, which everybody knows is a disaster." Straus said that schools in districts that have been affected by the downturn in the oil and gas economy might have to be shuttered. "We had a plan to bridge that. Unfortunately the Senate had other priorities." He attributed the failure to Patrick's "fixation on vouchers."

I asked Straus about the clash between business and cultural conservatives, which was tearing the Republican Party apart, both in Texas and nationally. He quoted William H. Seward, Lincoln's secretary of state, who described the forthcoming Civil War as "an irrepressible conflict." The prejudices unleashed by the election of Donald Trump were mixing with the already volatile elements of Texas politics. Given that Dan Patrick had been Trump's campaign manager in the state, there was bound to be a confluence of interests.

Referring to the bathroom bill, Straus said, "We came very close this session to passing a sweeping discriminatory policy. It would have sent a very negative message around the country."

"That's still possible, right?" I asked. Couldn't the governor just put forward his own bill and threaten to veto any amendments?

Straus agreed, but noted, "The legislature is not obligated to act upon his agenda items within the thirty-day period. And the governor would have the option to call as many thirty-day sessions as he would like."

"So it could stay in committee and not get voted out?"

Straus smiled.

The session was the most fractious in memory, and the bad feelings stirred up in the capitol will linger long after the lawmakers return home. Immigrant communities are fearful, lawmakers are vengeful, and hatemongers feel entitled to spread their message. And the bitter battle among Texas Republicans wasn't yet over. Governor Abbott called a special session, to convene on July 18, and set forth a list of twenty items that he said required action. Most of them could have been passed in the regular session; none of them were a priority for him before the session began. In addition to the bathroom bill, his list of demands included education vouchers, caps on state and local spending, and new abortion restrictions. He asked for a thousand-dollar pay raise for public-school teachers, which the local school districts—not the state—would likely have to pay for. "I expect legislators to return with a calm demeanor, and with a firm commitment to make Texas even better," the governor declared.

Straus was not intimidated. He told me, "We're under no obligation to pass anything."

★

REPUBLICAN POLITICAL CONSULTANT Karl Rove sometimes drops in on my regular Monday breakfast. He's a notorious figure in liberal Austin, a status he seems to relish. He's also a historian and writer, which is what draws him to our table. The week after the regular session closed, he sat down with us and we talked about how Texas turned red.

Rove attributed the turnover, in part, to migration. "People moved to Texas from somewhere else in the country, and that started to turn the urban areas Republican." The new Texans arrived with different political histories. My own family was part of that migration. My father was an Eisenhower Republican when we moved to Dallas in 1960. The Kennedy-Nixon campaign was under way, and Daddy was strongly for Nixon, although I think my mother secretly voted for Kennedy. She was always quiet about her politics. The Republicans didn't make Dallas a right-wing stronghold—it was already very conservative— but it became the first city in Texas to turn red, in 1954, when it elected Bruce Alger, a real-estate developer and political extremist, to Congress.

Suburbs sprang up to accommodate the massive growth in Texas in the postwar decades, and they tended to be more like one another than like the cities they surrounded. Everything was new: the churches, the schools, the shopping centers, even the trees. "Think about Williamson County, or better yet, Collin County—these were cow pastures in the seventies," Rove said. "You used

to be able to go to Frisco"—in Collin County—
"and there was one stoplight in it. Now it has ten
high schools."

Unlike the cities, the suburbs were largely middle class and overwhelmingly white. There was a
great sorting out, which left the cities poorer and
more concentrated with minorities. The suburbs
were organized around families who were seeking
affordable homes and good schools. Suburbanites
tended to have white-collar jobs, which meant
that they were less likely than laboring Texans to
belong to a union. They were more religious, often
intensely so, belonging to massive evangelical congregations. All of these suburban characteristics—
their relative affluence, their domination by white,
non-union, churchgoing families—coincided with
the core demographics of the emerging Republican majority.

Rove also pointed to another factor—"the se-
quential flow of parts of rural Texas into the Republican column." That process began in West
Texas in 1978, then moved to the eastern and central parts of the state. By 1994, "rural Texas had
moved from being solidly Democratic to solidly
Republican."

"That was where the progressives were, in the
old days, right?" I asked. "What changed in their
condition that caused them to turn Republican?"

"They were not so much progressives as they

were populists," he replied. "And populists think the system's rigged against them. They went from being economic populists, who thought the system was rigged against the little guy, to social and conservative populists, who thought that government was the problem."

"And also, the effects of the Civil War finally wore off," Bill Brands observed. "But when the national Democratic Party embraced civil rights, then the Southern Democrats decided this is no longer my party."

"The Democrats lasted longer in Texas than elsewhere in the South because the party remained relatively moderate," said Rove. Under Governor Ann Richards, however, "the Democratic Party took a hard left turn." It was Rove who engineered her downfall.

"What accounted for her popularity?" Steve asked.

"She was the aunt you loved to see at the family picnic every summer," Rove replied. "Outrageous, say anything, do anything." At the beginning of the Bush campaign, Richards had a 67 percent approval rating and more than $4 million in her war chest. George W. had lost one congressional race and had no experience in politics, but thanks in part to Rove's political mastery, Bush beat the incumbent governor 53.5 percent to 45.9 percent, the widest margin of victory in twenty years.

Karl Rove was born in an elevator in Denver, on Christmas Day 1950. He was one of five children. He would later learn that his father, a geologist, who left the family on the Christmas Day that Karl turned nineteen, was actually not his real father—he had adopted the two children that Rove's mother had in a previous, secret marriage. She was an unstable woman who eventually took her own life. According to reports, Louis Rove Jr., Karl's stepfather, lived the remainder of his life as a gay man. Karl was close to him until he passed away in 2004.

Karl grew up in Colorado, Nevada, and Utah, and he imbibed the Republicanism of the Rocky Mountain West. At age nine, he stuck a Nixon bumper sticker on his bike, only to be attacked by a neighborhood girl who made her Democratic preferences known by giving him a bloody nose. It was his first political fight.

He attended the University of Utah, although he never graduated; his focus was on getting elected president of the College Republicans. It would prove to be a legendary campaign. Managing the vote on Southern campuses for Rove's presidential bid was Lee Atwater. The two of them would one day reshape American political campaigns—Atwater, most notably, as campaign manager for George H. W. Bush in his brutal victory over Michael Dukakis in the 1988 presidential campaign; and Rove, with his involvement in George W. Bush's two gubernatorial victories, in 1994 and 1998, and his presidential elections in 2000 and 2004. But their first victory was getting Rove elected, in 1973, in the rawest political contest the College Republicans had ever seen. Both Atwater and Rove came away with a reputation for using dirty tricks to win.

Rove moved to Texas in 1977, at a time when the demographic changes in the state had not made themselves felt politically. But he was keen enough to recognize the trend. He was twenty-six years old, baby-faced, with wispy blond hair and pinkish skin. He went to work for George H.W., who had lost two races for the U.S. Senate but had formed a political action committee in preparation for an unlikely presidential run. John Tower was a Republican senator from Texas, but no other Republicans occupied statewide office. That changed the following year, when Bill Clements, a gruff and extremely wealthy oil-services provider who had been Nixon and Ford's deputy secretary of defense, got elected as the first Republican governor in Texas since Reconstruction. He ran against John Hill, the courtly former attorney general and chief justice of the Texas Supreme Court. Steve, who once profiled Clements, observed then, "Nobody really wanted a gentleman as governor of Texas when it was possible to have a roughneck. On election day the world as Texas had known it for a hundred years came to an end." Clements hired Rove to be his chief of staff.

In 1981, Rove started a direct-mail business in Austin and began running campaigns in Texas. Many of the earliest Republican victors in Texas owe their success to him. Rove also turned his attention to down-ballot races that the Republican Party had never taken seriously. In 1988, he consulted on the successful campaign of Kent Hance for the Railroad Commission, a powerful agency that, despite the name, actually regulates the oil-and-gas industry. That same year, he got Thomas R. Phillips elected to the Texas Supreme Court (yes, we even elect judges in Texas). Although Republicans were still just getting established in the state, "we won in a landslide twice when Karl was helping me," Phillips told me. Moderate and conservative Democrats began following voters into the Republican Party, and Rove was there to get them elected. Rick Perry, for one, served three terms in the Texas House as a Democrat, and even campaigned for Al Gore in his 1988 presidential bid, before changing parties the following year. With Rove's guidance, he became agriculture commissioner in 1990. Eventually, Rove would elect seven of the nine justices, both Texas senators, the land commissioner, the lieutenant governor—nearly every statewide office had a Rove Republican inside it. "What he did in twenty-five years is remake the political face of Texas and give shape and substance to a ruling political class," Bill Miller told me. In 1994, Texas elected its last statewide Democrat. "It was a complete rout of a political party," Miller said.

I asked Karl where he thought the Republican Party in Texas, which he had done so much to create, was headed. "Look at the House," he said. "Jonathan Stickland and the Freedom Caucus are a minority faction. The only reason they got that much traction this session is that Joe [Straus] didn't have his act together." He pointed out that there is still a bipartisan tradition in the legislature. This was true even under the extremely conservative Speaker Tom Craddick, who was overthrown by the coup that put Straus in the Speaker's chair. "Joe's election, I hope, portends the future," Rove said, "where you have a reasonable Republican who's backed by reasonable Democrats"—with the partisan extremists pushed to the sidelines.

★

ABOUT 1,100 NEW LAWS went into effect after the 2017 legislative season. Among them: children under the age of sixteen will no longer be allowed to marry; faith-based adoption agencies will be permitted to deny placing children with gay parents; and Texans can now openly carry swords, a welcome development for the samurai in our midst.

The special session of the legislature that Governor Abbott called was a disappointing end for cultural conservatives, however, concluding without property tax reform, a compromise on school finance, or the bathroom bill. Dan Patrick blamed Joe Straus. "Thank goodness Travis didn't have the Speaker at the Alamo," Patrick said. "He might have been the first one over the wall." The state did commit to continuing to study the high rate of maternal mortality, at the same time passing new restrictions on abortion and doing nothing to improve access to health care. The special session passed a law limiting local ordinances on trees, although it was not as comprehensive as the governor had wanted. Large cities will be required to hold elections for residents in areas targeted for annexation. These measures were part of a larger attempt to disempower cities, which Dan Patrick said were responsible for all the problems in America. The reason: "Our cities are still controlled by Democrats." He cheerfully observed, on the Fox Business Network, that "almost a thousand Democrats were defeated running for the local state houses and state senate and governors and lieutenant governors . . . We own the turf state by state, and Texas leads the way."

Not addressed by the legislature was the low quality of education in Texas, which is near bottom nationally in most measures of overall achievement. Texas spends $10,000 a year per student—$2,500 below the national average—an indication of where education stands in terms of the state's priorities. Racism may play a role in the steadily decreasing state support for public schools, but whatever the motivation, the workforce of the future has already been handicapped.

Texas also ranks low in terms of its infrastructure—the roads, dams, pipelines, parks, railroads, energy systems, wastewater treatment, and drinking water that modern civilization relies upon. It's not just a matter of aging structures and poor maintenance. For a state that is projected to double in population in thirty years, Texas has done little to prepare itself. For all of the boldness that Texans often boast of, there is timidity about confronting the challenges in front of us. But that's not the direction the social conservatives who rule the state are facing. They instinctively look backward, to a time when homosexuals were unseen, minorities were powerless, abortion was taboo, business and industry were largely unregulated, and science stood respectfully in the shadow of religious belief. Texas is not alone in its assault on diversity, nor in its determination to shove government out of civic life, but without high-quality education and modernized infrastructure the knowledge-based industries of the future will find other states, and other countries, in which to plant themselves. The refusal to face these challenges head-on seems to me not only imprudent but decidedly un-Texan.

Joe Straus received a vote of no-confidence by his own chapter of the Republican Party in San Antonio, a gesture repeated in a number of other caucuses in counties around the state. The ostensible reason was Straus's failure to advance the Texas GOP platform. That platform includes demands that the U.S. government surrender all of its authority over abortion back to the states, and that until then federal laws permitting abortion be ignored; that U.S. senators be appointed by state legislatures, rather than elected by the citizens; that the IRS, Environmental Protection Agency, the Department of Education, and a number of other federal agencies be abolished or defunded; that traffic-enforcement cameras be removed; that a photo ID be required of all voters; that the U.S. Supreme Court ruling permitting gay marriage be overturned; that Social Security be phased out; that federal gun laws be ignored; that the Federal Reserve System be abolished and precious metals be reinstituted as the standard for the U.S. dollar; that the minimum-wage law be repealed; that the U.S. withdraw from the United Nations and from international trade agreements, such as NAFTA; and that a high border wall be built along the Mexican border, wherever it is deemed "effective and cost-efficient." This document is a template for the future agenda of the Republican Party not just in Texas but in the nation.

Straus seemed to give the rebellion in the party caucuses little thought. He promised to run for a record-breaking sixth term as Speaker. Then, on the morning of October 25, he held an impromptu press conference in his office and announced that he would not seek another term. "I didn't want to be one of those people who held on to an office just because he could," Straus said. "There are new players and they deserve to have their voices heard."

Perhaps he was bowing to the inevitable. The House Republican Caucus was pushing a plan that would allow them to designate the candidate for the post, making Democratic votes irrelevant. Straus's enemies were exultant. "We did it!!! Speaker Straus is gone," Jonathan Stickland tweeted. "The future of Texas has never looked brighter." Julie McCarty, the president of the NE Tarrant County Tea Party, a statewide organization headquartered in Fort Worth, took credit for Straus's departure. "No, I will not allow Straus to waltz off in celebrated thanks for his 'service,'" she wrote on her Facebook page. "I will be David. I will mount Goliath's head on a sword—the saber I was awarded by Empower Texans for being a grassroots hero—and I will dance! I will display this victory for all to see, for the birds to peck at, for my fellow warriors to recognize God's hand in delivering our enemy and to be motivated that God is not done yet, for others who wish to follow in Goliath's footsteps to be warned what awaits them."

# ELEVEN

# Borderlands

Mexico defines Texas in a way that no other state experiences with any other nation. We are like a couple still living next door to each other after a particularly bitter divorce. Imagine the wealth and power that would have been Mexico's had Texas remained a part of it—a genuine rival to the gringo colossus. Our history and our populations are intermingled and complexly mirror each other. You'll find paired cities strung like beads on either side of the river: Del Rio and Ciudad Acuña, Laredo and Nuevo Laredo, McAllen and Reynosa, Brownsville and Matamoros. El Paso and Juárez are the ones most closely aligned. El Paso Street crosses the international bridge and becomes Avenida Benito Juárez. Physically, it's one city, straddling a political and cultural divide that has never been bridged.

Growing up in Texas, I was always aware of our festive and treacherous neighbor next door. As a young reporter, I wrote about the narcotics trade, and came to appreciate the peril that my Mexican colleagues experienced while covering the crime and corruption in their country. They were often under death threats, and many were actually killed. An Austin writer friend of mine was shot in Mexico City when his cab was hijacked. One can't understand Mexico without acknowledging the violence that is part of the atmosphere.

Octavio Paz, the great Mexican poet, once cataloged the differences he observed between his country and mine. "The North Americans are credulous and we are believers; they love fairy tales and detective stories and we love myths and legends," Paz writes. "They are optimists and we are nihilists—except that our nihilism is not intellectual but instinctive, and therefore irrefutable. We are suspicious and they are trusting. We are sorrowful and sarcastic and they are happy and full of jokes. North Americans want to understand and we want to contemplate. They are activists and we are quietists; we enjoy our wounds and they enjoy their inventions."

There is another distinction that Paz draws—this one between the North American's avoidance of death and the Mexican's willingness to contemplate horror: "The bloody Christs in our village churches, the macabre humor in some of our newspaper headlines, our wakes, the custom of eating skull-shaped cakes and candies on the Day of the Dead, are habits inherited from the Indians and the Spaniards and are now an inseparable part of our being."

The first time I went to Mexico was on a family trip to the little fishing village of Topolobampo, on the Pacific Ocean, in the state of Sinaloa. We flew to El Paso, then caught a bus to Chihuahua City, and from there took the train across Copper Canyon, in the heart of Tarahumara Indian country. I was sixteen; my sisters, Kathleen and Rosalind, were fourteen and eleven. This was the summer after the Kennedy assassination. I remember that because when we were at dinner one night in Mexico an American couple at the table next to us overheard us talking about Texas, and asked where in Texas we were from. When Daddy said, "Dallas," they got up and just left their meal sitting there.

Before the trip, I had a startling nightmare, one of the worst dreams I've ever had in my life. I was on an airplane, and suddenly I was floating above my seat. I looked around to find my mother, and saw her head come off. The next morning, I was sufficiently upset to tell Kathy and Roz about it. None of us had ever had a dream come true, and anyway we were children, and what did we know about Mexico? So we went.

On the way home, we retraced our steps, catch-

ing the train again at Los Mochis and crossing
the Sierras to Chihuahua. Then we got on the bus
to Juárez.

I was trying to nap, with my head against the
window. The road was empty and the monotonous
bleached landscape stretched out from nowhere
to nowhere. It started sprinkling, and the drops
shot across the windowpane like bullets. We were
going really fast.

The road was wet, and when the driver came
to a curve he didn't even begin to make it. Suddenly, we were off the road, bouncing in our seats.
Weirdly, the driver never slowed down. I heard
later that he was sixty-five years old and had had
his license for only two weeks, which might have
accounted for the fact that he didn't simply stop
and back up. Instead, he tried to navigate the bus
back to the road, in a big loop through a field,
going at the same wild clip, flying past cactus and
over boulders. Ahead was a bridge crossing a dry
arroyo. There was a slanted concrete abutment
at the base of the bridge, which the driver hit,
launching the bus into the air.

It was then, as I was hurled into the luggage
rack, that I looked back and saw my mother's wig
come off.

The bus flew across the road and landed with
such force that everyone over thirty broke their
backs. My sisters and I were the youngest passen-

gers, and although we were shaken, we were able to stand and walk.

We were in the middle of the Chihuahuan Desert. There were maybe forty injured passengers. No cars on the road, no way to call an ambulance, nothing to do but wait for the next bus.

The adults were splayed out on the floor or on their seats, groaning in pain. Daddy was stoic, but I could see he was suffering. My mother had also broken her breastbone and was gasping for breath. The driver was the most gravely injured. I later heard he went to prison. When the next scheduled bus finally came, about four hours later, we rode another hundred miles or so to Juárez, every bump in the road eliciting agonized choruses from the wounded passengers. It was sobering to hear the adults weeping. I didn't speak Spanish at the time, and I didn't understand why the police wouldn't let us take our parents to the hospital in El Paso. It turned out that accidents are often treated as crimes in Mexico, and we were all being held as witnesses.

★

I RETURNED to Juárez after Thanksgiving 2016. Mónica Ortiz Uribe, a freelance radio reporter in El Paso, accompanied me as we walked across the international bridge. "I like living in a place that allows me to experience both sides of myself," she told me.

The Rio Grande here is little more than puddles inside a concrete culvert, nearly all the water having been diverted to farms on both sides. What is left runs through an irrigation canal paralleling the river. Mónica pointed out where a U.S. Border Patrol agent, who was on bike patrol, shot a fifteen-year-old boy just across the river, about sixty feet away, in 2010. According to American authorities, the boy was with a group who were throwing rocks at the agents, a frequent complaint. Because the bullet crossed an international boundary, the case is legally complicated. (The U.S. Supreme Court recently heard arguments as to whether the agent who shot the boy can be sued, and returned the case to the Fifth Circuit Court of Appeals.)

The cartel wars in Juárez made it the most dangerous city in the world between 2008 and 2012, even worse than Baghdad. More than 10,000 people were slain during that period. When Mónica and I visited, Juárez was experiencing another killing spree, with nearly a hundred murders in October alone. Throughout Mexico, the homicide rate had surged 18 percent over the previous year. Everyone on both sides of the river was on edge.

Downtown Juárez was desolate. Mónica pointed out the pink crosses on the lampposts. Since the 1990s, hundreds of Juárez women, most of them teenagers, have been kidnapped, many of them in plain sight on the streets where we were standing. Some of their bodies have turned up in mass graves. Each of the crosses on the lampposts represents one of the missing women. "Now you can hardly find a streetlamp without one," Mónica remarked. "Women are still disappearing to this day, dozens every year."

Meanwhile, across the river, El Paso bills itself as one of the safest cities in America. Border towns are typically crammed with local cops, U.S. Marshals, Border Patrol agents, and members of the Texas National Guard. Sometimes, however, bullets from gunfights in Juárez fly over the border. In 2012, a woman was pushing a stroller in downtown El Paso when a stray shot hit her in the leg. Bullets from Mexico also struck a building at the University of Texas branch in El Paso, and another broke a picture frame in the city hall.

I checked into the Camino Real Hotel in downtown El Paso. My memory was that I had stayed here with my two sisters after the bus wreck, while our parents were still in the hospital in Juárez, but as soon as I arrived I realized that I had never been in this hotel before.

I'm fascinated by the ways in which memory fails us, how vivid incidents can be distorted or lost—or "repressed," to use Freud's term. I had never forgotten the bus wreck or the sight of my

parents in the Mexican hospital entirely encased
in body casts. But there were details that had
dropped away after fifty years. I recalled that I
had to hire a lawyer to get a writ that would let
my parents leave Mexico. One of the first words
I learned in Spanish was **abogado**. But I was at a
loss about why I couldn't remember the hotel.

I called my sisters.

"We were never in El Paso," Roz told me. "We
were always in Juárez." She thought we were there
for a week or ten days after the wreck. The hotel
wouldn't let me make an international call to contact people who could help us, so we were trapped.
"You finally went to a bank and told them that
your father was a banker, too, and they let you use
the phone," Roz said.

That must have been when I called our family
doctor, Robert Cox. He came down on a private
plane to ferry our parents back to Dallas. Dr. Cox
was a giant, about six feet seven or eight, and he
towered over the Mexican doctors in my parents'
hospital room. He had asked me to find an extra-
long bed at the hotel for him, which I couldn't do.

Kathy remembered that he came with a wad
of dollars, which he spread around in the hospital
and at the border to ease us all out of the country.

"Why did I have this memory of being at the
Camino Real?"

"I think there's another hotel by that name in

Juárez," Kathy said. "I remember because I stole the room key."

She was right. As soon as she mentioned the key, I recalled the baronial keys, and the archways and Saltillo tiles of the hotel we had actually stayed in. Kathy asked if I would repay the hotel for the stolen key. Apparently, it had weighed on her conscience all this time.

Kathy told me another thing that I had forgotten. On the flight home, Dr. Cox called the three of us together, as Mother and Daddy lay sedated on their gurneys. "He told us that our parents were going to be invalids for the rest of their lives," Kathy said. It may have had something to do with their bodies atrophying inside those body casts. "He said we might not even be able to finish high school."

You'd think I would have remembered that.

When we got to Baylor Hospital in Dallas, the casts were cut away and our parents were encouraged to move around. They wore braces for a long time, but they recovered. I wonder what happened to all those other passengers.

★

DOWNTOWN EL PASO IS in the middle of a renaissance. The city had been devastated by the implementation of the North American Free Trade Agreement—NAFTA—in 1994, which eliminated most tariffs between the United States, Canada, and Mexico. Until then, much of the city's economy derived from the garment industry, but those jobs jumped over the border into maquiladoras—the factories that are allowed to import certain materials for assembly or manufacturing and then return them to the United States as finished products. The goal of NAFTA was to draw Mexico into the high-wage economies of its northern neighbors and turn the entire North American continent into a single market. The Mexican president at the time, Carlos Salinas de Gortari, said it would transform his country's economy, so that it would "export goods, not people."

Donald Trump has decried NAFTA as the worst deal ever, and it's true that the agreement has had a mixed record for the United States and Mexico. In 1993, the balance of trade showed a narrow $1.7 billion U.S. surplus over Mexico; by 2016, after more than twenty years of NAFTA, that surplus had swung to a $64 billion deficit, the highest it has ever been. About 350,000 auto-workers lost their jobs in the United States, while about 430,000 such jobs were created in Mexico. Texas alone lost nearly 50,000 jobs in the two decades after NAFTA's passage, about 18,500 of them in El Paso. Some economists argue that the American jobs would have been lost in any case, because of globalization and automation, and that, in fact, the linkages with cheaper labor in Mexico gave American automakers an advantage in dealing with China. In any case, the percentage of Mexicans living below the poverty level— about 46 percent of the population—remains at roughly the same level it was when the trade deal was passed, and unemployment has actually risen. Almost two million Mexican farmers have been put out of work, unable to compete with their industrialized American counterparts. That has driven many of them to cross the border seeking better jobs. Cheaper goods have kept inflation down in the United States, but wages have also been slow to grow. Both countries have witnessed unprecedented levels of income inequality.

"I completely understand the fear that comes from NAFTA—we lived it," Veronica Escobar, then a county judge in El Paso, told me. "When the manufacturing left after NAFTA, El Paso became a ghost town." Now, she says, "we've reinvented ourselves." El Paso has adapted in part by servicing the maquiladoras across the border. There's a new medical school and a children's hospital in town. Hundreds of millions of dollars are being invested in renovating landmark buildings downtown. But the manufacturing jobs never returned. Seven out of the top ten employers in the city are telemarketing call centers. Across the river in Juárez, three hundred maquiladoras make parts and equipment for Bosch, Foxconn, Flextronics, Delphi, Lear, Boeing, Sumitomo, and other multinational corporations. Meanwhile, Mexico has raised the minimum wage to seventy pesos a day—less than four U.S. dollars.

I got a tour of El Paso with Max Grossman, a professor of architectural history and a member of the local historical commission. He's a trim man with a snap-brim fedora, like a film noir character. "In 1920, El Paso was the largest city between Dallas and San Francisco," Max said, as he pointed out some of the highlights of the city. The Plaza Hotel, formerly a Hilton, was where seventeen-year-old Elizabeth Taylor stayed before she was briefly married to Conrad Hilton Jr. In the window of the oldest building downtown, now a pawnshop, was the blackened mummified trigger finger of Pancho Villa, the Mexican revolutionary general, which was on sale for $9,500. Nearby was the office building where the gunslinger John Wesley Hardin had his law practice before he was shot in the back in a saloon. "El Paso was legendary for its lawlessness," Max said happily. There were the handsome concrete Caples Building, where Francisco Madero planned the Mexican Revolution, and the CVS pharmacy, formerly the Elite Confectionary, where Pancho Villa indulged in strawberry sodas and peanut brittle. Afterwards, we had dinner next door to a hotel where John Dillinger spent the night.

★

MÓNICA AND I DROVE OUT to a well-known crossing spot in the desert just west of El Paso. A massive fence was under construction. There are already nearly seven hundred miles of fence along the two-thousand-mile U.S.–Mexico border, as a result of the 2006 Secure Fence Act, passed during the George W. Bush administration. This stretch was not yet completed.

It was dark and cold. As we crossed the railroad track, we ran into a couple of Border Patrol agents, who told us it had already been a very busy night. "We caught two different groups of forty to fifty people, and another group of twenty," one of the agents said.

The next day, Mónica and I rode with another Border Patrol agent, George Gomez. He grew up in the region, at a time when the border was completely open. "I would go out to shoot jackrabbits with a BB gun," he said, as we passed through the sandy hills. "I'd see hundreds of people coming across on a daily basis. They'd be landscapers, carpenters, maids. In the evening, you'd see them going back. El Paso was basically an open border." There was a barrier then, of sorts—a cable running through upright railroad ties—but people just stepped over it. Folks on both sides thought of themselves as citizens of the border, as if it were a region, not a boundary. The border was what they had in common; it united them and made them distinct from their countrymen farther away.

In many respects, that's still true. Whenever I'm on the border, I hear the resentment against authorities whose job is to enforce the laws. Because of the language skills required, a large portion of the Border Patrol workforce is Hispanic. Many border people see them as traitors. "They despise us, really," Gomez told me. Kids throw rocks at them. Cartels sometimes issue a "green light" to assassinate particular officers. When Gomez is off duty and people ask what he does for a living, he tells them he's an assistant baseball coach.

In 1984, in response to a large influx of immigrants, the United States put up a chain-link fence that offered negligible deterrence. "Sometimes we'd apprehend the same individual three or four times a day," Gomez said. In the mid-1990s, the Border Patrol began cracking down, but the migrants created strategies to defeat the new enforcement—for instance, by forming a mob of dozens or hundreds, then charging all at once across the border and scattering every which way. "We'd catch the kids and the grandmas," Gomez said. Once, while he was acting as a canine handler at a checkpoint, he uncovered a migrant who had been upholstered to resemble a captain's chair in a van; if it hadn't been for the dog, no one would have noticed.

Despite the recent increase in illegal crossings, the trend has been declining drastically for a decade. "In 2006, in the El Paso sector, there were 122,256 apprehensions," Gomez said. In 2015, apprehensions dropped to 14,495, before rising again. "El Paso prosecutes every individual who comes in," Gomez told me as we headed west on I-10. "They are going to be jailed, if even for a day."

The average stay in the immigration detention centers is about thirty days, but those who challenge their deportation typically remain in detention for months or even years. According to Gomez, those who have gotten court dates a year or two in the future often disappear into America. "Right now, there's no way of tracking them. They just get lost." The backlog in the immigration courts is about two years.

Historically, the vast majority of detainees are Mexican citizens, but in 2014 the balance shifted to Central Americans, including an alarming increase in unaccompanied minors. Gang violence, in El Salvador, Honduras, and Guatemala—among the most violent countries in the world—has created a spike in asylum seekers. "A fifth of the population of El Salvador is now living in the U.S.," another guard told me. Nearly 45,000 migrants from Guatemala were picked up in Texas in the first eight months of 2016. Many of them speak only Indian languages, confounding immigration officials and legal services.

Gomez took us up on a hilltop above a landfill. We were now standing in the southeast corner of New Mexico. From there, we had a clear view of the Texas-Mexico border as it runs toward the gray mountains. There were two parallel highways, I-10 on the American side and Carretera Anapra–San Jerónimo on the Mexican side. The sprawling suburbs of Juárez mirrored the American community to the north. As we watched, a Union Pacific freight, double-stacked with shipping containers filled with goods from the maquiladoras of Juárez, headed west toward Los Angeles.

Between the two countries runs the new fence, like an industrialized Christo installation. There are actually two kinds of fences—one for vehicles, which is really just a metal rail running between concrete-filled pylons; and one for pedestrians. It is eighteen feet high and covered with a fine mesh that makes it difficult to get a grip. Yet people still come through. "They use rope, grappling hooks, ladders, garden hoses—some even use screwdrivers and scale it like Spider-Man," Gomez said. But once a person gets over the top, he has to jump down, risking a broken leg or a jammed knee. Drug smugglers usually drive through the desert, where the fence is low; sometimes they use plasma cutters to slice through the barrier rail and then carefully weld it back together and erase the tire tracks. The towering pedestrian fences pose a greater challenge for vehicles. "They'll use ramps," Gomez says. One time he saw a Jeep that was stranded on top of the fence; it had to be lifted off by crane.

From our perch on the hilltop, Gomez pointed out the glint of the windshields of Border Patrol agents in strategic vantage points, lying in wait. One was stationed in a parking lot at a shopping mall; another was near a cypress tree in a spot informally called Two Cup because the homeowner always offers coffee when he sees an agent. Torre's Windmill was named after an agent who was injured. Backpacker's Corner is a spot on the slope of Mount Cristo Rey on the horizon. There are sensors buried all around, high-intensity stadium lights, and usually helicopters swooping overhead. Still, thousands continue to cross the Texas border every month.

Undocumented migrants who make it into Texas are trapped inside a ribbon about fifty miles wide, defined by checkpoints—twenty-three of them—on every road leading away from the border. They call that strip between the border and the checkpoints **la juala,** the cage. Many choose to stay within that perimeter, unwilling to go back to Mexico or to take the risk of venturing farther into the United States. Often their families are just a few miles away in Mexico.

I spoke to Will Hurd, who represents the massive Twenty-third Congressional District, which stretches from the west side of San Antonio to the edge of El Paso. His district is larger than most states east of the Mississippi, and contains 820 miles of Texas's border with Mexico. A former undercover CIA agent who now serves on the intelligence committee in the House, Hurd is the first black Republican elected to Congress from the state, although the district is 70 percent Hispanic. He is also one of the few Republicans in Congress to speak against the construction of a wall. "The cost is estimated to be anywhere between twelve billion dollars to forty billion dollars," he said, citing a study by the Massachusetts Institute of Technology. "The entire U.S. intelligence budget is fifty-three billion dollars." He agrees that in densely populated areas, a physical barrier makes sense, but he thinks the hundreds of miles of remote Chihuahuan Desert would be better protected, and far more cheaply, by sensors and drones.

Hurd does not believe that a wall would stop the flow of drugs from Mexico into the United

States. "It's a fifty-billion-dollar business, and you're not making that amount of money by sending cocaine across the border in some kid's book bag. You're bringing it across in vehicles, in fixed-wing aircraft and submersibles. The wall doesn't address that." He says it is more effective to work with Mexican police and intelligence counterparts, focusing on drug kingpins, in order to stop the flow of narcotics before it reaches the U.S. border. But such close cooperation depends on good relations between the two countries.

Hurd is especially worried about the future of NAFTA. "Mexico is Texas's number-one trading partner," he says. If NAFTA were to be overturned, Texas would be especially hard hit. "The trade imbalance is only one indicator of the relationship. It doesn't take into account the service industries. It doesn't take into account the people from Monterrey who come to San Antonio to shop. Our relations are too complex to boil down to a single number."

★

"THERE ARE TWO NARRATIVES about what the border is," Fernando Garcia, the founder of the Border Network for Human Rights, told me. "The farther away you are, the more chaotic and violent it appears, but when you live at the border, there is a different reality." Alarmed by the increasing militarization along the border and the abuses that were taking place against undocumented migrants, Garcia began organizing the immigrant community and informing people of their rights. He says he has found a surprisingly willing partner in the El Paso Sector of the Border Patrol, which reviews every case of abuse that Garcia's organization collects, and as a result, complaints have decreased substantially.

One of the projects Garcia has worked on with the Border Patrol is called Hugs Not Walls. For a few brief minutes, families on both sides of the Rio Grande line up. Those on the American side—many of them undocumented immigrants—wear blue T-shirts, and those on the Mexican side wear white. Then, at a signal from the Border Patrol, they walk down the sides of the culvert into the muddy riverbed. Many of them are weeping even before they meet, then they fall into embraces and take photos. Four hundred families were brought together in the first two events. A third "hug" took place in February 2017, days after the newly inaugurated President Trump issued an executive order to build a wall on the border.

I spoke to several women who participated. One had been living in El Paso and hadn't seen her father and siblings for sixteen years. Another woman said she and her husband had been living together in El Paso for twenty-seven years until he was arrested for drinking and driving and was sent back to Mexico. A third woman has a daughter who is one of the "dreamers" who grew up in America and hopes to gain citizenship. "Our situation is precarious under the new administration," the woman said. "We're living in the shadows now."

One can't live in Texas without being aware of those shadow people. They tread a line that the rest of us scarcely acknowledge. At any moment, everything can be taken away, and they are thrown back into the poverty, violence, and desperation that drove them to leave their native lands and take a chance living an underground life.

I thought about the sanctuary cities bill in September 2017, when a 28-year-old Mexican national, Juan Coronilla-Guerrero, was assassinated in a gang-ridden town in central Mexico. He had been living in Austin with his wife. He was picked up at the Travis County courthouse in March, when he responded to misdemeanor charges of assault and possession of marijuana. He was one of those whom Sheriff Sally Hernandez had refused to hold for federal immigration authorities because he had not committed a sufficiently serious offense. His wife had warned a federal judge that her husband would be killed if he were sent back to Mexico. Other Mexican nationals detained by U.S. immigration authorities have pleaded to be deported anywhere other than across the Texas border, where the Zetas, one of the most brutal of the drug cartels that run much of Mexico, lie in wait for them, routinely kidnapping them for ransom, but often winding up killing them instead.

The violence and criminality does spill over the border. "In the last five and a half years in Texas," Dan Patrick told Fox Business News, "we've apprehended over two hundred and twelve thousand criminal aliens. We've charged them with nearly six hundred thousand crimes, including over a thousand murders, six thousand sexual assaults, ninety thousand other crimes, hundreds of kidnappings. We have to stop sanctuary cities, secure the border, and make America great again."

I have spent much of my professional life writing about terrorism. I believe in secure borders. There is good reason to worry about having a vast class of people inside our country who are made criminals simply by their presence. I understand but do not condone their actions. We are complicit in their suffering, however. We take advantage of their weakness, their lack of standing or recourse. The shadow people provide the cheap labor that border states, especially, depend upon. They are not slaves, but neither are they free.

## TWELVE

# The High Lonesome

You don't get to Wink, Texas, by accident. It's sixty miles west of Odessa, tucked below the corner of New Mexico, on a two-lane blacktop passing through the aptly named hamlet of Notrees and a town called Kermit after the son of Theodore Roosevelt who once came to hunt antelope. Seven miles south of Kermit is Wink. It is one of the many near-ghost towns stranded by an oil boom that came and went. In the 1920s, thirty thousand people lived here. Wink was a den of gambling and prostitution, run by the Mob. Those times are long gone, like tumbleweeds blown away in the wind. Wink now is as close to nowhere as you can get and still be on pavement.

Downtown is made up of a handful of buildings, mostly shuttered, except for a one-story cinderblock structure sporting the word "Museum." It's this modest building that draws pilgrims like me.

On the front door of the Roy Orbison Museum

is a number to call if you want to be let in. Walter Quigley answered and said he'd be right over.

"Do you smell that?" Walter asked, as he unlocked the door. He pointed to the awning above us. "Bats," he said. "There was a gap up there and several hundred of them got into that space. When they flew out the other evening, I sealed it up, but evidently there are still a bunch in there."

Inside the single-room museum was a small collection of artifacts and photos of Roy at different stages of his life, along with album covers and posters. Above the door was a beat-up guitar that Roy once played, which had been hanging in a friend's garage for forty years. As a teenager, Roy was dumpy, pale as a biscuit, and nearly blind; in high school, he began dyeing his cottony hair black so he didn't look like an albino. Still, he was picked on incessantly. "The students here would treat him so rotten dirty," Walter said. "I won't repeat what they said to him."

Walter put on a CD of one of Roy's albums. There's so much pain and longing in those songs— "Crying," "Dream Baby," "Oh, Pretty Woman," and especially "Only the Lonely"—you can feel the rejection pulsing through his soaring, spectral voice, which filled up the little museum, along with the occasional squeak of a dying bat.

After I moved to Texas, I became a musician. I was thirty-eight and a half years old, and deter-

mined to play "Great Balls of Fire" on my for-
tieth birthday. It was the hardest thing I've ever
done. I'm still taking piano lessons, and although
I'll never be a great player, I'm in a band, called
WhoDo. We play blues and rockabilly. Our set
list is populated with songs by Texas musicians,
including Stevie Ray Vaughan, Muddy Waters,
Buddy Holly, T-Bone Walker, and of course the
great Roy Orbison.

> **Only the lonely**
> **(dum-dum-dum-dumdy-doo-wah)**
> **Know the way I feel tonight**
> **(ooh-yay-yay-yay-yeah)**

That song came out in 1960. I was in the seventh grade in Abilene, Texas. I had never heard
anything exactly like it—Roy's operatic three-
octave voice on a country ballad, married to doo-
wop, and infused with the existential solitude of
the West Texas plains, an unhappy man with a
thrilling and unmistakable voice, our Edith Piaf.

One of my bandmates, Brian Turner, who sings
Roy's version of "Mean Woman Blues" to close out
our show, had tipped me off to ask Walter about
the sacred relic, the object of the pilgrim's journey.
Walter hesitated, then reached under the display
case and pulled out a wooden box, wrapped in a
sweatshirt. Inside the box were Roy's trademark

tinted eyeglasses, black plastic frames with bifocal lavender lenses. I put them on.

⋆

WHEN I WAS in high school in Dallas, my friends and I would drive around aimlessly for hours, mesmerized by a late-night broadcast on WRR called **Kat's Karavan**. It played early rhythm and blues, otherwise known as "race music," by such great Texas bluesmen as T-Bone Walker, Lightnin' Hopkins, and Lead Belly. You can draw a line from those musicians to Janis Joplin, who took the Texas blues and used it to supercharge rock and roll. Another trajectory would go from R&B through mariachi to arrive at Selena, or through pop to discover Beyoncé. Texas is a great scrambler of cultural forms.

My piano teacher, Floyd Domino, is a boogie-woogie master. He has two Grammys, and he's played with George Strait, Willie Nelson, Waylon Jennings, and many other country stars. He is known for mixing Oscar Peterson with Western swing. He's been teaching me now for two decades. I'm talentless but persistent.

I know classical pianists who can trace their training through their teacher and their teacher's teachers all the way back to Beethoven. I asked Floyd where our tradition comes from. "Al Stricklin," he said.

As Floyd tells it, Stricklin, from Antioch, Texas—the Antioch that is in Johnson County (there have been as many as fifteen Antiochs in Texas)—was a self-taught jazz pianist who was influenced by hearing Earl "Fatha" Hines and his smooth Chicago-style swing on the radio. In 1927, when Stricklin was working at a radio station in Fort Worth, three musicians came in for an audition. One of them carried a fiddle in a flour sack. He introduced himself as Bob Wills from Hall County, in the Panhandle.

"What kind of music do you play?" Stricklin asked.

"Different," said Wills.

Wills promised he would come back and hire Stricklin as his piano player one day when he formed a real band. In the meantime, Wills and his players formed the Light Crust Doughboys, backing up Pappy O'Daniel on his radio show. They were wildly popular, but O'Daniel was a tyrant, and Wills had a drinking problem. After O'Daniel fired him, Wills formed another band that became known as the Texas Playboys. In 1935, Stricklin joined the group. The fusion of Chicago jazz, frontier fiddle, and the blues that Bob Wills learned from his black playmates in the cotton fields constituted the fundamental elements of Western swing. My own band once got to play with Johnny Gimble, who was a fiddle player in the Playboys. I felt that I had been inducted into a fraternity that I didn't really qualify for.

I asked Floyd what characterizes the "Texas" sound. "First of all, it's riff-based," he said. Riffs are brief musical figures that are stated and restated and explored over different chord changes. Musicians talk about being in the "pocket," which Floyd explains is "not a spot, it's an area. Texas music tends to be played on the backside of the groove." You can hear that in the blues shuffles of the Vaughan brothers, T-Bone Walker, Johnny Winter, ZZ Top, and Red Garland—a kind of relaxed, almost-too-late stutter step.

Floyd grew up in Berkeley, California, in an academic Jewish household, but his ear was captured by the sounds of Western swing. To the despair of his parents, he ran off and joined a band, Asleep at the Wheel, led by Ray Benson, then in Oakland, which was dedicated to keeping that music alive. Bob Wills was their inspiration, and Al Stricklin became Floyd's mentor. Willie Nelson invited the band to move to Austin in 1974.

Floyd's real name is Jim Haber. The stage name was thrust upon him by a couple of his Asleep at the Wheel cohorts who had analyzed his style of playing—which, in their minds, was a combination of Floyd Cramer, the father of country piano, and Fats Domino, the New Orleans R&B king. "When Ray introduces you tonight, he's going to call you Floyd Domino," one of them said. It was supposed to be an experiment, but as soon as Jim walked off the stage, everyone started calling him Floyd. It just stuck. A decade later, when Floyd was touring with Waylon Jennings, he decided he wanted his real name back. The production manager called the band together and told them, "Floyd's real name is Jim, and from now on, that's what he wants you to call him. Ain't that right, Floyd?"

★

JOE ELY, a singer-songwriter friend of mine, marched me through an immense Walmart in Lubbock. We walked toward the rear of the store, past the appliances and ladies' clothing, until we arrived at the diapers. Joe turned to the baby strollers and said, "Here, right here, was Buddy Holly's house."

Lubbock and the stretch north through the Texas Panhandle produced so many great musicians. Waylon Jennings came from Littlefield, Jimmy Dean from Plainview, the Gatlin Brothers and Tanya Tucker from Seminole. Lubbock itself produced Sonny Curtis, Mac Davis, Delbert McClinton, Gary P. Nunn, Lloyd Maines and his daughter, Natalie—there's a long list of singers who continue to make music that comes out of the cotton fields and oil rigs and somehow spreads all over the world. Joe is part of that tradition. He reminds me of Bruce Springsteen, whom he's toured with; he's a roots rocker who sings about the people he grew up with, making anthems out of their lives. His songs blend country and honky-tonk and Mexican corridos into a distinctive regional sound. You often hear him playing with his fellow Lubbock musicians Jimmie Dale Gilmore and Butch Hancock, in a group called the Flatlanders. He is also part of Los Super Seven, along with Freddy Fender, Lyle Lovett, Flaco Jimenez, and a changing cast of other, mostly Texas musicians. I sometimes sing one of Joe's songs, "Fingernails," with WhoDo.

Joe and I rode down Broadway, the redbrick main street, past the only skyscraper in Lubbock, the twenty-story Great Plains Life Building, which sat empty for years after being hit by a tornado in 1970. "You can see it's still a little twisted," Joe pointed out. There's a vacant lot where his father's Disabled American Veterans Thrift Store used to be, across the street from where several Mexican dance halls in the old warehouses once stood. "I was a young kid, but there was music on every corner," Joe said, "with accordions and **bajo sextos** and even horn sections. There couldn't be bars because Lubbock was dry."

I asked Joe what made Lubbock such a musical

town. "I don't know about others, but I think all the emptiness made me want to fill it up," he said.

We drove out to the cemetery and got a groundskeeper to show us Buddy Holly's modest grave, a flat tombstone, the inscription spelled "Holley," his actual family name. There were several guitar picks left there by visiting musicians. "I brought the Clash here when they played Lubbock," Joe recalled. "We stayed all night in the graveyard, until the sun came up, sitting around, singing songs, drinking beer." Joe and I marveled at the brief span of Buddy's life, 1936 to 1959; he was twenty-two years old when he took that fateful airplane ride with Ritchie Valens and the Big Bopper on a snowy night in Iowa. "All his recordings were done over a period of eighteen months," Joe said. "His early stuff was bluegrass, and then rockabilly came along. It was Elvis and Carl Perkins that inspired him."

We headed out Highway 84 to the Cotton Club, a roadhouse fifteen miles outside of town. The club has gone through many hands, and burned down several times. Joe himself owned it for a while. It's a one-story clapboard building, an elongated shack, really, but at one time it was considered the most important venue between Dallas and Los Angeles. Johnny Cash, Tex Ritter, Fats Domino, and Benny Goodman appeared there.

Bob Wills performed every Friday night. Then in 1955, a cultural tornado arrived in the form of Elvis Presley.

The daughter of the club owner used to let young musicians, like Buddy Holly and Mac Davis, slip in through the kitchen to hear Elvis whenever he came to play. Waylon Jennings and Roy Orbison were transfixed by his performances. Elvis married country music to rhythm and blues—race music—and turned on a sexual faucet that drenched the Baptists and Church of Christers in unholy waters. After hearing Elvis, Buddy Holly went home and wrote his first rock-and-roll song, "Not Fade Away." We still play it in our band.

"See, this is the back door," Joe said as we approached the club from the grass parking lot. "Elvis's Cadillac would've been right about here. Supposedly, he signed some girl's panties and her boyfriend beat him up and stuck a rag in the gas tank and burned up his Cadillac."

Joe recalled another Lubbock musician who went to high school with him, Norman Odam, a gawky kid who would stand on the stoop of the schoolhouse, at 7:00 a.m., before classes began, and sing at the top of his lungs. Kids would throw pennies at him, which Odam gathered for his lunch money. He began calling himself Legendary Stardust Cowboy. He actually recorded a few songs with Mercury Records, including "Paralyzed." "It's three minutes of screaming at the top of his lungs, played on a G7 chord," said Joe. "It nails you to the wall. T Bone Burnett was on drums. They made some test pressings and sent them to the Dallas stations, and within a week it was getting more play than the Beatles." Legendary Stardust sank as quickly as he rose, but his persona influenced David Bowie, who modeled his Ziggy Stardust character on him and actually covered a couple of his incoherent songs.

That evening, Joe played a solo acoustic set at the Cactus Theatre in downtown Lubbock. The place was filled with friends and fans, and Joe was in a ruminative frame of mind. "Growing up in Lubbock, you had to sorta make your own entertainment," he said, and the audience laughed knowingly. "My parents had friends who owned the dry-cleaning store. We'd go out to the lake for a picnic after church, and then we'd go in the back door of the dry cleaners and they'd let us kids try on other people's clothes. There was no greater thrill. I wish I had a song about that."

★

I DROVE SOUTH, descending from the high plains into Post, the erstwhile utopian community established by the cereal maker C. W. Post at the turn of the twentieth century. He was defeated, like so many others, by the absence of rain, although he used to set off dynamite charges on the mesas every ten minutes for several hours a day with the goal of pulling moisture out of the sky. One can imagine the effect on the other utopians.

It feels ominous to drive through West Texas with a clean windshield. Road trips always used to be accompanied by the incessant splatter of death. We'd pass through clouds of lovebugs, those perpetually copulating critters, which coated the windshield in a greenish sheen; and then the grasshoppers would hit, in blobs of orange-yellow goo. Painted ladies and miller moths and June bugs contributed their own colorful innards. Wipers only made things worse. The whole front of the car would be peppered with insect carcasses, and the Texas sun baked them into a buggy frittata. They were hell to wash off; I remember scrubbing the grille and never getting it clean enough. Truckers, especially, would protect their radiators with mesh shields. Bugs were simply part of the Texas air.

Now, when I collide with a bug, I'm surprised. I can only speak for Texas, but the absence of insects seems to be a part of a general diminution of life. The fence lines along our roadsides used to be ornamented with scissor-tailed flycatchers, those elegant acrobats, so rare now that the insects have disappeared. Steve remembers the sound of turtles being scrunched as tires rolled over them; this was at a time when so many were crossing the road it was hard to thread a route through them. The inventory of life forms is being funneled down to a roster of hardy pests. We're living in a world of mosquitos, roaches, fire ants, starlings, rattlesnakes, and feral hogs. In fairness to the animals, I suppose I should add humans to the top of the list.

Snyder is home to the **White Buffalo** statue in front of the courthouse. The white buffalo is a kind of totem for me. In 1955, the same year Elvis came to the Cotton Club, I was in the third grade in Ponca City, Oklahoma. There was a seminal episode of **The Adventures of Rin Tin Tin,** in which Rusty, the orphan who was being raised by a troop of soldiers at Fort Apache, saves the life of an Indian. As every boy my age knew, if you save an Indian's life, he's obliged to follow you around until he can return the favor. The Indian in question happened to be on a spirit quest, searching for the white buffalo. I was deeply stirred. The next day in music class, before the bell rang, our teacher asked us each to stand up and say what we were going to be when we grew up. After the movie star, the private detective, and the hairdresser, I rose and said I was going to follow the white buffalo. The hoots I got from my classmates made me feel like Ted Cruz at the Republican convention.

There really are white buffalo—most are albinos—and one was shot by a famous buffalo hunter, J. Wright Mooar, on October 7, 1876, just outside Snyder. Tens of millions of buffalo were exterminated by hunters at the end of the nineteenth century, in equal parts for the hides and to deprive the Indians of their food source. A plaque in front of the **White Buffalo** statue says that Mooar personally killed 22,000 of them, "a record probably unsurpassed." An exhibit in the museum quotes a settler in the region: "The bones were so thick in some places that one could walk upon them some distance without touching the ground."

Although white buffalo are extremely rare—only fifty are said to exist in the world—they are mysteriously abundant on some of the exotic game ranches in Texas. At the Ox Ranch near Uvalde, you can shoot one of their fifteen white buffalo for $25,000 to $30,000, depending on the size of the animal. The ranch's website notes: "According to the National Bison Association, it is estimated that only one of every 10 million births results in a White Buffalo!" You can also shoot an addax, an endangered antelope; or a dama gazelle ("the largest and rarest gazelle in the world"—only five hundred known to exist); or many of the magnificent animals whose heads grace trophy rooms around the state. "When hunting these rare animals at Ox Ranch, you may choose from these hunting methods: from a Blind, Spot and Stalk, Bow Hunting, Pistol Hunting, Rifle Hunting, or Safari Style!" The site cheerfully adds that the white buffalo is sacred to many Native American tribes. "Their presence is a sign of spiritual rebirth and better times ahead."

I know this sounds grotesque to non-hunters, but these exotic game ranches serve as a repository for animals that may be extinct in the wild. "There are now more Arabian Oryx on Texas hunting ranches than in the rest of the world combined!" the website boasts. By the way, if you are there to shoot a white buffalo, the ranch will throw in a free hog hunt. You can stalk your prey with night-vision glasses, or you can choose to hunt from a blind, which sounds more congenial. "This Blind Has a TV That Receives Live Game Camera Footage, DirecTV, a Poker Table, Air Conditioning, and a Fully Stocked Bar."

★

STEVE DROVE UP from Austin and met me at the Dixie Pig in Abilene. We both lived in Abilene as kids, and although we didn't know each other then, our lives were like rails of track running in the same direction. We wonder why we never met earlier. We could have been friends so long ago.

I went to public school in Abilene and Steve went to St. Joseph's Academy, which has long since been torn down. Steve wanted to see if he could find the site where it once stood. I wanted to go by my old neighborhood as well. We passed Alta Vista Elementary, the handsome redbrick building where I entered fourth grade. It was closed in 2004, but at least it was still standing. We went around back of the schoolhouse, and Steve took my picture in the spot where I was struck by lightning. I had been playing with some kids, and suddenly we were all sprawled on the ground like tenpins. I think the lightning must have hit the metal gutter and shot through the downspout near where we were standing. I was at an age when close calls didn't have the mortal resonance they do now. Steve also claims to have been the victim of a lightning strike, although he was still a fetus when his mother was shocked during a storm while washing dishes. He can't expect full credit for that.

The house I lived in, on Amarillo Street, is also still standing. I was pleased to see how nicely it is cared for. There's a sign on the back fence saying that the house is now a member of the Society for the Preservation of Quaint Old Homes. When we lived there, the house was white, and nearly every year after a dust storm I'd have to wash it. More sensible owners have painted it a sandy color. My father had planted magnolias on either side of the door, which were still there the last time I passed by, thirty years ago. Now they're gone, replaced by two oaks that tower over the house. The passage of time was made shockingly visible. I knocked on the door, but nobody was home. I wondered if the cork floor in the den was still scarred from my games of mumblety-peg.

Steve and I stopped in at the Grace Hotel, once the fanciest spot in town. Steve had set a scene in one of his novels there. The Grace is now a museum, and there happened to be an exhibit of Abilene in the 1950s, exactly the time when we lived there. There were mannequins wearing the clothes our parents would have worn—sack dresses and tropical shirts, in Popsicle colors of lime and orange—and appliances that had been in our kitchens. It was strange to see your own life and times laid out in front of you in a museum exhibit. "If you think about it," Steve said, "when we moved here we were as close to the Indian wars as we are now to the day we were born."

As we were exiting the exhibit, we came upon a street map of Abilene in 1955. I called Steve over and pointed to St. Joseph's Academy. It was directly across the street from my elementary school.

I drove back to Austin, under a Turneresque sunset with a gibbous moon rising from a bank of pink clouds. A herd of Black Angus cattle moved like shadows in the places where the buffalo once grazed. I thought about how unintentional most of life is. Part of me had always wanted to leave Texas, but I had never actually gone. Sometimes we are summoned by work or romance to move to another existence, and for me those moments when there is no reasonable alternative to departure have always been joyful, full of a sense of adventure and reinvention. Staying is also a decision, but it feels more like inertia or insecurity. Most of the time I live in a state of vague discontent, tempted by the vision of another life but unwilling to let go of the friends and daily habits that fill my time. When I am in other states or countries, I'm always aware of being in exile from my own culture, with all its outsized liabilities. I wish I lived in the mountains of Montana or on the Spanish Mediterranean. I wish I had a condo in a high-rise overlooking Central Park, with a piano by the window. These thoughts have been at play in my imagination for decades. Now here I was, on a darkening highway in Texas, with so much more road behind me than what lay before.

★

IN 2015, I received a Texas Medal of Arts Award, along with a lot of people I have long admired, including the Gatlin Brothers, playwright Robert Schenkkan, and Jamie Foxx. At the reception, the head of the Texas State Cemetery passed through the crowd, noticing name tags. I saw him eyeing

Dan Rather and T Bone Burnett. Then he approached me with a smile and said, "We're looking forward to hosting you."

Several lifetime achievement awards had come my way recently. I was inducted into the Hall of Fame at Woodrow Wilson High School in Dallas, joining another list of notable alums, including a couple of Heisman Trophy winners, an Olympic gold medalist, and the guys who invented the margarita machine and the corny dog—contributions to Texas culture I could never hope to match. It was nice to be honored by people I cared about, although I couldn't help hearing that drumroll of departure.

Of all the eccentric honors that Texas can bestow on its citizens, however, admittance to the state cemetery is in every way the ultimate. It's the Texas version of Arlington National Cemetery. The list of famous Texans interred there includes Stephen F. Austin, Barbara Jordan, and several once-well-known authors. Those who have been accepted but are still alive, like Steve, are listed as "pending." It had been suggested that I should let my availability be known, and I had done so.

"But my application got turned down," I told the cemetery chief. "I heard that Governor Perry vetoed me."

"Surely not!"

"That's what I heard."

Perry and I had had a tiff a few years before, in his first months as governor. I was once again the emcee of the gala for the Texas Book Festival. I noticed that Perry didn't show up. "He's probably at a public high school leading the prayer," I cracked, referencing a recent unconstitutional incident on the part of the new governor.

The next day, the director of the festival informed me that word of my remark had gotten back to Perry and he was demanding an apology.

"But it was a joke!"

"I know that, but the governor took offense," she pleaded. "Now his office is threatening to withhold the use of the capitol for the festival. We'll have to close down!"

Golly. I wrote the governor, saying I was "so sorry." He wrote back right away, claiming that he had been raising money for paralyzed children, not snubbing the festival. He signed it, "Prayerfully, Rick."

At the arts reception, the cemetery chief urged me to reapply. He reiterated that the governor would certainly not have stooped to such a mean-spirited action. In any case, we had a new governor, who had just given me a medal, so my chances were improved.

I wasn't so sure I would reapply, however. Nothing says commitment like a burial plot.

# THIRTEEN

# Far West, Far Out

I used to think Marfa was a kind of practical joke that West Texans were playing on cultural elites. It's remote even for Texas. The nearest airports are in El Paso and Carlsbad, New Mexico, each two hundred miles away. The landscape is okay if you like scrubby hills and plains of yellow grass. And yet aesthetes come from all over, lured by the minimalist vibe the place embodies.

Whenever I'm in Marfa I feel like I'm in a **Twilight Zone** episode and something really strange is about to happen. One winter evening, when Roberta and I passed through town on our way to Big Bend, we saw a skunk sauntering down the sidewalk of the main street. He had the place all to himself. He affected an air of proprietorship as he navigated past the Hotel Paisano, where James Dean, Rock Hudson, and Elizabeth Taylor stayed in 1955, when they were filming **Giant**. During a classic West Texas hailstorm, Hudson and Taylor raced around with buckets to catch ice for their Bloody Marys. We lost sight of the skunk as he approached the pink wedding-cake courthouse in the center of town.

That night we drove east of town on U.S. 67 to see the Marfa Mystery Lights. Against the shadowed outline of the Chinati Mountains, odd yellow and white lights darted about, merging and dividing, disappearing, then reappearing seconds later in a different spot. They seemed to be dancing, which added to the air of enchantment. There have been numerous explanations—gas from petroleum deposits, optical illusions, electrical discharges from crystal formations—the most plausible being that they are reflected lights from the highway. James Dean was reportedly so fascinated by them that he bought a telescope. Your perceptions of what is real or at least normal get tested.

The artist Donald Judd rented a house in Marfa in 1971, "due in part to the harsh and glib situation within art in New York and to the unpleasantness of the city," he wrote. He was also on the run from any form of government, and far West Texas was as close to anarchy as he could get. "I chose the town of Marfa (pop. 2,466) because it was the best looking and the most practical," he wrote.

He wound up buying an abandoned army base that had been a detention center for German prisoners of war. There were a number of barracks and two massive brick sheds that had been used to repair tanks and artillery pieces. Judd filled the sheds with rectangular aluminum boxes of the exact same dimensions, differing only in the ways in which they are subdivided. One box is bisected by a vertical panel, another by a slanted panel at a sixty-degree angle, and so on—a hundred geometric variations on a single theme. The glare off the boxes made it difficult to see inside; it was like looking at water through the reflection of a bright afternoon.

Judd noted that as an artist he was primarily interested in space, and he designed this immaculate environment to eliminate the distraction of color or whim. He claimed to have invented the concept of an "installation," by which he meant the use of an entire room to present his concept. The rectangular theme of the boxes was echoed in the etched-concrete floor, the coffered ceiling, the windowpanes, and even the weathered bricks. Looking through the windows at the bleached-out field, one sees larger, concrete boxes replicating similar choices. They are well made and dignified but also look like leftover shipping containers.

Roberta adores Donald Judd. "I appreciate the spareness and severity of the lines in concert with the spareness and severity of the surroundings," she explained, as we wandered among the concrete boxes outside in the blinding sunlight, which Roberta called "an essential part of the art." She was so caught up she didn't notice the shimmering whipsnake sliding through the grass at our feet.

I admired the exactness of Judd's enterprise, although it was hard to square his fixation on order with his anarchic politics, or the cultish following that has sprung up in the two decades after his death. When we checked into our hotel, there were Donald Judd books for sale at the front desk, and even bumper stickers asking WWDJD? What Donald Judd would do was a question I had never asked, but the Marfans were deeply interested in the answer.

We walked over to the new Robert Irwin installation, a U-shaped building. One wing is painted black, the other is white, and they are transected by scrims that filter the light. Rectangular windows at specific intervals admitted trapezoidal patches of sunlight onto the concrete floor. Through the windows I could see farmsteads and telephone poles. Doves were cooing. A piece of tin roof was flapping in the breeze. I wondered what art even was. Donald Judd in 1986:

A definition of art finally occurred to me. Art is everything at once. Insofar as it is less than that it is less art. In visual art the wholeness is visual. Aspects which are not visual are subtractions from the whole.

Which means what?

★

A PAINTER FRIEND of ours in Marfa, Julie Speed, bought the old jail and turned it into her studio. While she and her husband, Fran Christina, the former drummer with the Fabulous Thunderbirds, were renovating the place, Fran jackhammered out a portion of the wall, which was fourteen inches thick. "He came in all covered with cement dust," Julie recounted. "He told me he had found a leg bone in the wall."

" 'Oh, a deer leg bone,' " Julie surmised.

" 'No, a human leg bone.' "

Julie insisted that it must be a deer tibia and that Fran was confused.

" 'Well, Julie, it was wearing a boot,' " he said.

Julie speculated that since the walls were poured around 1917, the leg might have belonged to a U.S. cavalryman in General Pershing's army, which was chasing Pancho Villa at the time. Perhaps the soldier got shot in the leg and it had turned gangrenous and had to be sawn off, she suggested. "They are about to bury it, but then someone remembers, hey, they're pouring cement for the new jail today, so let's throw the leg in there so the coyotes don't dig it up."

She consoled herself with this thought as Fran buried the leg, reciting some Latin he recalled as an altar boy in Rhode Island. Only later did she consider that the rest of the body might still be inside the wall.

Julie's art is like Judd's mainly in its obsessiveness. Sex, violence, and religion are her constant themes. Many of her human figures have three eyes or an extra nose. She mixes Mexican folk art and Japanese woodcuts with Italian Renaissance portraiture, making work that is both gorgeous and bizarre. Her art reminds me of Hieronymus Bosch's in its singular, haunting vision. Julie now wears her hair in three asymmetrical gray braids, topped by a beret.

We had a drink on the "cloud balcony" that Julie and Fran built to watch the sky. The clouds in the high desert sail past like galleons. It's the most beautiful sky you've ever seen. As soon as the sun went down, Venus switched on like a searchlight.

I asked Julie what she thought of Judd's and Irwin's art. She placed them in the "Because I Say So" school of conceptual art, which began with Marcel Duchamp and the Dadaists. "They do have a way of making you focus on the world and seeing it in a different way," she said.

I thought about how, when we came out of the Irwin installation, the shadows of a barbed-wire fence on the sidewalk were so striking that Roberta took a picture—art being made by the noticing of it.

I think Julie feels at home in Marfa in part because of the weirdness. She told us a story that obviously delighted her. A couple of blocks away from her house, a thirty-two-year-old man, Christopher Michael Cobos, allegedly beat his wife and was attempting to run her over when family members and passersby pulled her out of the street. Juan Lara, a Marfa cop, arrived just as Cobos was fleeing in his Chevy pickup. Officer Lara turned on his siren and gave chase. Cobos suddenly stopped, threw his pickup into reverse, and rammed the police car, disabling it. Lara radioed for assistance. A state trooper took up the high-speed chase on Highway 90, which runs beside the Union Pacific railroad tracks. A train was heading west at the same time. Suddenly, Cobos veered off the highway into the pasture, aiming his truck for a spot on the tracks just ahead of the oncoming train. His timing was off; the train collided with the pickup full force and sent it flying over the top of the locomotive and landing upside down.

The trooper was astounded to see that Cobos was still alive. An ambulance arrived to take the badly injured man to the hospital in Alpine, but in the middle of the ride, Cobos came to and attacked the EMS attendant. The ambulance driver radioed for assistance. Another state trooper forcibly subdued Cobos, and they got him to the hospital.

The next morning, Officer Lara and another cop drove Cobos back to Marfa to be arraigned. They took the precaution of having him in handcuffs. The county judge, Cinderela Guevara, received the Marfa maniac in her third-floor office in the lovely pink courthouse. She opened the window for some air, and Cobos leaped out, headfirst. Fortunately, recent rains softened the impact. By now, Cobos had been in a car wreck, been hit by a train, gotten in a fistfight with a state trooper, and plunged three stories out of a courthouse window. He was airlifted to a hospital in Odessa with a full menu of broken bones and damaged organs.

I later heard that his wife dropped the charges.

★

SOUTH OF MARFA IS the road to Big Bend, one of the least-visited national parks in the country, and also one of the most glorious. On the way, there is a pleasant resort, Cibolo Creek Ranch, built around several old forts inside the crater of an extinct volcano. Roberta and I once stayed there in the off-season, midsummer, and spent our time chasing hummingbirds and the adorable vermilion flycatcher. In more temperate weather, the ranch has served as a getaway for celebrities, including Mick Jagger, Tommy Lee Jones, and Bruce Willis. In February 2016, an Austrian hunting society, the all-male International Order of St. Hubertus, named after the patron saint of hunters, gathered there. Among them was seventy-nine-year-old Supreme Court justice Antonin Scalia, who was found dead in bed one morning. Scarcely an hour after his death was announced, Senate majority leader Mitch McConnell said that he would refuse to confirm any nominee to the Court that President Obama put forward. It seemed to me that the country had just taken another big step in the direction of Texas.

Big Bend was the site of one of my most satisfying journalistic triumphs. I had come here in the early 1980s with Wann Langston Jr., a cranky old professor of vertebrate paleontology at UT. I was very fond of Wann, although his students were plainly afraid of him. I traveled around the state with him and a group of his doctoral candidates looking at bone beds and fossil deposits in Cretaceous limestone for an article I was writing about prehistoric Texas. Up near Glen Rose, we stopped at a cow pasture where, in 1947, Wann, then a young graduate student himself, had found a variety of dinosaur bones. It's a rich area for paleontologists. The dinosaur tracks you see in the American Museum of Natural History in New York were excavated from the nearby Paluxy River. According to Wann's field notes, the bones he noticed so long ago were located near a petrified stump, but he had come back three times over the years and had never been able to locate the bones or the stump.

We all fanned out. I'm not good at finding things. It's a skill that requires looking past the surface of normality for the little inconsistency. One of the sharp-eyed students finally discerned the petrified stump, which appeared at first to be simply a mass of shattered rock but on closer examination was revealed to be exquisitely faceted, like a cubist painting.

Suddenly one of the students cried "Hallelujah!" and we all raced over. A rancher had recently driven a bulldozer through the scrub oaks to make a road, and in the roots of the upturned trees, like giant radishes, were dinosaur bones. Once you recognized them, they seemed to be everywhere, on the hillside and in the creek bed. It was a thrilling day.

When we got to Big Bend on that trip, Langston was joined by several other distinguished paleontologists from the university who were looking for remains of the Texas pterosaur, a huge flying reptile. Langston was famous for his "eye for bone," but we had spent a long, hot day with nothing but sunburn to show for it. We finally regrouped on a knobby hilltop. I was standing in a circle with the finest paleontologists in the state. I asked Wann to tell me again exactly what we were looking for. "Well, it looks like a rock, but it's striated," he said.

"Like this?" I said, picking up an object that was literally at his feet.

"Well, yeah," he said. "That's the knee bone of a hadrosaur."

"Would it go with this?" I said, picking up another object that completed the rest of the knee.

I know it's not earthshaking.

★

ROBERTA AND I STOPPED in Presidio to pick up some burritos, which we ate at Fort Leaton, amid bare mesquite trees and the lethal-looking Texas buckthorn. West Texas is dotted with old military garrisons that were established to advance white settlement in Indian country. Fort Leaton was actually a trading post, belonging to an infamous scalp hunter named Benjamin Leaton. After acquiring the property in 1848, he began selling weapons to the Apaches and Comanches in exchange for settler cattle that he arranged for them to steal. Such were some of our noble pioneers who conquered the West.

At the time Leaton bought the "fort," it was on the bank of the Rio Grande, which is now a mile away—another problem with building a wall along the Texas border, which is defined by the deepest channel of the river.

Roberta and I hiked an ancient riverbed called the Closed Canyon Trail, in the state park next to Big Bend. As it happens, this trail is the setting for the final scene of Rick Linklater's film **Boyhood**. The lead character, Mason, has grown up and heads off to Sul Ross University in Alpine. He meets a girl. They hike the Closed Canyon, under towering stone walls that twist one way and another, so that you can never see far ahead, like life itself. You know that they are falling in love and they are leaving their childhood behind.

Roberta and I had a similar romance. We met in college, at Tulane University, in an archaeology class. I was interested in her the moment she walked in—late to class, unapologetic, wearing a purple dress with a scarf at her neck, her chestnut hair tied in a bun. Miss Murphy. That was fifty years ago.

She grew up in Mobile, Alabama. Her father was a doctor. They lived in a clapboard country house on an estuary called Dog River. She used to sit on the dock and catch brim for breakfast.

Both her parents were alcoholics, and the most responsible member of the household was the maid, Rosena Lipscomb, who lived on a bean farm farther up the river. Rosena used to row to work until the alligators got too troublesome.

Roberta's father, Dr. Murphy, was a genteel racist, like so many of his station, but Rosena was the person who really raised Roberta. It was the central contradiction of her life. The civil rights movement was just beginning. Rosa Parks refused to give up her seat on the bus to a white man in Montgomery, Alabama, sparking the bus boycott in 1955, and thrusting a young pastor in that city, Martin Luther King Jr., into leadership. Many of the signal events in the movement—the Freedom Riders, the March on Montgomery, the Birmingham church bombing, the march across the Edmund Pettus Bridge in Selma—took place in Alabama, and formed a backdrop for Roberta's childhood.

She went to Murphy High School, named after her grandfather who had been superintendent of schools. In 1963, she was an Azalea Trail Maid, which got her photograph on the front page of the Mobile newspapers twice that year. The first picture was a group shot with Governor George Wallace, who is clearly flirting with her. The second was on November 22, in the afternoon paper. The headline says "Pres. Kennedy Is Shot," with a

brief story—six paragraphs—but the photo is of
Roberta and another Azalea Maid who are said to
be vying to be queen of the festival. It's the much
longer article.

We were married in Athens, Greece, where
Roberta had studied during a year abroad, and we
lived our first years together in Cairo, where we
taught at the American University. There were no
diplomatic relations between the United States and
Egypt at the time, so we were thrown in among an
eccentric group of expats—about the only Americans in the entire country—teaching adolescents
only a few years younger than we were. Those first
two years of marriage in Cairo were some of the
most pleasant days in our lifetime together, except
for the absence of air-conditioning.

We spent the next decade looking for home.
For six months, we lived in a little A-frame lake
house in Quitman, Texas, about two hours east
of Dallas, that my parents owned. We grew veg-
etables; Roberta made cobblers out of the black-
berries on the fence line; I caught bass and catfish
in the lake. This was during the Euell Gibbons
craze. Roberta had read his book **Stalking the
Wild Asparagus**, which exalted the pleasure of
foraging for food, and she loved to prowl through
the pastures for various weeds, some of which
were poisonous if eaten in the wrong season. She
always told me they were dandelions. In the eve-

ning we'd eat on the deck and watch the sunset as flying squirrels soared between the pin oaks. They're nocturnal and terribly timid. It's said that if you corner one, it will die of fright.

I was writing about my experiences in Egypt, in what I expected would be my first article for **The New Yorker**. I styled it "Letter from Cairo." The day I finished it, I walked out to the road, raised the red flag on the Rural Free Delivery mailbox, and sent the manuscript off, along with my dreams of instant acclaim. Somehow, the manuscript went from the mailbox in East Texas to editor William Shawn's office in Manhattan, and back again, in what seemed like a single day. There was a card enclosed, the first of many I would receive from various magazines, politely rejecting the article I'd spent months writing. At the bottom, in a neat hand, was a single word: "Sorry."

We lived briefly in Durham, North Carolina, where Roberta worked in the Duke library, sorting books in Greek and Latin (she was a classics major), then for a couple of years in Nashville, where I wrote for **The Race Relations Reporter** and Roberta worked as a bookseller; and then seven long years in Atlanta, where I freelanced and she sold books. We never felt that we had landed and wondered if there was any place that was somehow right for us.

I suppose many people live in places they're not

especially attached to, or that they actively hate. Marriages are like that as well. There's a high level of discontent even in enduring relationships, together with long periods of stagnation and moments of shocking intimacy. You acquire a private library of memories. Arguments are born that last for the rest of your lives among the touchstones of joy and revelation. The commonalities draw you together or suffocate you.

And then children come.

Gordon was born in 1976. He weighed more than ten pounds and was delivered by cesarean section. After all the Lamaze classes, I was crestfallen to be ushered out of the delivery room, leaving Roberta alone at the supreme moment of our lives. I remember when my father arrived to see the new baby, and we stood in front of the nursery window, looking at the little creatures with blue or pink bows in their hair. Gordon was the biggest baby in the hospital, I boasted. My father remarked that his first child was also big. I took some pride in knowing that my baby was bigger than his, even though his baby was me.

We bought our first house in Atlanta, which had been built by the people who owned the brick company. We rented out the top floor while we renovated the bottom. The two of us hung new ceilings and rewired the place. We put in a garden, and I learned how to can. Gordon helped me make tortilla pizzas while Roberta got a master's degree in early childhood education.

When I got a job offer from **Texas Monthly**, we were both ready to leave Atlanta. Within weeks after we moved to Austin, Roberta declared that she never wanted to live anywhere else. We had arrived in a community of writers and artists with lots of young children; we had a sense that we were finally onto something. Roberta and I bought another duplex. At last I had a steady job. Roberta began teaching kindergarten. Life was affordable, if a little provincial. Still, I was restless.

Our second child, Caroline, was born a year after we moved to Austin. Because Roberta had already had one child delivered by C-section, the protocol was that the next one would have to be as well. Our new obstetrician had a more relaxed policy, and she let me remain in the delivery room. There was a surgical tent set up across Roberta's belly so we couldn't see the bloody business below. I was holding Roberta's hand when the doctor asked, "Larry, would you like to see Roberta's liver?"

I certainly would.

I went around the tent and stared at the long gash in Roberta's abdomen, and the organs that lay inside. Caroline was there, as yet unborn. I felt a shiver of mortality at the same moment that life was entering the world—a life that shuffled together our genes and those of our ancestors into something unique, something that only we could have made.

✦

LAJITAS IS a little resort town on a low-water crossing of the Rio Grande. Chisos Indians and Apaches used to cross here, until the Comanches ran them off. Now the town is mainly known for its mayor, a goat named Clay Henry. Actually, a succession of goats with the same name have occupied that high office. The current Clay Henry is a black-and-white goat that has been dehorned. The main task of all Clay Henrys is to drink the beers that the tourists buy at the Sunoco station next door to the goat pen. One of Clay Henry's predecessors was castrated by a disgruntled citizen who objected to his drinking on Sunday.

While I was there, a group of tourists came over to take a look, and one of them stuck a bottle of beer through the cage. The goat snatched it out of his hand and downed it in a single expert gulp. This happens dozens of times a day. Roberta refused to get out of the car.

That evening we had dinner with Betty Moore, a former colleague of mine at **Texas Monthly**. She is a petite blonde with intensely blue eyes. When she was head of production at the magazine, she agreed to make a brochure for a rafting company on the Rio Grande. She returned to Austin, but found herself weeping when she remembered the desert landscape and the sere red mountains on the horizon. Finally, she quit her job, moved to Terlingua, an old mining encampment near the park, and became a river guide. Her move prompted an exodus of other women from the magazine, all of them drawn to this remote, scarcely populated corner of the state. "It's not the same place I moved to," Betty complained. "There are just a lot more people."

The last census for Terlingua counted fifty-eight residents.

"There were only five women in town when I came," said Betty's friend Mimi Webb Miller. "And it was pretty lawless back then." Mimi was a debutante from a prominent family in Wichita Falls, and the niece of former Texas senator John Tower. When she moved to Terlingua, she became the mistress of a notorious drug lord named Pablo Acosta. He was shot down by Mexican authorities in 1987, and Mimi was on the run for several years, with a $40,000 price on her head. "Daddy wasn't happy about that," she said.

Roberta and I were staying at Mimi's eclectic inn, La Posada Milagro, with bottle trees and blue Christmas lights lining the flagstone paths and doorways all aslant. An old Mobil Oil Pegasus sign leans against a fence. Down the hill is a coffee shop where everybody shows up in the morning, and nearby is the Terlingua Trading Company, with its spacious front porch, where Terlinguans gather in the evening to play music and watch the sunset. "Sometimes you hear the most interesting conversations," Betty says, "and other times it's just a bunch of drunks." There's a resident guitar on the porch and an impressive assortment of hula hoops. A sign admonishes, No Dogs on the Porch, which seems to be the only rule in town.

Modern Terlingua, if you can call it that, is embedded in the ruins of the mining village that occupied this place from the late nineteenth century until the 1940s, when the price of quicksilver collapsed. You can see the remains of the former community in the stone walls of the old ghost town. The cemetery is filled with the graves of the Mexican miners, many of whom had fled the revolution across the river only to die of mercury poisoning from the processing of the ore. Others were on the losing end of a gunfight. By and large their graves are simple stacks of rocks with two sticks nailed together in a cross, but you also see the wild artistic impulse that runs through everything in this anarchic society. The ornamental Mexican graves are adorned with beads and candles and artificial flowers. The later Anglo arrivals in the graveyard are less dignified, festooned with flags, totems, sculptures, gimme caps, dolls, mounds of beer bottles, and coins of small denominations.

✫

"YOU GET EXCITED and I get worried," Roberta observed, as we bounced across the ruts of a jeep road in Big Bend. We had been repeatedly warned about bears, and the evening before we had come upon a mountain lion crossing the road just in front of us. It's true I was excited.

I had been thinking about how trusty our old Land Cruiser was. It could climb a mountain if I asked it to. I bought it seventeen years ago and, except for routine maintenance, it has been in the shop for repairs only one single time. I feel very loyal to it. I started thinking about the trustiness of some of my esteemed possessions. My bike. A pair of shoes I've had resoled several times. I asked Roberta what her trusty objects were. She mentioned a silver necklace I gave her for Christmas years ago. It seemed we were far apart on definitions. On the other hand, I suppose each of us considers the other trusty, according to our understanding.

We came finally to our campsite at the foot of Pine Canyon. Before us were the towering red walls of an ancient caldera. It was remote and desolate, but the majesty of the place made us quiet for a while.

It had been a long time since I'd set up a camp. Memories of many wilderness trips we had taken before, in parks and forests all over the West, came into my mind. Our first camping experience as a family was in Colorado. Gordon and Caroline were ten and five. I had purchased a giant family tent, a dining canopy, a lantern, a Coleman stove, and a folding picnic table, and I hadn't taken any of them out of the boxes until we arrived at night in Rocky Mountain National Park. Somehow, we set them all up. The next evening, it stormed, and we huddled around the lantern inside the tent playing Chutes and Ladders.

Now the kids were grown, and Roberta and I had gotten out of the habit of camping. I suppose we've been waiting for our grandchildren to get old enough to enjoy spending the night on the ground, with mosquitoes and ticks, when it's too hot or too cold. I have always believed that memories have to burn a little to make an enduring place in your heart.

After lunch we hiked into the canyon, through a mile of grassland. Roberta has asthma, the legacy of getting pneumonia three times while she was teaching. Illness is a tax on teachers, especially at the elementary level. She was once chosen Teacher of the Year at her school, but I finally begged her to stop. It was just too hazardous. Now many of her students are grown. She still runs into them in restaurants or grocery stores. She was one of those teachers everybody remembers.

We passed a young Hispanic family sitting in the shade of a stand of juniper. There were two jumpy boys under the age of five. Their lovely young mother had the kind of merry eyes that disappear when she smiles. She pulled back a scarf to show us the baby she was nursing. When we parted, Roberta said, "I'm not going to complain anymore."

Farther up the trail, a group of bird-watchers had their binoculars focused on some finches in the bushes. They were hard-core and proud of it. We compared notes about what they had seen. I said the only bird we had spotted not on their list was a silky-flycatcher.

"That wasn't a silky-flycatcher you saw, it was a black-tailed gnatcatcher," one of the women insisted, invoking her authority as a member of the Audubon Society in Williamson County.

"Well, it was small and black and had a very prominent crest," I said.

"They don't have crests," she said, not giving an inch.

★

THE PATH ABRUPTLY BECAME steep, the temperature dropped, and rocks on the trail were moist and slippery. Then we came to the end, a rock face two hundred feet high, with black stains where water leaked down onto the clay-colored boulders below.

On the way back to camp we had an argument about the color of the Mexican jays we saw along the trail, flitting into the oaks and catching the sun like stained glass. Roberta suggested they were turquoise, fully aware that we have never agreed on what color that is. I thought they were azure. "No, the sky is azure," she said. I'm at a disadvantage where names of colors are concerned. As a little girl, Roberta treasured her box of sixty-four Prang crayons, and she remembers all the shades. She finally decided the jays were "iridescent teal."

Back at camp, I boiled a pot of water on our camp stove and poured it into a dehydrated backpacker meal—lasagna—as well as a tasty apple crisp. We drank wine and watched the mesas bleed into the evening sky. Just before dark, a black-billed cuckoo perched on an agave stalk and joined the concert of mountain chickadees. The Big Dipper came into view above the horizon. It wasn't even seven o'clock and it felt ridiculous to go to bed, but it was dark and getting cold. We climbed into the tent and zipped it shut. We had brought along wool hats and long johns, so we were warm enough, but I had forgotten how hard the ground could be.

In the middle of the night, I had the unwelcome realization that I would have to take a crap. I grabbed a flashlight and unzipped the door as quietly as possible, then crawled outside. The mountains in front of me were etched in black against the starry backdrop. There was no moon. The Dipper had risen almost directly overhead. A satellite traced its slender arc against the constellations. There was a physical sense of being pressed down by the starlight, as if it had weight, a gravitational force. Even without the flashlight I could see a path through the prickly pear into a nearby ravine.

My father once told me that he had a religious experience while taking a crap beside a trout stream. He was not the kind of man to talk about bodily functions, and I was so surprised I failed to ask what the revelation was. I so wish he had told me. Martin Luther, who was obsessed with scatology, recorded that he had been on the toilet when he received one of the central inspirations of Protestantism, that salvation is achieved through faith alone. It was then that he was "born again." I have never had such a moment, but under these stars revelation once again seemed possible. In every generation until mine, most of humanity lived with the night sky. As people began moving into cities and using more illumination, the sky gradually disappeared. There must be a corresponding loss of wonder without the stars to remind us where we stand in creation.

When I got back to the tent, Roberta was awake, and she stuck her head out to look at the sky. "Oh, my God!" she said.

At dawn, there were two jackrabbits sitting in our campsite. They loped off a couple of yards and continued to stare at me, seeming to pass some ironic commentary between the two of them. Roberta emerged when the coffee was ready— Starbucks Instant, a miraculous improvement on the boiled grounds of olden days. We broke camp and headed down to Rio Grande Village, at the southeastern border of the park.

There, we hiked up a promontory and stared across the river at the little Mexican village of Boquillas, with its adobe houses in sherbet colors, "like Candy Land," Roberta observed. You used to be able to take a boat across for lunch, but since 9/11 you need a passport to return, and we'd forgotten ours.

I noticed a couple staring into the water under a boardwalk that spanned a marsh. "Rio Grande perch," the husband said, pointing to a pair of striking greenish-gray fish with bright cream-colored spots. "It's the only cichlid native to Texas." He was a petroleum engineer but had studied freshwater marine biology as an undergraduate at Texas Tech. The female perch had swept out a circular nest in the mud with her tail, while the male was diligently patrolling the perimeter. These perch mate for life, which is rare in the animal kingdom—among the few examples are prairie voles, sandhill cranes, macaroni penguins, black vultures, and pot-bellied seahorses. The list is pretty short. It raises the question of whether love exists outside of human society, or is it just a comfortable habit that some creatures fall into.

We ate lunch under an impressive stand of palms, beside the remnants of an old health camp. We had changed into swimsuits to soak in the old hot springs on the very edge of the river. There used to be a bathhouse here, but now only the foundation remains. It felt good to get clean after camping and hiking. The hazel-colored Rio Grande beside us had been refreshed by waters from the Rio Conchos, which flows through the Mexican state of Chihuahua. I could easily have tossed a pebble into Mexico. I got out of the hot bath and slipped into the river, which was swift and bracing.

★

THE DREAM OF WALLING OFF Mexico has a long history. "The United States Government intends to build a high fence of nearly a thousand miles along the Rio Grande in Texas to keep the 'wetbacks' out, the Mexican workers," Donald Judd wrote in 1992, in one of his fanciful rants.

It already has huge balloons to watch the drug business. Having learned from this scale and inflation, they plan to inflate a tent over Texas so that the military planes can fly in peace. The noxious gases of the sewage sent from New York to Texas will keep the tent inflated . . . The map of Texas has an interesting shape and is a symbol so that a vast bulbous tent shaped like Texas will look impressive as you fly toward it, more so than the Dallas skyline. It can be air-conditioned too. There will have to be an orifice for the Dallas Fort Worth Airport, an eye of Texas.

I worry that the Trump administration might start building the wall in Big Bend simply because the federal government already owns the land. One evening we had hiked through Santa Elena Canyon on the other side of the park, where the walls on the Mexican side rise to 1,500 feet, and the light at sunset reminded me of the heroic western paintings of Albert Bierstadt. I tried to envision a wall down the center of the river. It seemed like a prison for nature.

It's true that undocumented immigrants cross over in Big Bend; in 2016, the Border Patrol picked up 6,366 people who it believed had entered the country illegally in the park sector, and seized 16 pounds of cocaine along with nearly 42,000 pounds of marijuana. These are very small figures compared with those for other sectors along the border, but they are not negligible. When Roberta and I were choosing campsites, there were some at the very tip of the bend in the river that had been off-limits because of the illegal traffic across the border. They had suddenly become available because the authorities considered them safe, now that enforcement had become so much stronger, proving that there are ways of policing the border without defacing one of the most beautiful parts of the state.

When we came out of the water, we ran into Jesse Manciaz and Peter Owen, members of the Carrizo/Comecrudo tribe. Jesse had a medicine-man pouch and a necklace of bear claws around his neck. There was an eagle feather in his hatband, indicating his status as a warrior (he's a Vietnam veteran). Peter wore a snappy little porkpie hat.

"We're meeting people to talk about the wall," Jesse told me, explaining that their tribe inhabited both sides of the river. They were used to crossing freely. Now they were threatened with partition. He said it was hard to get the message across. "People think there are no more Indians in Texas," Jesse complained.

Peter suggested that was because Mexican Americans don't know who they are. "They're actually Indians."

There were some ancient pictographs on the

cliff face above us. It was a mystery how they got there. They were impossible to reach without twenty-foot ladders. West Texas is full of such inscrutable emblems. Some are thousands of years old; some of the more recent ones show the arrival of the conquistadors. You can sometimes make out buffalo and snakes and recognizable animals, but the ones we were looking at were symbols and enigmatic figures. Roberta thought she discerned an owl. "The owl has always been a messenger," Jesse said. But through our field glasses we could see that there was some projection from the body of the creature. "Maybe a phallus," Peter conjectured. "A lot of these were painted as puberty rituals." He mentioned another pictograph just outside the park with a phallus that appears to enter a vagina when the light is right. "It's life, you know." I was thinking that teenagers have the same preoccupations no matter where they stand in history.

On the way back to the parking area, we ran into another birding couple. I mentioned to them the dilemma faced by the Indians who would be divided by the wall. "People think America is supposed to be some big open country and everybody can do as they please," the husband said irritably. His wife added, "I don't see what's wrong with it as long as it's on their side of the river."

We drove to Del Rio and got in just after dark.

Already, the stars had been erased from the sky. We went to dinner at Manuel's Steakhouse. The Academy Awards were being broadcast on a giant TV. Then we went back to the Hampton Inn. It felt good to be in a bed again. In the morning, I turned over and reached for Roberta's breast. I could feel her heart pulsing in my hand.

# FOURTEEN

# Among the Confederates

In the last week of July, Roberta and I, along with Steve and his wife, Sue Ellen, went over to the state cemetery to pick out our plots. It's off East Seventh Street in Austin, in what used to be a blue-collar Latino neighborhood but has become increasingly upscale, with bars and restaurants giving the hipsters plenty of opportunity to contemplate their mortality.

There had been rain the night before, and the grass was vivid and glistening. We rode around in a golf cart, sizing up the real estate. On Monument Hill, only one gravesite had been selected, now occupied by Eugene Cernan, a former NASA astronaut who was the last man on the moon. I interviewed him once; he told me that he had written his daughter's initials—TDC, for Teresa Dawn Cernan—in the moon dust. He also uttered the last words on the moon, as he fired up the lander vehicle to rejoin the orbiter: "Okay, let's get this mother out of here." Cernan wanted to be on top of the Monument Hill so he could be as close to the moon as possible.

Nearby is the grave of another explorer, the French sailor found in the wreck of the **La Belle,** the only remnant of the disastrous 1686 expedition of René-Robert Cavelier, Sieur de La Salle. The ship, with the sailor's skeleton intact, had been hidden in the silt of Matagorda Bay for three hundred years when archaeologists discovered it, along with a pewter cup inscribed "C. Barange"—perhaps the sailor's name. Among the war memorials is one to the "Nine Men of Praha," in memory of the soldiers from a little Texas town who died in the Second World War, all the young men in that village.

On top of Republic Hill is a statue of Stephen F. Austin, the founder of Texas, who also brought slavery into the colony, dooming his creation to so much iniquity and turmoil. Clustered around Austin's grave are assorted governors and politicians. George W. Bush will be the first president buried here, when his turn arrives, as well as Rick Perry and Dan Patrick. There's Robert McAlpin Williamson, "Three Legged Willie," who had a wooden leg but still managed to fight in the Battle of San Jacinto and later serve in the Republic's congress. Dan Moody is here, the youngest governor in Texas history; he broke the back of the

Ku Klux Klan, which was a dominant force in Texas in the 1920s. As attorney general, Moody also brought down the corrupt governor James E. Ferguson, and his wife, Miriam, who had succeeded him in office—our first woman governor. She made a place for herself in Texas lore when she campaigned against bilingual education, allegedly exclaiming, "If English was good enough for Jesus, it's good enough for the schoolchildren of Texas." In the indiscriminate society of the graveyard, Ma and Pa Ferguson lie almost head to heel with Dan Moody.

I accept that my life has already been lived. It has been a provincial life in many ways, intersecting only occasionally with history and the people who made it. I've always chosen to remain a step away from the center of the action, which for me would have been in the bustle of Manhattan or the corridors of power in Washington or the bungalows of Hollywood studios. They are all lives that beckoned to me. Each of them might have been more fulfilling than the one I chose. Instead, I've lived in a culture that is still raw, not fully formed, standing on the margins but also growing in influence, dangerous and magnificent in its potential. I have been close enough to those beguiling alternative lives to drink in the perfume of temptation. And yet, some maybe cowardly instinct whispered to me that if I accepted the offer to live elsewhere, I would be someone other than myself. My life might have been larger, but it would have been counterfeit.

I would not be home.

There are friends already here. Bud Shrake, a writer we all loved, lies next to his girlfriend, Ann Richards, the former governor. Ann's epitaph quotes from her inaugural address in 1991: "Today we have a vision of Texas where opportunity knows no race, no gender, no color—a glimpse of what can happen in government if we simply open the doors and let the people in." Bud's epitaph reads, "So Far, So Bueno."

We rode down the path, past the white headstone of former Texas legislator Bill Kugle, who wanted all eternity to know "He never voted for Republicans and had little to do with them." The black granite monument of Barbara Jordan, the first African American Texan elected to the U.S. House of Representatives, simply says, "Patriot." At the bottom of the hill, in stark, orderly rows, are the graves of two thousand Confederate soldiers. Above them, on a shady hillside, is the memorial to their commanding officer, Albert Sidney Johnston, a hero of the Texas Revolution and one of the greatest Confederate generals, who fell at Shiloh.

There was a spot near Johnston where we lingered. One could still see Stephen F. Austin on the top of the slope, with his hand reaching out in our direction. I felt a little light-headed. We all came to agreement rather quickly.

I had made my choice.

# Acknowledgments

Texas has been well served by the reporters who struggle to hold our political and business leaders accountable. That is especially notable in a time when the press is under assault, and reporters often assailed personally, by the most powerful people in our state and country. I am fortunate to have many friends in the press, a number of whom were vital in the preparation of this book. Mimi Swartz, of **Texas Monthly** and **The New York Times,** has been a wise and buoyant counselor, not only for this project but throughout my career. She was an invaluable guide to her adopted city of Houston. Robert Bryce, an author and senior fellow at the Manhattan Institute, gave me useful guidance on the oil and gas industry. Robert Wilonsky, a city columnist for **The Dallas Morning News,** reacquainted me with my old hometown. Mónica Ortiz Uribe, a freelance radio reporter, shared her two cities—El Paso and

Juárez—with me. Historian Lonn Taylor gave me a useful overview of West Texas. Manny Garcia, Houston bureau chief for **The New York Times,** graciously hosted me in the midst of deadlines brought on by Hurricane Harvey. And of course my friend Stephen Harrigan is a resource I have been calling upon for nearly forty years.

Steve and I are two of the foursome that meets for breakfast on Monday mornings, an ongoing conversation that has brought me considerable education and much delight. Many of the ideas I explore in this book were first broached over coffee and pastries with Steve, Gregory Curtis, the former editor of **Texas Monthly,** and historian H. W. "Bill" Brands.

In 2009, a new publication started in Texas, one that has done more than any other organization to inform citizens about the politics of our state. John Thornton, a venture capitalist in Austin, along with Evan Smith, then the editor in chief of **Texas Monthly,** and Ross Ramsey, then the editor and owner of **Texas Weekly,** joined forces to create an all-digital platform called **The Texas Tribune.** I don't know of any other state that has the depth of political coverage that the **Tribune** has been able to supply in Texas. Certainly, no other state needs it more.

David Danz's illustrations wonderfully capture the diversity and spirit of Texas.

Once again, Jan McInroy cast her scrupulous eye over the copy. When I get a manuscript back from her, I'm always a little abashed at the mob of errors that she has rounded up and placed under grammatical arrest. I am also grateful to my fact-checkers. At **The New Yorker**, Tammy Kim, Fergus McIntosh, and Rozina Ali checked the article "America's Future Is Texas" (July 10 and 17, 2017) that gave rise to the current book. David Kortova and Elizabeth Barber checked "A Tale of Three Wells," which was published in the January 1, 2018, **New Yorker** as "The Glut Economy." Emily Gogolak, a **New Yorker**–trained checker, moved to Austin in time to examine the rest of the manuscript. Welcome to Texas, Emily.

Some of the other work in this book, mainly in the chapter "Culture, Explained," appeared in **Texas Monthly** ("Remembrance of Things Primitive," February 1993).

I am enviably supplied with extraordinary professional support: Ann Close, my longtime editor at Knopf; Andrew Wylie, the world's best agent; and Daniel Zalewski, who has been my editor and supporter at **The New Yorker** for many years, and I hope for many more. It was the editor of that wonderful magazine, David Remnick, who asked me to "explain Texas"—I think because he couldn't understand why I live here. I hope this book answers the question.

## A NOTE ABOUT THE AUTHOR

Lawrence Wright is a staff writer for **The New Yorker** and the author of nine previous books of nonfiction, including **In the New World, Remembering Satan, The Looming Tower, Going Clear, Thirteen Days in September,** and **The Terror Years,** and one novel, **God's Favorite.** His books have received many prizes and honors, including a Pulitzer Prize for **The Looming Tower.** He is also a playwright and screenwriter. He plays the keyboard in the Austin-based blues band WhoDo. He and his wife are longtime residents of Austin, Texas.